Contemporary
Jewish
Philosophies

William E. Kaufman

Contemporary
Jewish
Philosophies

PUBLISHED BY
RECONSTRUCTIONIST PRESS and BEHRMAN HOUSE, INC., N.Y.

Library of Congress Cataloging in Publication Data
Kaufman, William E
    Contemporary Jewish philosophies.

    Bibliography: p.
    Includes index.
    1. Judaism—20th century—Addresses, essays,
lectures. 2. Jewish theology—History—Addresses,
essays, lectures. 3. Judaism—United States—Addresses, essays, lectures. 1. Title.
BM565. K36   181'.3   75-30761
ISBN 0-87441-239-0
ISBN 0-87441-238-2 pbk.

ⓒ Copyright 1976 by William E. Kaufman
Published by Reconstructionist Press
and Behrman House, Inc., New York

Manufactured in the United States of America

Design by Marsha Picker

To the memory of my parents

CONTENTS

Foreword

With pride and pleasure, the Reconstructionist Foundation offers this work by Rabbi William Kaufman to the reader who is concerned with Jewish religious thought. The subject and the writer are well matched, for Dr. Kaufman, by virtue of his education and temperament, is highly qualified to deal with theological formulations, and especially with efforts to apply the insights of Jewish religious thought to the problems and purposes of the contemporary generation.

William Kaufman is a graduate of the Jewish Theological Seminary, where he earned the title Rabbi; he received his Ph.D. from Boston University in Philosophy. He now serves as spiritual leader of Congregation B'nai Israel in Woonsocket, Rhode Island. He is a member of the Editorial Board of the *Reconstructionist* magazine, and contributes to various publications.

Several years ago, when Rabbi Kaufman was kind enough to consult with me regarding a book he was planning to write on Jewish thought, it occurred to both of us that the contemporary Jew was seeking "meaning," not only in his life and the life of society, but in Jewish life in particular. In response to this burgeoning demand for clarification and guidance, a virtual renaissance of Jewish thought has been achieved.

Unlike the generation before the Holocaust, the generation following it has produced a series of thoughtful and scholarly writers, who have turned their attention to the fundamentals of human existence. Jewish life, prior to that time, we observed, had generated organizations and institutions, and had developed individuals whose major concerns had been philanthropy, the upbuilding of Zion, resisting anti-Semitism, and perfecting the art of "community relations." But an uneasy feeling prevailed.

Despite frenetic activity, Jews experienced emptiness, purposelessness; they had lost the will to be Jews and, in some tragic instances, the will to live at all. Surely the Holocaust was the great watershed, and subsequent to it, writers like Richard Rubenstein, Emil Fackenheim and Arthur A. Cohen emerged to cope with the spiritual consequences of the monstrous tragedy. Adumbrating this spiritual crisis, men like Franz Rosenzweig, Leo Baeck, Martin Buber, and Mordecai Kaplan had opened new vistas of Jewish thought; but it took the Holocaust to engage the attention of the new generation.

The outpouring of theological and philosophical writing was, indeed, unprecedented. Book after book appeared, and some were widely read. But—and this is the crux of our discussion—it appeared as though each writer took no cognizance of any other. With few exceptions, there seemed to be little intellectual intercourse between a philosopher and his colleagues. Each one set forth his own views; and the reader was unaware of any common framework in which all of them were functioning. The reader was offered a variety of views (see my *Varieties of Jewish Belief*, and *The Condition of Jewish Belief*, edited by Milton Himmelfarb), but there was no apparent exchange between any two.

What was lacking, we concluded, was a critique of all the major expressions, from Rosenzweig to the latest contributors to the subject, by a single writer who would establish an intelligible framework within which to explicate and to evaluate what was available to this generation of concerned persons.

Hence, the present volume. Whether the reader shares Rabbi Kaufman's preference or not, he or she will recognize the value of this perspective on the fashioners of contemporary Jewish thought, for that perspective enables the reader to establish the relations between one thinker and another within a clearly defined outlook.

We hope that this volume will stimulate students of religion, and lay readers, to explore the world of religious thought, and will help them to formulate a concept of God, man, and the Jewish people that will answer the needs of the mind and the heart.

Ira Eisenstein
President, Jewish Reconstructionist Foundation

Preface

The present work is a systematic critique of the theological and philosophical views of the major Jewish thinkers of the twentieth century. The amorphous state of contemporary Jewish thought requires, I believe, a more disciplined approach than heretofore undertaken. My purpose is accordingly thematic rather than historic. My concern is with movements of thought, the explication of ideas, the development of arguments and the justification of conclusions.

Hence my emphasis is on the trends of thought represented by the various thinkers studied. Obviously, it would be impossible to encompass all the theologies of contemporary Jewish thinkers in one volume. A criterion of selection is therefore necessary. Accordingly, my selection of the thinkers to be studied has been governed by the following criterion: Which Jewish thinkers in the twentieth century best illustrate the theological options open to the contemporary Jew? Admittedly, some of the thinkers to be discussed are still alive and their thought is still in process. Hence, my emphasis is on the arguments they have developed in their works up to the time of this writing.

Thus the pattern of this book is one of challenge and response. Its purpose, among other things, is to activate the mind of the reader to the vital issues of Jewish theology in our time. My method is Socratic rather than dogmatic. I am interested more in raising questions than answering them. Animating this work is my belief that the unexamined Jewish life is not worth living.

To those who have inspired me to examine contemporary Jewish thought, I am deeply indebted.

My special debt is to Dr. Ira Eisenstein, President of the Jewish Reconstructionist Foundation, whose careful editorial work has guided me throughout this arduous intellectual journey. His clarity of thought and his profound understanding of the needs of the writer and the reader have been an intellectual adventure to me.

I also wish to acknowledge the inspiration of Dr. Mordecai Kaplan, who showed me the possibility of an intellectually defensible understanding of Judaism.

I am grateful as well to Professors Nahum Glatzer and Ernst Simon, who kindly answered my queries about the theology of Franz Rosenzweig. I am indebted to the Jewish Theological Seminary of America for providing me with the Judaic background to undertake this task. For enriching my philosophical background, I am grateful to my doctoral advisors at Boston University—Professors Peter Bertocci and Erazim Kohak. I owe much to Rabbi Ludwig Nadelman for his many helpful suggestions.

I wish to thank Miss Agnes Gibbons, our congregation secretary, for typing the first draft of the manuscript and Mrs. Sandra Whipple for typing the final drafts.

I wish, also, to thank the members of Congregation B'nai Israel, who constantly encouraged this venture.

And to all the staff of Behrman House for their practical guidance—a special thank you.

My greatest debt is to my wife, Nathalie and our children, Ari and Beth, whose love has enabled me to persist in the writing of this book.

Woonsocket, R. I.   William E. Kaufman

Part 1 The Challenge of Contemporary Jewish Thought

1 Introduction:
The Crisis of Meaning

The purpose of this book is to present and evaluate the theological views of the major figures in contemporary Jewish thought. I am writing this book because I believe that the modern American Jew faces a crisis of meaning. And this crisis is inextricably bound up with the present precarious situation of organized religion.

Organized Religion versus "the Religious"

Ours is an age when the foundations of organized religion are crumbling. But, paradoxically, this does not mean that the present intellectual and emotional climate is not conducive to "the religious."[1] If by the "religious" we mean a heightened quality of experience, the search for new dimensions of life, the quest for deeper levels of consciousness—we can generally assert that

3

many intellectually sensitive people are genuinely seeking new ways of religious understanding.

Prominence of the Term "Transcendence" and Its Significance

This quest is typified in literature by the prominence of the term "transcendence." Open a philosophical or theological journal, glance through a book on present-day religious thought, even peruse a work on literary criticism—eventually you will stumble on the word "transcendence." "Transcendence" is an extremely ambiguous term. On the one hand, it is employed to mean the enlargement of personal horizons, the process of overcoming one's limitations. On the other hand, it is used to denote *that which transcends us*—and commonly designates what a self-conscious intellectual would in common parlance (and not in a scholarly journal) refer to by the term "God." The prominence of the term "transcendence" in contemporary literature is a vivid manifestation of modern man's religious quest. And the ambiguity of its usage, which we shall attempt to unravel throughout this book, typifies the spiritual confusion of our time.

Our principal aim is the emergence of clarity out of this confusion. This is the significance of the term "critique" in our study. By "critique" we mean an attempt at clarification—a therapeutic process—and not an invidious and destructive intellectual game.

This critique, then, is meant to be constructive—or better, *reconstructive of contemporary Jewish thought.* For it is our belief that despite its confusing and chaotic character, the very quest for transcendence is a salutary development. It signifies that modern man is in search of ultimate value. He is striving to find *meaning* for his life—a meaning more inclusive and more compelling than the immediate gratifications of money, pleasure, and security. The age-old ultimate questions still haunt man: What conception of God can I accept? What is the relation of God to the universe? How shall we conceive the relation of man to God? There is, in short, a deep-seated metaphysical urge in human beings that cannot be stifled.

The Contemporary Religious Problem and the Jew

But the search for a meaningful religious orientation in today's world is an unusually difficult one. What is the problem? What is the crux of the difficulty? It is not a problem of scarcity but of overabundance. The problem lies in the proliferation of salvation cults that are mushrooming throughout America, such as Zen Buddhism and Transcendental Meditation. Dazzled by the bewildering array of salvation cults, modern man does not know which way to turn.

The modern Jew is not isolated from his environment. Since the emancipation, the challenges of the environment constantly impinge upon him. He can no longer divorce himself from the cultural matrix by returning to the ghetto.

Even so the reader will undoubtedly object—salvation is not a *Jewish* concept. How then can today's salvation cults affect the Jew?

The problem here is one of semantics. To be sure, salvation is not a Jewish concept if it is taken to mean a deliverance from the bondage of the world. But if it is understood in a wider sense —as the fulfillment of the human potential—it is most assuredly a Jewish concept and an *essential human need*. And it is this need that is the source of religion as a social phenomenon: "Religion is a natural social process which arises from man's intrinsic need of salvation or self-fulfillment."[2]

handy - dandy?
isn't an easier
answer at hand
i.e. in Jewish
traditions of
Messianism?

An Analogue in the Past

Can we find an analogue in the past to the contemporary religious problem as it confronts the Jew? It is evident that the contemporary problem is not similar to the dilemma the Jew faced in the age of Moses Maimonides in the twelfth century. At that time, there was one dominant universe of discourse—Aristotelianism. Aristotelianism, with its view of God as First Cause, seemed to conflict with the anthropormorphisms in the Bible that depicted God in human form. Maimonides therefore attempted to reinterpret these anthropomorphisms so that they would not conflict with Aristotelianism. The problem Maimonides sought to resolve was thus sharply drawn: the reconciliation of Jewish tradition with Aristotelianism.

The problem today is hardly so clear-cut. Hence, a more illuminating analogue is the challenge Saadya confronted in the tenth century. His was an age of moral, spiritual, and intellectual confusion—very much like our own. A plethora of sects and schools abounded. The contrast between the ages of Saadya and Maimonides is epitomized in this description: "The bewilderment which characterized his own age is due not so much to the conflict between one particular creed of philosophy and the traditional faith, as to the impact of so many rival creeds and philosophies upon the minds of his contemporaries."[3] Substitute ways of salvation for "creeds and philosophies" in the above passage, and we have our present age.

The Modern Jew and the Need for Salvation

It follows that if Judaism does not satisfy this intrinsic human need for salvation or self-fulfillment, the religiously sensitive Jew will seek salvation in other areas and in other ways, and many have already done so. Hence it is crucial that today's Jew have a clear idea of the various contemporary interpretations of what Judaism has to say, of what it means, and of its significance for his life. In a word, if the modern Jew is not to be swept along in the maelstrom of contemporary life, he must be fortified with a knowledge of the theological options and alternatives that are open to him.

Salvation, Theology, and Judaism

But what relation does theological understanding have to self-fulfillment? After all, isn't Judaism purely a way of life?

In the first place, Judaism is a way of thinking as well as a way of life. The issue in religious life today is not belief *per se* or action *per se*. Rather it is the *integration* of belief and religious practice: What action symbols strengthen my will to live? What beliefs can pragmatically affect my actions? The separation of belief and action as if they were two separate compartments can only result in a schizophrenic Judaism. Furthermore, to speak of Judaism as a way of life where belief takes second place is to render an intellectual injustice to Judaism.

In the second place, if beliefs are to guide life, they must be refined, purified and clarified. Such clarification is the task of theology, broadly understood.

Traditional versus "Open" Theology

In its traditional sense, theology is the systematic statement of the beliefs in a given community. Religion, as a phenomenon, is the datum, the given. As a natural social process, religion is prior to theology. Theology has generally been a second-order activity —a reflective summary of the religious beliefs of a particular group. As such, it has consisted of an attempt to weave these beliefs into a coherent pattern so as to establish the distinctiveness of a particular religion. Understood in this light, traditional theology has often taken the form of a defensive maneuver—a systematic presentation of the religious beliefs of a particular group with a hidden agenda of showing their superiority to those of other religions. This kind of theology as apologetics rightly deserves the stiff criticisms voiced against it.[4]

Another characteristic of traditional theology is its systematic character. The negative feature of this aspect of theology is its tendency to congeal the fluidity of religious expression into a closed, fixed system.

Theology, in this sense of a systematic, monolithic and "once and for all" statement of beliefs, cannot capture the evolutionary development of Jewish thought. Judaism, as the evolving religious civilization of the Jewish people, cannot be embraced by one systematic theology.

Is it not therefore appropriate to jettison this particular conception of theology, especially with respect to Judaism? There is, after all, no *a priori* reason for identifying theology with a closed system. For this reason, let us explore the possibility of an open theology—a theology of clarification rather than a dogmatic theology.

The very etymology of the term "theology" supports this interpretation. "Theology" derives from the Latin *theos* meaning "God" and *legein* meaning "to speak." Hence theology means speaking or discourse (*logos*) about God. An open theology would therefore designate a clarification of our ways of speaking about God. Since it is the height of arrogance to assume that the last word has been spoken on this matter, since man's search for a discovery of the Divine is a never-ending process contingent upon the development of human knowledge and insight, a contemporary theology can never be closed but must always be open to new experience shaped and clarified by the collective human mind.

Theology and Philosophy

If theology connotes a refinement and clarification of our ways of speaking about God, a precondition of such discourse is the elucidation of language and experience. This is the principal function of philosophy today.

Philosophy, originally meaning "love of wisdom," is no longer synonymous with abstract and abstruse metaphysics. By and large, philosophers today are engaged in a process of the clarification of meanings.   ? Locke?

One major trend in contemporary philosophy is the analytic study of language. The pioneer of this approach, Ludwig Wittgenstein, conceived of philosophy as the battle against the bewitchment of our intelligence by the use of language. Words are all too often a source of confusion rather than a source of enlightenment. This is especially true of the philosophy of religion. We only have to reflect on the misunderstandings generated by such terms as "revelation," "supernaturalism," and "process" to become aware of the need for clarifying the meaning of the terms we use.

Another major movement in contemporary philosophy is existential phenomenology—referring to the clarification of the structures of human experience. It is very tempting to regard human experience as a buzzing, booming confusion. On the contrary, as the Gestalt psychologists have demonstrated, our experience is structured. We discern patterns; we do not merely sense discrete particles of experience. The structure of natural human experience is cogently illustrated by the following statement of a philosopher of science:

> We find the eye highly structured for color discrimination, for perception of edges and contours. Similarly, the ear is highly articulated for discriminating relations of pitch and loudness. The regular rhythms of breathing, of heartbeat, of sleeping and waking, of hunger and satiety, connote structure in the very conditions of life.[5]

Add to this the capacity of the human mind to intuit conceptual patterns in experience. The rudimentary concept-formation of the child who learns the concept "animal" and the scientist who discovers a law of nature—both demonstrate the unique capacity of the human mind to discern meaning in existence. And existential phenomenology is precisely the study of the meaning and structure of human existence.[6]

Common to both of these major trends in philosophy, therefore, is the clarification of meaning—be it linguistic or experiential.

Since the present crisis in Judaism is one of meaning, it follows that an open philosophical theology offers a promising avenue of deliverance from the intellectual confusion that reigns in our midst.

The Need for Theological Reconstruction

The reflective contemporary Jew stands at a crossroads. Dubious of the traditional categories, he seeks new modes of thought. And the need for a reconstruction of contemporary Jewish thought is not merely academic. It is existentially vital. The following tragic situation is a vivid illustration.

A middle-aged man dies suddenly, leaving a wife and college-age sons. Her emotion is a complex mixture of grief and anger. She has a target for her anger. It is an anthropomorphic conception of God. She knows no other idea of Divinity. The concept she has is that of a cosmic puppeteer, a God who pulls the strings of life and death, of fortune and disaster. It is the Deity of the traditional High Holy Day liturgy—the God who keeps a ledger of life and death, who decides who shall live and who shall die. Why, she asks, did this "merciful" God take my husband at so young an age?

The bereaved sons are intellectually as well as emotionally shaken. Their father was a model of conduct to them. Their conception of the justice of God is shaken to its foundations. Their belief in the truth of the traditional theological doctrines is shattered.

More precisely, their sense of the inner consistency of their religious beliefs has been undermined. Their concept of the applicability of religious teachings to human experience has been challenged. And their belief in the pragmatic value of religious ritual and prayer is seriously undermined.

It is my passionate belief that unless people are aware of alternate theologies, a tragedy can simply demolish a naive faith. And the damage may be irreparable. Unable to regain their pristine faith, such people are likely to dismiss Judaism as an antiquated relic irrelevant to their lives.

Jewish college students especially are often astonished to learn that alternative conceptions of God exist. Conversant with the latest trends in scientific thought, their religious view is quite frequently fixated at a childhood level. They may be familiar with the theory of relativity; but their God-idea may be that of "the old man in the sky." Their religious development, in short, has not kept pace with the enlargement of their horizons in other areas of life.

Hence they are often amazed to learn that there are thinkers who do not conceive of God as a being or entity but as power, process, or Being itself. This is not to imply that these latter conceptions do not pose difficulties of a different order of complexity. My point is rather that there is an existential and not merely an academic need for a reconstruction of contemporary Jewish theology. (For) it is a matter of the utmost importance for life itself.

The method of this reconstruction involves the clarification of alternative theologies and their examination in terms of the criteria of inner consistency, empirical or experiential reference, and pragmatic value. In the following chapter we shall develop and explain these criteria. We shall endeavor to show that Jewish thought cannot exist in an insulated) vacuum—in an autonomous realm immune from the canons of meaningful discourse. We shall illustrate the present lack of clarity in contemporary Jewish thought and begin to traverse the road back to clarity. As we embark on this voyage, I trust that it will become clear to the reader that criteria or standards of intelligibility are necessary for all statements—Jewish or otherwise.

At this point, one preliminary possible objection can be anticipated. It may be argued that human beings are not consistent and that life is deeper than logic. In answer to this objection, it must be stated categorically that the foibles of human nature are no excuse for sloppy thinking. The basic premise for all thinking worthy of the name is the integrity of the human mind. If we are to abandon the ideal of intelligibility, we might as well dismiss all efforts of the human mind to discover truth as futile. For without intelligibility, there is no meaning. And it is intuitively evident that the crisis of meaning which has been the subject of this chapter can only be met by meaning itself. This book is a quest for the illumination of meaning in contemporary Jewish thought. The basis of this quest is a renewed faith in the human mind. It is time to stem the flight to irrationality and to return to the ideal enunciated by Ralph Waldo Emerson in his memorable statement: "Nothing is at last sacred but the integrity of your own mind."[7]

NOTES

1. See John Dewey, *A Common Faith* (New Haven: Yale University Press, 1934), Chapter 1, where the author distinguishes between religion and "the religious."

2. Mordecai M. Kaplan, *The Meaning of God in Modern Jewish Religion* (New York: Reconstructionist Press, 1962), p. ix.

3. *Three Jewish Philosophers,* introduced and edited by Hans Lewy, Alexander Altmann, and Isaak Heinemann (New York: Meridian Books, 1961), translator's introduction to Saadya's *Book of Doctrines and Beliefs,* p. 12.

4. See, for example, Walter Kaufmann, *Critique of Religion and Philosophy* (New York: Harper and Brothers, 1958).

5. Marx W. Wartofsky, *Conceptual Foundations of Scientific Thought* (New York: The Macmillan Co., 1968), p. 317.

6. As will be noted in detail later, one of the negative features of Jewish existentialism is its failure to make sufficient use of the valuable method of phenomenology employed by many existentialist thinkers.

7. Ralph Waldo Emerson, "Self-Reliance," in *The Complete Essays and Other Writings of Ralph Waldo Emerson,* edited by Brooks Atkinson (New York: Random House, Inc., 1940), p. 148.

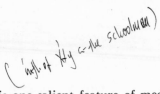

('not' of Hy c= the schoolmen)

If there is one salient feature of medieval Jewish philosophy,
it is the quest for clarity. Although the medieval universe of
discourse seems foreign to the modern mind, one cannot deny
the imposing intellectual edifice that was built. Just as a medieval
cathedral exemplified the ascent to perfection, so medieval Jewish thought was a search for intellectual perfection. Terms such
as "substance" and "accident" were defined, arguments were pro-
pounded, and a consistent methodology was employed.

analogy not
in effective
statement

To explore the world of contemporary Jewish thought is to
enter a different domain. Instead of precision, we find vagueness
and ambiguity. Arguments are replaced by categorical assertions.
It is, in short, an undisciplined field.

Our first task is to make a preliminary survey of this unculti-
vated territory. Our ultimate aim is its cultivation and reconstruction.

The Present State of Jewish Thought d ?

In 1966 the editors of *Commentary* magazine compiled a symposium of contemporary Jewish thought. This symposium consisted of restatements of the basic concepts of Judaism and their relevance to the modern age. This collection of essays has been published in book form under the title *The Condition of Jewish Belief.*[1]

In his introduction to this book, Milton Himmelfarb, a contributing editor to *Commentary*, describes his reaction to these statements: "What impression does this symposium give of the present state of Jewish thought? In general, that there is far less theological ferment than among Christians and that there are few new ideas about Judaism."[2]

If Himmelfarb's comment is disturbing, the reasons he offers for his assertion are even more disquieting: "I am not a follower of Buber, but once, when everybody at one seminary was sneering at Buber-*mayses* (a pun on the Yiddish *bobbe-mayses,* old wives' tales), I almost wanted to enlist on Buber's side. They were obviously sneering at the theological enterprise itself, and rabbis should know that a sneer is no refutation. Historically, some Jewries were more theological than others. The more advanced the culture they lived in and the more vigorous its philosophical life, the more they had to theologize. Medieval Spanish Judaism was more theological than Franco-German Judaism, Maimonides more than Rashi. In those terms, we live in Spanish and not Franco-German conditions, and we too need theology. How much? More, I would say, than we are getting."[3]

I am in complete agreement with Himmelfarb's feeling that we need more theological thinking on the current scene. We are first, however, compelled to ask: Why the sneer at the theological enterprise itself? Was it due to an attitude of *pan-halachism* or religious behaviorism—that Judaism is purely revealed law? Or was it due to an intellectual laziness, a reluctance to think or to question one's cherished beliefs? The former attitude ignores the *Agada*—the rich theological and imaginative corpus of Jewish thought. The latter attitude is one of intellectual arrogance.

It is my contention that if contemporary Jewish theology is to become an intellectually respectable enterprise, such arrogance and complacency must give way to intellectual modesty. Intellectual modesty is a willingness to limit our claims to what we

can know from human experience. It involves an openness to
new insights. And it signifies the importance of the challenge of
a variety of ideas.

It is this emphasis on the varieties of Jewish belief as a healthy
phenomenon which is one of the merits of Reconstructionism.
An analysis of these "varieties" will help us to further explore
the present state of Jewish thought.

The Varieties of Jewish Belief

The Reconstructionist movement is animated by the contention that "in the Judaism of today and tomorrow, diversity of
theologies must be recognized as both inevitable and desirable."[4]
Indeed, it is precisely this latitude of belief, this diversity in
theological thinking, that is the hallmark and *sine qua non* of
religious liberalism. And unless thinkers are encouraged to develop new and unique approaches to Judaism, the liberal spirit
dies and is replaced by religious dogmatism. It is, therefore, the
merit of Reconstructionism to emphasize the present diversity
of thought as good.

Nevertheless, an important qualification must be stated. Diversity of thought does not mean that all Jewish theologies and
philosophies are equally valid. Diversity of thought must not be
an excuse for arbitrary assumptions and the abandonment of
argument.

This point may seem too obvious to emphasize. Unfortunately,
to many minds it is neither obvious nor self-evident. And the
reason for this lies in a hidden set of assumptions implicitly
maintained by many theologians.

The basic thrust of these assumptions is that all thinking must
ultimately rest on an irrational commitment. Hence, one has the
right to believe whatever he pleases.

These implicit assumptions have been stated concisely in the
following three propositions:

> (1) for certain logical reasons, rationality is so limited that
> everyone has to make a dogmatic irrational commitment;
> (2) therefore, the Christian has a right to make whatever
> commitment he pleases; and
> (3) therefore, no one has a right to criticize him for this.[5]

It is clear that anyone who holds to these premises, either
explicitly or implicitly, will doubtless maintain that argumentation and the quest for clarity are pointless. Such a person will

simply say: "Believe what you want to believe. That is the end of the matter."

It is also clear, however, that if such premises are accepted, the death knell is sounded for religious liberalism. For religious liberalism is inseparable from religious humanism; and the standard of humanism is respect for the integrity of the human mind. This respect implies the right to ceaseless criticism, the demand to make ideas clear, and the ideal of the open mind.

The dogmatic irrationalist, at this point, may object with the following rejoinder: Does not the liberal thinker himself entertain an irrational commitment—to wit, the commitment to rationality? And in the light of the chaotic state of our world, is not this commitment itself irrational?

This argument rests on a glaring *non sequitur*. From the chaotic state of human affairs, the ubiquity of war and strife, the irrationality of human behavior, the dogmatist derives the conclusion that a commitment to rationality is itself irrational. In fact, however, precisely the opposite conclusion follows. Is not the appeal to irrationality itself part of the problem of contemporary life? Does it not silence and stifle man's impulse to improve the human situation?

After all, reason is still man's noblest characteristic. The capacity to reason, as Maimonides insisted, is the divine image in man. This does not suggest that religion is purely a rational phenomenon. There are nonrational factors involved in religious belief such as intuition and faith. My point is simply that these nonrational factors must not be regarded as irrational or contrary to reason. By the supremacy of reason, I mean the openness of all beliefs to criticism according to rational criteria, whenever such criticism is justified.

Moreover, this by no means implies that the irrational, emotional, and aggressive impulses in man must not be squarely faced. But glorifying these impulses is not reckoning with them. Of course, Freud discovered the turbulent sea of unconscious feelings of hatred and aggression. But Freud also delineated the method of psychoanalysis to deal with them. And his underlying belief was: "Where the id was, there shall the ego be." Submission to the irrational in man is human bondage; only in the victory of reason is human freedom.

The argument of this section can now be summarized. The variety of contemporary Jewish theologies is good. But recognition of the necessity for variety does not mean that all approaches are equally valid. Nor can this diversity serve as an excuse for dogmatic irrational commitment and lack of clarity. Man's greatest gift is his mind; and destiny intended man to use it.

In Pursuit of Clarity: Two Concepts of Transcendence

It is now time to illustrate the need for clarity in contemporary Jewish thought. And there is no better vehicle for this purpose than a selection of various uses of the term "transcendence." Take, for example, the following passage on the nature of transcendence:

> Transcendence is not imposed. Transcendence is a directional valent of mundane existence. It is a domain, a province, an unfulfilled and contentless nothing; it is not, however, a mere emptiness, that is, an emptiness unrelated to and discontinuous with the busy occupation of immane existence, a thrust out and beyond the conditions of nature. It is empty only in the sense that it is not filled by nature, however much our natural existence alludes to its content, suggests it, indicates it. Transcendence is not equivalent, therefore, to the supernatural. Where transcendence is an epistemological gesture, a nothing which surrounds and buffers the heavy atmosphere of everyday life, supernature is filled emptiness, a substantial presence which is at the superficies of transcendence. In effect, we transcend toward the supernatural. The supernatural is the goal of transcendence.[6]

The author of this passage, Arthur A. Cohen, is one of the well-known Jewish theologians of our time. I shall therefore devote considerable attention to his thought at a later stage in this book. At this point, my intention is to comment briefly on the above passage because it exemplifies both the strengths and problems of a great deal of contemporary Jewish thought.

Its positive feature is the rich texture and poetic quality of the language. The words are highly suggestive and evocative. One cannot help but be impressed by the majesty of the language; and also one has the feeling that something terribly important is being said.

The problems arise when we attempt to understand precisely what is being said. Here the passage itself is in need of commentary and clarification. The question thus suggests itself: Is it the author's intention to be elusive as well as allusive? The answer is unequivocally in the negative. Cohen emphatically states: "All thought is directed toward clarification."[7] The irony, therefore, is that this clarification is itself in need of explication, for it presupposes an understanding of such complex concepts as "transcendence" and "supernatural." Hence, for the layman, the following paraphrase of this passage would be essential:

Arthur Cohen treats "transcendence" as a dimension of human existence. Transcendence, in his usage, refers not to God but to certain aspects of human existence which allegedly point beyond themselves to God. This particular usage of transcendence rests upon the following assumption: Human experience is not simply a brute encounter with a given datum. There is a basic tendency in human perception and imagination to transcend, or go beyond, the given datum.

To illustrate: I see a tree. But I see not only the tree. I look beyond the tree and see it superimposed against the background of the landscape. Further away in the distance, I see a glimmer of the sea. I can even catch a glimpse of the horizon of the sea. And in my imagination, I wonder what lies beyond the horizon. This sense of wonder leads me to think of the horizon as that which points beyond itself to a different order of reality.

For Cohen, transcendence is that dimension of human existence, nourished by the imagination and by feelings of awe and wonder, which transcends or points beyond itself to an alleged reality "beyond nature." This reality "beyond nature" is the supernatural.

By means of the above commentary, the reader can begin to ask such questions as these: Do all men possess this capacity for transcendence? Can the phrase "beyond nature" be given an intelligible meaning, and according to which criteria? Is it empirically meaningful? What is its pragmatic value?

My purpose at this juncture has been to show the need for clarification and the kind of clarification necessary for an understanding of contemporary Jewish thought. Moreover, the preliminary discussion of Arthur Cohen's concept of transcendence demonstrates vividly the need for criteria of evaluation.

Another more common usage of transcendence is illustrated by Steven Schwarzschild:

> To be sure, the God of the Hebrew Bible is preeminently a transcendent God, i.e., a God who is above and beyond the world, a God who is not identical with but "larger than" the

world. But at the same time He is not disconnected from the world. To the contrary, He is in, with, and for the world. . . .[8]

Here transcendence is used not as a term descriptive of human experience but as an adjective qualifying the nature of God. Here again a phrase is used which is clear to the writer but may by no means be clear to the reader. What does it mean to say that God is above and beyond the world? Is God above the world in the same sense that the ceiling is above my head? And what does "larger than" mean? Surely, the author does not mean to imply that God is corporeal—that He occupies space. Surely he wants this phrase to be taken as a metaphor. Or does he? One does not know precisely what this writer wants to say. And that is just the problem.

Here too the need for criteria stands out in bold relief. The point is quite simply this. How are we to distinguish meaningful from nonsensical talk about God? In order to answer this question, we must first determine what the distinguishing features of meaningful talk are.

The Criterion of Inner Consistency

If a statement is to be meaningful, it must first be self-consistent. The statement "It is raining and it is not raining" is self-contradictory and therefore meaningless. Why is it meaningless? Because logically, from a contradiction, any conclusion whatsoever follows. For this reason, a self-contradictory statement is a meaningless statement.

This criterion has special relevance for theological discourse. Quite often, theologians indulge in the language of paradox. A paradox is an assertion which is seemingly contradictory but, in an ultimate sense, is held to be true. Perhaps the best example of paradox is the Christian doctrine of the Trinity: There is One God and yet He is three persons.

Many thinkers have glorified the paradox. From Tertullian who said *"Credo quia absurdum est"* ("I believe because it is absurd") to Kierkegaard whose existential faith was predicated on the paradox of the Incarnation, the recourse to this mode of approach is a recurrent phase in theological discourse.

Is a paradox, then, that which in any other realm would be a contradiction? Does the concept of paradox imply that religious thinking is *sui generis*—not subject to the canons of logical discourse?

Paradox is a result of dealing with concepts which bring our reflective capacities to the limits of their capabilities. Let us honestly admit that our finite human minds are limited in any discourse about God. Yet there is what I would call an intellectual imperative to stretch our cognitive powers as far as possible before resorting to the language of paradox and its allied concepts of mystery and ineffability.

Religious thinking is not a hermetically sealed compartment immune from all canons of meaningful and logical discourse. Yet it does possess a certain distinctiveness in that it deals with ultimates. In dealing with ultimates, we ought to use the criterion of inner consistency as steadfastly as possible and not resort to the language of paradox and mystery until and unless our conceptual apparatus fails.

The problem is that not a few thinkers begin with paradox, mystery, and ineffability. Ineffability is itself an illustration of paradox: it refers to a mystical experience that one is incapable of describing in words. The real paradox is that mystics are generally quite profuse in their language describing what presumably cannot be put into words.

Moreover, the mystic frequently claims that his experience of God is completely beyond human understanding. Here we must differentiate between the term "God" and the reality of God. The preconceptual reality of God is admittedly a mystery. But once we use the term "God," we have begun to "corner" the mystery. Language and concepts have many uses: they define, describe, differentiate. Once we use a term, we have differentiated an experienced reality. To use terms, to describe experiences— and to claim at the same time that what one is describing is completely beyond human understanding—is surely self-contradictory.

In a word, my claim is that it is much too easy to begin with paradox, mystery, and ineffability. It is analogous to an admission of defeat before we begin.

We have been endowed with minds. The intellectual imperative demands that we use them to the best of our abilities. Are we to abdicate the use of our minds in dealing with the noblest enterprise of man—the quest for God—for transcendence?

The criterion of inner consistency must therefore be our guide as we make the perilous ascent. Only as we approach the summit, after we have made an intellectual climb—only then have we the right to relinquish our cognitive powers.

The Empirical Criterion

A statement is alleged to be meaningful if it deals with something that can be seen, felt, touched, imagined, conceived—in a word, experienced or capable of being experienced.

We have already touched on the difficulty involved in a concept of a transcendent God above and beyond the world. Let us explore the difficulty further.

The preposition "above" has a legitimate usage in referring to spatiotemporal objects: "The airplane is above my head" is a legitimate usage. "The ball soared above the outfielder's head" makes sense. Why do these statements make sense? Because they deal with empirical, experiential, verifiable facts.

Compare these statements to the following: "X is above the world." If by world, we mean the planet earth, then the statement could conceivably refer to Apollo 12. But when theologians talk about God being above the world, they generally mean "the universe."

Now, what possible sense can it make for a human being to speak of an "X" above or beyond the universe? It presumes, for one thing, a total knowledge of the universe—which we lack. It presumes, as well, a naive concept of the universe or nature as a box or container. In short, this concept does not even do justice to the mystery and vastness of the universe itself.

The point I am making is that the statement "X is above the world" is of a different order than "The airplane is above my head."

"X is above the world" not only does not deal with experienced reality, it is doubtful that it deals with reality as capable of being experienced.

This is an example of how important the empirical criterion is in dealing with theological statements.

The Criterion of Pragmatic Value

There is no movement in contemporary philosophy more improperly maligned and more misunderstood than pragmatism. It is generally equated with the simple-minded doctrine: "Something is true if it works." Needless to say, such a doctrine makes a mockery of the notion of truth.

The real meaning of pragmatism is far more subtle and rich. Its basic thesis is that one must consider the significant consequences of a belief for human life. Does a belief render life more meaningful, more worthwhile? Does it foster man's nobler impulses? Does it generate hope for man?

These questions are terribly important in evaluating a concept of God. All too many concepts of God render man a submissive, servile, and cringing creature. Typical of this is the German theologian Schleiermacher's definition of religion as a "feeling of absolute dependence." Here is psychological dependency, which the mature man must outgrow, elevated to a cosmic plane.

Many thoughtful people have rejected the concept of God because they have imagined Him as a kind of invisible monarch demanding obsequious obeisance from his serfs. Can we blame people for rejecting such a concept?

How different is a concept of God which elevates man, which fosters his independence! How much nobler is a humanistic religion *with* God—a God who calls man to arise and stand erect and be independent! How much more value is there to a concept of God which brings out the best and not the worst in man!

This is quite sufficient to show how important it is to gauge the pragmatic value of a conception of God. It makes a great deal of difference for a man's life whether he believes in a tyrannical concept of God or in God as a power that makes for self-reliance.

The question most frequently asked concerning belief in God is: What difference does it make? One's conception of God, I have tried to show, makes a great deal of difference in one's life.

Are These Criteria Compatible with Judaism?

Since this is a work on contemporary Jewish thought, one must ask whether these criteria are compatible with Judaism. It has been frequently argued, for example, that Judaism occupies a unique position in the history of culture: it is *sui generis* and not subject to general or universal categories. The following considerations, however, count against an *a priori* immunity of Judaism from universal criteria.

To begin with, it is important to note that "Judaism" is not a univocal term. In truth, there is not one monolithic intellectual structure which we can call Judaism. In fact, history shows that there have been a variety of Judaisms. For example, the Judaism of Job was different from the Judaism of Jeremiah. The Judaism of Maimonides was different from the Judaism of Rabbi Akiba. In a word, there is no one single concept of Judaism. Judaism is rather a multivalent term; it is a mosaic of different and various patterns. The evolving religious civilization of the Jewish people is the totality of every creative endeavor undertaken by Jews. No one concept can capture its variegated tapestry.

Hence the question of the compatibility of these criteria with the Judaic modes of expression raises the further question: Whose mode of expression? Hillel, Maimonides, or Joseph Karo? Therefore, raising the question of the "Jewishness" of a particular concept is like fishing for minnows in the sea.

Secondly, it is important to forestall another "category mistake" that is frequently made. One may object that the use of such a criterion as "inner consistency" is a Greek and not a Jewish concept. Here it is important to note that Greek thought, like Judaism, is not a one-dimensional thought pattern. Not all Greek writers were rational. Nor were all Jews antiphilosophical. The title of Professor E. R. Dodds' book *The Greeks and the Irrational*[9] ought to disabuse one immediately of such facile generalizations.

Furthermore, how can any student of the Talmud deny the role of "inner consistency" in its methodology? The following description by Harry A. Wolfson of the Talmudic method underscores the Talmudic student's quest for clarity which is not at all dissimilar from the kind of approach we wish to introduce to contemporary Jewish thought:

> Confronted with a statement on any subject, the Talmudic student will proceed to raise a series of questions before he satisfies himself of having understood its full meaning. If the statement is not clear enough, he will ask, What does the author intend to say here? If it is too obvious, he will ask again, It is too plain, why then expressly say it? If it is a statement of fact or a concrete instance, he will then ask, What underlying principle does it involve? Statements apparently contradictory to each other will be reconciled by the discovery of some subtle distinction, and statements apparently irrelevant to each other will be subtly analyzed into their ultimate elements and shown to contain some common underlying principle. . . . And there is a logic underlying this method of reasoning. It is the very same kind of logic which underlies any sort of scientific research, and by which one is enabled to form hypotheses, to test them, and to formulate general laws. . . . Just as the scientist proceeds on

the assumption that there is a uniformity and continuity in nature, so the Talmudic student proceeds on the assumption that there is a uniformity and continuity in human reasoning.[10]

It is this assumption of the uniformity and continuity of human reasoning that is the basis of the criterion of inner consistency.

One cannot deny also that the criterion of empirical or experiential meaningfulness has functioned in Judaism. Take, for example, the important role of experience in much of Biblical thought:

> The prophet Hosea bewailed the fact that Israel lacked the knowledge of God (Hosea 4:6) in the sense of appreciative experience of what God meant to Israel. . . . Likewise the Psalmist affirms that God is near to all who call Him, who invoke Him in truth (Psalms 145:18). Indeed he advises us to experience the reality of God, assuring us that we will find Him to be good.[11]

Add to this the Psalmist's exhortation: "Taste and see that the Lord is good" (Psalm 34:9). One cannot deny the constant appeal of the Biblical authors to the test of experience.

Finally, it cannot be denied that the criterion of pragmatic value has functioned in Judaism. The assessment of the consequences of an ideal, a practice, a law, an idea has been a factor of no small importance in Jewish life. Witness, for example, the Talmudic dictum: *Pok Hazi Ma D'ama Diber*—"examine what the public is practicing." Another example is even more apposite. In answer to the question as to the proper way of man, Rabbi Simeon said: *"Haroeh et Hanolad"*—considering the consequences of one's actions. (Ethics of the Fathers 2:13.)

Finding support in the massive and multivalent tradition of Judaism for these criteria is not, however, the most significant point. Far more significant is the willingness to recognize that the advance and progression of Jewish thought can only by furthered by constant critique and intellectual reconstruction. Jewish intellectual isolationism must give way to the willingness to evaluate Jewish thought by the universal canons of rational discourse.

The belief that Judaism is an autonomous world of its own, not subject to reason or criticism, must be discarded if contemporary Jewish thought is to become a disciplined and respectable field of inquiry.

The Need to Question

In the following chapters, I shall examine such theological options in contemporary Jewish thought as Jewish existentialism, liberal supernaturalism, covenant theologies, and neonaturalism.

In examining the writing of a particular thinker, I shall ask these questions:

What did the author intend to say?

Did he say it clearly?

How does he justify his statements, and what are his arguments?

Are his statements consistent with one another?

What aspects of human experience elucidate his theory?

What is the pragmatic applicability of his theory?

Only if these and similar questions are asked, is there hope for a greater contemporary Jewish thought in the making.

NOTES

1. Editors of Commentary, *The Condition of Jewish Belief* (New York: The Macmillan Co., 1967).
2. *The Condition of Jewish Belief*, p. 4.
3. *Ibid.*, pp. 5–6.
4. Ira Eisenstein, ed., *Varieties of Jewish Belief* (New York: The Reconstructionist Press, 1966), p. v.
5. William Warren Bartley III, *The Retreat to Commitment* (New York: Alfred A. Knopf, 1962), p. 90.
6. *Varieties of Jewish Belief*, pp. 33–34.
7. *Ibid.*, p. 31.
8. *Ibid.*, p. 246.
9. Berkeley: University of California Press, 1948.
10. Harry A. Wolfson, *Crescas' Critique of Aristotle* (Cambridge: Harvard University Press, 1929), pp. 25–26.
11. Mordecai M. Kaplan, *The Religion of Ethical Nationhood* (New York: The Macmillan Co., 1970), pp. 20–21.

Part 2 The Worlds of Jewish Existentialism

3 Franz Rosenzweig:
Toward an Existential Jewish Theology

We are now ready to begin our discussion of those Jewish thinkers who represent the major trends in contemporary Jewish theology. The first of these trends which we shall examine is Jewish existentialism.

What Is Existentialism?

Existentialism is a movement in modern philosophy which stresses the priority of individual human existence over objective and abstract thinking. As such, existentialism is a revolt against those forms of philosophy which tend to embrace the individual in an all-encompassing conceptual scheme, thereby denying the uniqueness of each particular life. This theme is illustrated by a story told by Sören Kierkegaard, the nineteenth-century Danish philosopher and forerunner of the existentialist movement.

Kierkegaard tells of "an absent-minded man so abstracted from his own life that he hardly knows he exists until, one fine morning, he wakes up to find himself dead."[1]

Kierkegaard's story brings out the salient features of existentialism. First, as the name of the movement indicates, its primary concern is individual human existence. Second, it maintains that human existence is too individual and idiosyncratic to be captured by abstract general concepts. On the contrary, human existence can be understood only from within. Third, central to existentialism is the theme of authenticity—that is, each man is to a large extent the author and creator of his mode of existence.

For this reason, the individual is responsible for what he makes out of his life. Any attempt of man to deny his freedom and responsibility—such as blaming his environment or genetic background—is inauthentic. In short, man is what he makes himself to be. This is the meaning of the existentialist dictum "existence precedes essence"—namely, each individual, through his own existence, fashions his own essence or nature. Human nature is not something fixed or predetermined. The existing individual is responsible for his own nature. Thus, existentialism is a radical negation of any kind of determinism that would rob man of his freedom and responsibility.

Furthermore, the existentialist deals with themes that would seem to be the province of the psychologist rather than the philosopher. Since the focus of the existentialist is on individual human existence, he describes the feelings individuals have—no matter how irrational they may be. In this connection, many existential philosophers employ the method of phenomenology. Phenomenology is a description of human experience as it is felt by the subject, without reference to the question of the objective validity of these feelings. To illustrate: the phenomenologist is interested purely in describing the feelings of the paranoid who perceives people pursuing and persecuting him. He is not interested in the relationship of these feelings to objective reality. Objective reality is thus *bracketed* or temporarily suspended. Only experienced reality is considered.

Now the feelings that existential phenomenologists describe are often of a morbid nature: anxiety, guilt, and especially feelings about death. Existential philosophers do not treat death merely as a natural fact. Their concern is with how the individual faces up to the prospect of his own eventual death.

This subjective treatment of death is the starting point of the philosopher whose thought we now examine—Franz Rosenzweig.

Biographical Perspectives

In the *Commentary* symposium alluded to before, the editor of the collection arrived at the following conclusion: "The single greatest influence on the religious thought of North American Jewry, therefore, is a German Jew—a layman, not a Rabbi— who died before Hitler took power and who came to Judaism from the very portals of the church."[2] The thinker referred to is Franz Rosenzweig (1886–1929). And the singular position of Franz Rosenzweig in contemporary Jewish thought is due in large measure to the dramatic quality of his life.

Rosenzweig's life, expressed in his own terms, was a "hygiene of return"[3] to Judaism, a rediscovery of his Jewish religious identity. He was born December 25, 1886, in Cassel, Germany—an only child to Georg and Adele Rosenzweig. His parents were cultured and affluent. But their Jewish life was marginal and nominal. Virtually the only positive Jewish influence on the young Rosenzweig was that of his great uncle, Adam Rosenzweig (1826–1908).[4]

The affluence of Rosenzweig's family enabled him to pursue variegated intellectual and artistic interests. He studied medicine for two years. In 1907 he shifted to a major in philosophy and history, accompanied by studies in theology, art, literature, and the languages of classical antiquity. In 1912 he received his doctorate. His dissertation was entitled *Hegel and the State*.

The year 1913 was a crucial one in Rosenzweig's life. During the first part of the year, he turned to yet another field of study —jurisprudence. At this time he came into contact with an old friend, Eugen Rosenstock, who was a lecturer on medieval constitutional law at the University of Leipzig.

Rosenzweig was impressed by his friend's interest in theology. Even more important, Rosenzweig was moved by the religious fulfillment Rosenstock had found by his conversion from Judaism to Protestantism.

Rosenstock challenged Rosenzweig to the very core of his being. As a result of his dialogues with Rosenstock, Rosenzweig was led to a critical either/or situation. These dialogues precipitated an existential crisis in Rosenzweig's religious life.

The crisis culminated in an all-night conversation of the two men on July 7, 1913. Rosenstock convinced Rosenzweig that his theological position was untenable. Philosophically, the cultural relativism Rosenzweig espoused at that time was no match for Rosenstock's firm and consistent faith in revelation. With respect to religion, Rosenstock compelled Rosenzweig to acknowledge that his Judaism was "a kind of personal whim, or at best, a pious romantic relic of the posthumous power of a dead great uncle."[5]

Being a serious intellectual, Rosenzweig was not content with such a half-hearted religious identity. He therefore resolved to become baptized as a Christian. Nevertheless, as a student of history, Rosenzweig desired to enter the Christian faith in the way prescribed by the New Testament Epistle to the Hebrews. Accordingly, Rosenzweig decided that he would convert "in the way in which the New Testament Epistle to the Hebrews speaks of the conversion of the entire Jewish people, observing the Torah until the moment of conversion frees him, as in the view of the Church it does, from the duty to perform its mitzvot (commandments)."[6]

In accordance with this procedural condition, Rosenzweig decided to attend High Holy Day services in preparation for his conversion. It has been maintained that Rosenzweig had a religious experience of conversion—but not to Christianity. At the Day of Atonement service in a small synagogue in Berlin, it has been claimed that Rosenzweig underwent a profound spiritual experience. Rosenzweig's disciple, Nahum Glatzer, emphasizes the transformation this alleged experience wrought in Rosenzweig's orientation: "Rosenzweig left the service a changed person. What he had thought he could find in the church only—faith that gives one an orientation in the world—he found on that day in the synagogue."[7]

It is singularly important to note that the nature of the religious experience itself is not described, but only its transforming effect. This reluctance to communicate the most personal, the most private, aspects of his experience, we shall find, is a recurrent theme in Rosenzweig's thought. It is, moreover, perplexing when we consider the significant role that experience will play in his theology. Nevertheless, it is possible to reconstruct, from Rosenzweig's letters, some of the considerations that might have led to his decision to remain a Jew.

Thus, in a letter to his cousin Rudolf Ehrenberg, Rosenzweig contrasted the situation of the Christian who can reach the Father only through Jesus with that of the Jew "who does not have to reach the Father because he is already with him."[8]

Another letter, this time to his mother, and written twelve days after Yom Kippur, is more revealing: "You will have gathered from this letter that I seem to have found the way back about which I had brooded in vain for almost three months."[9]

This letter indicates that Rosenzweig's attendance at High Holy Day services need not be interpreted as a procedural condition for conversion. Rather, Rosenzweig's visit to the synagogue may have been a way of working out his inner conflict concerning his Jewish identity. Nor is it necessarily the case that his decision to remain a Jew was the result of a sudden religious experience on the Day of Atonement. It seems more plausible to suggest, as the letter indicates, that Rosenzweig was contemplating this decision for a period of time prior to the Day of Atonement. And on the Day of Atonement, the cumulative effect of his deliberations was crystallized in his decision to remain a Jew.

The important phrase in the letter is "the way back." In spite of his theological attraction to Christianity, stimulated by Rosenstock, Rosenzweig undoubtedly possessed an inner sense of his own ancestral roots and heritage. Thus the way out of the conflict between Judaism and Christianity was, finally, an effort to find his own way back to Judaism.

The rest of Rosenzweig's life was therefore devoted to elaborating a philosophical and theological rationale to enable the alienated Jew to find a way back to Judaism. Rosenzweig discovered in existentialism a philosophical mode to delineate this "hygiene of return." He developed this conception in his magnum opus *The Star of Redemption,* written on postcards from the trenches in World War I. He further adumbrated his ideas in such essays as "The New Thinking" and "The Builders," and in his voluminous correspondence.

After the war, he devoted his energies to putting his ideas into practice by heading the famous *Lehrhaus* in Frankfurt—an institution devoted to adult Jewish education and designed specifically to inspire intellectually alienated Jews with the will and the ability to rediscover Judaism by returning to the study of its authentic original sources.

Tragically, Rosenzweig was struck by a severe paralyzing illness in 1922. His heroism and his persistence in his writing from this time until his death in 1929 are among the reasons for the supreme position Rosenzweig occupies in contemporary Jewish thought.

Unfortunately, this very "cult" of Rosenzweig has beclouded an objective approach to his work. It is doubly unfortunate since such hero-worship was one of the things that Rosenzweig most detested.

Therefore, an objective appraisal of Rosenzweig's work is a most important desideratum in contemporary Jewish thought. It is to that task that we now turn.

The Starting Point of Rosenzweig's Philosophy

Rosenzweig's thought begins with an affirmation of the irreducible fact of human individuality. This existential starting point is expressed in the following statement: "I really believe that a philosophy, to be adequate, must arise out of thinking that is done from the personal standpoint of the thinker."[10]

From Rosenzweig's personal standpoint, the individual's fear of death is the initial datum to be recognized. It is precisely the fear of death that places human individuality in boldest relief. On the basis of his own confrontation with death in the trenches of World War I, Rosenzweig realized that the consolations of idealistic philosophy—that the individual is part of a larger whole —cannot rob death of its sting. Despite such proffered consolations, Rosenzweig insists: "Man shall not shake off the anguish of earthly life; he shall *remain* in the fear of death."[11]

The starting point of Rosenzweig's philosophy is similar to that of Martin Heidegger. Heidegger, too, maintained that philosophy must begin with the individual's consciousness of his own mortality. Here we find a keynote of the existentialist approach to philosophy: human existence must be understood from within. No appeal to an abstract essence, such as Hegel's Absolute Spirit, can liberate man from his own inner anxieties about death.

Yet man tends to avoid facing the unpleasant reality of his own imminent demise. On reading an obituary notice, man thinks of death as something that happens to others, as an event in the world, as an objective fact but not as a subjective, ever-present possibility. Why, then, do the existentialists seek to remind us of the ever-present possibility not to be?

Such an awareness, Heidegger maintained, is the only path to authenticity. Once I become conscious of the fact that no one can die for me, I also am brought to the authentic consciousness that no one can live for me. I alone am responsible for myself. I can blame neither society nor my environment for my fate.

For Rosenzweig, too, bringing to light the individual's inevitable confrontation with death is the beginning of authentic philosophy. Because each man must die alone, it seems difficult for man to burst the bonds of his lonely subjectivity: "Only the single being can die, and everything mortal is lonely."[12]

So far, Rosenzweig's thought parallels the existentialism of Heidegger. But Rosenzweig is not content to remain with this loneliness. Unlike Heidegger, Rosenzweig's central problem and task was to forge a path out of the forest of human subjectivity. This path, however, had to be based on his own individual human experience, his own personal standpoint. Accordingly, Rosenzweig wrote: "To achieve being objective, the thinker must proceed boldly from his own subjective situation."[13] Rosenzweig's aim, then, was to discover a bridge from subjectivity to objectivity. How could such a bridge be erected? About one thing Rosenzweig was emphatic: it could not be discovered by pure thought. For this reason, Rosenzweig criticized the Absolute Idealism of Hegel.

Rosenzweig's Critique of Hegel

The central thesis of Hegelian philosophy is the unity of thought and being. Hegel's thought was a supreme attempt in the history of philosophy to conceive ultimate reality as truly and concretely knowable. According to Hegel's Absolute Idealism, reality can be understood as the gradual unfolding and development of God or Absolute Spirit in history. In this view, God or Absolute Spirit is the one true reality.

And the Absolute Spirit, being immanent in the historical process, is knowable at each stage of its development by the human mind. Underlying this philosophy are the conceptions that the truth is the whole; that the whole, at any given time, is knowable by the human mind; and that there is one fundamental subject or substance—Absolute Spirit.

Rosenzweig viewed Hegel as the culmination of the philosophic tradition. To Rosenzweig, traditional philosophy is monistic—that is, it seeks to derive reality from a single substance or principle. Explaining Rosenzweig's view of traditional philosophy, Julius Guttmann wrote:

> For traditional philosophy, it is self-evident that the world is a unity and can be derived from a single principle. From the time of Thales, who viewed water as the principle of being, to Hegel, who viewed Spirit as the one true reality, no one challenged this assumption, which goes on to deduce from this principle all of the modes of being.[14]

It is, of course, an oversimplification to conceive of "traditional" philosophy as monistic. For example, Democritus was a pluralist and Plato was a dualist. It therefore appears that Rosenzweig was reacting primarily against Hegel when he criticized the tendency of philosophers to inquire into the essence of things and to "reduce the essence of one thing back to the essence of another."[15]

In his critique of Hegelian essentialism, Rosenzweig followed the positive philosophy of Friedrich Schelling (1775-1854). Schelling's influence on the growth of existentialism is often overlooked. It is important to remember, for example, that Kierkegaard attended his lectures.

Schelling distinguished between two types of philosophy. Negative philosophy was the philosophy of essentialism. He called it negative because it abstracts from man's concrete situation to attain a conception of universals or essences—such as the essence of man or the essence of reality. Negative philosophy, however, does not uniquely characterize what is positively given. To speak of the essence of man, for example, tells us nothing about the fact that a given individual exists in space and time.

Positive philosophy, on the other hand, deals with the individual's actual situation in space and time. Schelling's positive philosophy is thus the forerunner of Rosenzweig's existentialism. And Schelling's method, which he called "higher empiricism"—an effort to describe the concrete experience of human beings—prefigures Rosenzweig's method of absolute empiricism.

To sum up: Reacting against the Absolute Idealism of Hegel, Rosenzweig found in Schelling's positive philosophy a mode of approach congenial to his interest in the individual and his life situation. Disenchanted with the concept of an Absolute Spirit, Rosenzweig preferred to begin more modestly, with man in his naked individuality. Following Schelling, he adopted what he thought to be a truly empirical approach to describe human existential reality—the method of absolute empiricism.

Rosenzweig's Method: Absolute Empiricism

Having disavowed pure thought or rationalism as an approach to reality, Rosenzweig sought an alternative method more in consonance with his existential approach to life. This method he called "absolute empiricism."[16]

By "absolute empiricism," Rosenzweig meant a pure and complete description of experience without conceptual constructions that fit given facts into the Procrustean bed of such preconceived notions.

This method represents an ideal toward which Rosenzweig strived. We shall find that, quite often, Rosenzweig seems trapped by the very conceptual constructions he seeks to avoid. He is quite obviously combatting his own inner predilection toward such conceptual constructions. What is singularly interesting, however, is the development of Rosenzweig's thought after he wrote *The Star of Redemption*. As his thought progresses, we find that he himself becomes more liberated from conceptualism and more capable of placing greater trust in the deliverance of his own experience. Moreover, as he becomes more immersed in Jewish sources, he becomes more interested in finding a praxis for life rather than a philosophical superstructure to underpin it.

In order to achieve his aim of an absolutely empirical philosophy, Rosenzweig relied on what he considered to be the sound common sense of a healthy individual. Instead of inquiring into the essence of things, the healthy individual is content to accept the facts as they actually are. For example, a philosopher seeking the essence of things would tend to view a chair as a manifestation of a metaphysical principle such as "matter." In contrast, Rosenzweig writes: "Common sense is content to know that a chair is a chair, and is unconcerned with the possibility that it may, actually, be something quite different."[17]

Second, the individual of sound common sense does not seek a universal synthesis. He is content to acknowledge plurality and multiplicity without striving to reduce them to a spurious unity.

Third, the individual of sound common sense is interested in the relation of things to each other—what they do and what is done to them. He is more concerned with the actual observable interaction of elements than with the phantom of unfathomable essences.

Fourth, the individual of sound common sense realizes that his knowledge is bound to time. Rosenzweig explains:

> The new thinking, like the age old thinking of sound common sense, knows that it cannot have cognition independent of time—though heretofore one of philosophy's boasts has been that it is able to do this very thing. One cannot begin a conversation with the end. . . . At every moment, cognition is bound to that moment and cannot make its past not passed, or its future not coming.[18]

In this passage, Rosenzweig is arguing that one cannot philosophize *sub specie aeternitatis*—under the aspect of eternity. Rather, a philosophy of sound common sense must remain close to the patterns of our actual experience, reflecting our daily temporal existence.

Again, it must be emphasized that the man of sound common sense with his method of absolute empiricism is an ideal which Rosenzweig projects and toward which he was working. He himself, as we shall see, fell prey to this very tendency to philosophize *sub specie aeternitatis,* relying very heavily on the concept of eternity in *The Star of Redemption.*

Rosenzweig's method of absolute empiricism, outlined here, bears a remarkable similarity to the radical empiricism of the American pragmatist William James. James, too, emphasized plurality and relationships rather than substance and essences. James insisted that to know something does not mean to know its essence but rather its function—how it acts and how it is acted upon.

James also emphasized the temporal nature of reality—that reality is a process, like a flowing stream, that cannot be fully captured and encapsulated by our mental concepts and constructions.

The principal target of James's criticism was also Hegelian philosophy. Thus, interestingly enough, the chief adversary in the philosophical drama of both Franz Rosenzweig and William James was the Hegelian Absolute. Unlike James, however, Rosenzweig's struggle with Hegel was more pronounced. Steeped in this Germanic mode of philosophizing, Rosenzweig, in his early thought, did not fully liberate himself from the Hegelian tendency to utilize conceptual construction. Thus, in *The Star of Redemption,* Rosenzweig utilizes a triadic arrangement of concepts, reminiscent of Hegel's tendency to use such triads as thesis, antithesis, and synthesis.

In short, Rosenzweig was a man of his time striving to liberate himself from the prevailing Hegelian philosophy of his age. Let us now follow Rosenzweig in this attempt.

The First Triad: God, the World, and Man

Rosenzweig's aim, as we have seen, is to develop a philosophy based on pure experience, on the facts as they actually are. What are these facts?

Rosenzweig is quite definitive on this point. The experience of the man of sound common sense, Rosenzweig maintains, discloses the presence of three elements of reality—man, the world, and God: "But experience, no matter how deeply it probes, will find only the human in man, the worldly in the world, and the godly in God."[19]

At this point, the most pressing question concerning Rosenzweig's thought arises: Why just these elements? Why not others?

A totally absolute empiricism, like that of William James, is open to an endless plurality of elements. Why, then, does Rosenzweig confine himself to just these three?

A preliminary answer to this question has already been suggested by Rosenzweig's tendency, reminiscent of Hegel, to think in terms of triads. But why this particular triad?

Again, it is important to note that Rosenzweig was steeped in German philosophy. Undoubtedly, he had thoroughly studied the philosophy of Immanuel Kant (1724–1804). Kant maintained that there are three "Ideas" which are mental representations of the unconditioned—of that which can be posited but whose essence cannot be known. These "Ideas" are regulative principles representative of the limits of possible experience. Kant held that there are three such "Ideas"—the soul, the world, and God.

It has been suggested that the philosophical basis of Rosenzweig's three elements is precisely this Kantian triad of concepts.[20] The only change Rosenzweig introduces is his substitution of "man" for "soul." And the reason for his change is precisely his effort to free himself from a philosophical abstraction such as "soul" and to replace it with the existential conception of man.

This hypothesis, I believe, has a great deal of merit. According to the Kantian philosophy, the essence of the soul, the world, and God cannot be known. So, too, according to Rosenzweig, the essence of the three elements cannot be known: "So far as their essence is concerned, God, the world, and man are all equally transcendent in regard to each other, and as to their reality, we cannot say what they are, only—but that belongs to a later chapter."[21]

Why would Rosenzweig posit three elements—God, world, and man—which cannot be known in themselves? The most plausible hypothesis is that he had in mind Kant's three "Ideas" and also the Kantian conception of the *Ding an Sich,* or thing-in-itself, which cannot be known by pure reason. Every philosophy needs a set of basic axioms or presuppositions. Being steeped in German philosophy, Rosenzweig more than likely utilized these conceptions as his presuppositions.

The problem is that this is hardly an empirical approach. Attempting to resolve this problem, N. N. Glatzer, one of Rosenzweig's leading disciples, admits that God, man, and the world are conceptual constructions, but are used by Rosenzweig as auxiliary concepts: "These are clearly conceptual constructions, a method from which Rosenzweig could not free himself, though he considered them to be mere auxiliary concepts."[22]

Glatzer has explained to the present writer what is meant by auxiliary concepts. To Rosenzweig, Glatzer explains, conceptual constructions were like crutches which an injured man uses until he learns how to walk on his own. Thus, in his book *Understanding the Sick and the Healthy*[23] (written in July 1921 shortly after *The Star of Redemption* had been published), Rosenzweig compared the speculative philosopher to a paralytic patient being cured by common sense and pure experience. This book is indispensable to an understanding of Rosenzweig's thought, for it provides a penetrating insight into Rosenzweig's polemic against speculative philosophy, his struggle against his own tendency in this direction, and his effort to reach what he considered to be the healthy plateau of common sense.

To summarize: Rosenzweig employs the terms God, world, and man as conceptual constructions, as aids, as tools with which to embark on his philosophical odyssey. But his ideal was a phi-

losophy of pure experience—which he considered to be the outlook of the man of sound common sense. Whether Rosenzweig
ever achieved this ideal—and whether this ideal is worth achiev-
ing—is a question which remains to be explored. Meanwhile,
we turn to Rosenzweig's path to this ideal—the new thinking.

The New Thinking

We have seen that, according to Rosenzweig, nothing can be
said about the essence of the three elements—God, the world, and
man. But we have also noted Rosenzweig's hint that although
their essence cannot be known, something can be said about
them. How can we speak about these elements if we do not know
their essence?

An analogy will help us to understand Rosenzweig's answer
to this question. When I have a conversation with another person, I do not have to know his essence in advance, to communicate with him. In order to communicate, what is primarily necessary is my earnest concern for the other. And if I really want
to establish communication in depth, an attitude of love for the
other person becomes important.

Rosenzweig places great stress on the concept of speech, of
dialogue. Although man cannot know the essence of God or the
world, he can enter into dialogue with them. This is the meaning of the new thinking: "In the new thinking, the method of
speech replaces the method of thinking maintained in all earlier
philosophies."[24]

How does speech differ from thought? Quite simply, thought
is a monologue, whereas speech is a dialogue. A dialogue is
characterized by risk, uncertainty, and adventure.

As Rosenzweig writes: "I do not know in advance what the
other person will say to me, because I do not even know what
I myself am going to say. . . . All this is quite beyond the comprehension of the thinking thinker, while it is valid for the
speaking thinker."[25]

Here we find the stirrings of a major trend in contemporary
Jewish thought—the philosophy of dialogue. The philosophy of
dialogue did not begin with Martin Buber's conception of I and
Thou. Nor did it begin with Rosenzweig. What, then, is the historical background of the new thinking—the dialogic philosophy? The following statement is a concise summary:

> The new thinking centered at first in the rediscovery of
> Feuerbach's *Principles of the Philosophy of the Future* and its
> thesis that the basis of truth is not the self-consciousness of an
> ego, but the interrelationship between Thou and I. . . . The
> new thinking was a phenomenon characterizing a whole genera-
> tion deeply impressed by the bankruptcy of the bourgeois-
> Christian world and the emptiness of the academic routine.[26]

Thus, according to the new thinking espoused by Rosenzweig,
what happens between people is more important than the solitary reflections of a scholar sitting in his ivory tower.[27] It is only
by listening to the other person that I can be illumined.

Transposing the new thinking into theological terms, its thesis
is that only by opening myself to the revelation of the Supreme
Other, can my soul be illumined. It is only by relationship
to an Eternal Thou that I can become I. Thus, dialogue with
the other person becomes the model for the relationship between man and God. It is to that relationship, as conceived by
Rosenzweig, that we now turn.

The Second Triad: Creation, Revelation, and Redemption

What, then, can be said about the relationship between the
three elements: God, man, and the world? In answer to this
question, Rosenzweig wrote: "God, man and the world reveal
themselves only in their relations to one another, that is, in
creation, revelation, and redemption."[28]

Rosenzweig here is elaborating a dialogic Biblical theology.
He maintains that it is precisely this relationship between the
elements that is unique in Judaism. To the Greek pagan consciousness, the three elements exist in isolation from each other
—the cosmos, the Olympian gods, and the lonely tragic hero.
The uniqueness of the Bible is that the three elements are
viewed as related.

The relationship between the world and God is signified by
the term creation: the relation is that of Creator to the created.
Rosenzweig is not asserting creation as a scientific fact. He is
not concerned with theories of cosmology. What he means by
creation is the continual dependence of the world upon God
for its support. Thus, creation is for Rosenzweig a continuous
activity of God, an incipient revelation of God to which the
world responds. Accordingly, Rosenzweig writes:

> What is creation from God's point of view can only mean, from the world's, the bursting forth of the consciousness of its creatureliness, its being created. . . . This is creature consciousness, the consciousness not of having once been created but of being everlastingly creature; as such it is something thoroughly objective, an authentic revelation.[29]

Rosenzweig's point is that whereas creation is "past for God,"[30] it is an everlasting present reality, akin to revelation, for the world. It is difficult to determine whether Rosenzweig means this statement as metaphor or as reality, as poetry or as truth.

As in so much of contemporary Jewish thought, Rosenzweig simply does not state how he means these assertions to be taken. Is he a panpsychist? That is, does he really believe that the world is animated, "conscious" of its creaturehood? When he says that the world is "everlastingly creature," is he asserting a doctrine of the eternity of matter? And note the epistemological audacity involved in the claim that what is present for the world is past for God!

A reply to such objections might be that Rosenzweig has moved from philosophy to theology—or, more exactly, that he stands between philosophy and theology. Yet the theologian, as well as the philosopher, owes the reader a clarification which is impossible to receive from such opaque pronouncements.

More interesting is Rosenzweig's view that creation is an incipient revelation, that creation gives rise to revelation. By this, Rosenzweig means that man's consciousness of his own creaturehood leads him to an awareness of God's love which, for Rosenzweig, is the essential meaning of revelation.

Revelation is the most important concept in Rosenzweig's theology. Rosenzweig found in revelation the bridge he was seeking from subjectivity to objectivity. As he wrote: "The theological concept of revelation must provide the bridge from the most subjective to the most objective."[31]

Revelation also supplies the bridge from philosophy to theology. Rosenzweig maintained that theology completes philosophy by providing the objectivity that philosophy, by itself, cannot obtain.

We noted previously that transcendence of human subjectivity is the key aim of Rosenzweig's thought. For him, revelation is the vehicle of transcendence.

Revelation, for Rosenzweig, denotes the relationship between God and man. The subject is dealt with in Book Two of *The Star of Redemption*. The full title of Book Two offers us a key to understand this concept: "Revelation or the Ever Renewed Birth of the Soul." And the opening words of Book Two, taken from The Song of Songs, provide us with the focus of Rosenzweig's theory of revelation: "Love is as strong as death." For Rosenzweig, revelation is the assurance of God's love, and that love gives birth to the human soul.

In order to understand this concept of revelation, let us focus first on the model of human love. Let us note some features of love.

First, the word love is virtually impossible to define. It connotes concern, care, devotion, and interest in the other as an other. All of these words describe. They do not capture the essence of love. The essence of love can be captured only in dialogue. In this private moment, love is something that happens to the two lovers—something private, incommunicable.

Second, an individual cannot exist without love. It is an established fact that an infant can die because of total absence of love. Moreover, experiments in sensory deprivation show that a person cannot maintain his sanity without contact with another.

Third, love enables individuals to surmount many obstacles in life which otherwise would crush them. The following life situation illustrates this point: A woman is about to enter the hospital for a major operation. Her husband has just lost his job. Their financial resources are virtually depleted.

Yet her feeling of her husband's love sustains her, when she realizes that there are many people in worse situations because their lives are without love. Thus, she says: "Life without love is the only real tragedy, for love gives me my sense of self-worth."

In this phenomenology of love in human life—its private character, its expression only in dialogue between lover and beloved, its power to sustain the beloved—are the human experiences which can serve as a model to illustrate Rosenzweig's theological concept of revelation as love between God and man.

First, Rosenzweig insists on the incommunicability of revelation to a third party. Just as the love between two lovers cannot be communicated to a third party, so the human experience of

God "is incommunicable, and he who speaks of it makes himself ridiculous."[32]

For this reason, Rosenzweig avoids attributing content to God's alleged revelation to the Jewish people at Sinai: "This revelation is certainly not law-giving. It is only this: Revelation. The primary content of revelation is revelation itself. 'He came down' (on Sinai)—this already concludes the revelation. 'He spoke' is the beginning of interpretation, and certainly 'I am.' "[33]

Rosenzweig here is advocating a nonpropositional view of revelation. What is revealed is not a series of statements or propositions issuing forth from a Divine source. What is revealed is simply God's love or God's presence, which is inexpressible. It cannot be communicated to a third party. Yet Rosenzweig believed that such experiences happened and continue to happen.

Second, man cannot exist without the love of God. Revelation gives birth to the human soul. Rosenzweig depicts man, before revelation, as dumb and mute. Revelation gives man the power to speak. As Rosenzweig writes: "Under the love of God, the mute self came of age as eloquent soul. This occurrence we had recognized as revelation."[34]

Third, God's love confers the individual's identity and sense of self-worth. Rosenzweig emphasizes the Biblical verse, "I have called thee by name: thou art Mine."[35]

To Rosenzweig, this verse shows that God initiates dialogue when he calls man by name. N. N. Glatzer has suggested to the present writer that what Rosenzweig is saying here is more than a metaphor but less than literal truth. What Rosenzweig means to imply, Glatzer suggests, is that human life is not an accidental collocation of atoms. Rather, human individuality has meaning, because it is a gift conferred by God.

Rosenzweig's theory of revelation is the most powerful aspect of his theology. It is aesthetically moving, conveying a feeling of the overpowering majesty of God and the depths of the human soul. Furthermore, it raises a very important problem: Does theology require an Archimedean point, an assumed or posited absolute standpoint beyond man with which to begin?

It is important also not to lose sight of other essential questions. Emotionally appealing as Rosenzweig's theory is, is it true? Must we, in our search for truth, abandon ourselves to an objective referent taken completely on faith or revelation? And how does Rosenzweig's conception of God's love fare when taken in conjunction with the problem of evil? Does it die the death of a thousand qualifications? And, most important, by positing revelation as an objective fact, has Rosenzweig abandoned the existentialist orientation with which he began? These questions will be discussed in the final section of this chapter.

Let us now consider the third concept of Rosenzweig's triad: redemption. Revelation instills in man the hope of redemption. When man becomes conscious of God's love, he experiences the love of his neighbor as a commandment. Love of God expresses itself in love for one's neighbor.

Rosenzweig sees implicit in man's love of his neighbor an ensoulment or vitalizing of the world. Love, for Rosenzweig, not only endows the other person with spirit. It ensouls the world. This ensoulment of the world is its process of redemption. Thus Rosenzweig writes that "the world . . . becomes animated with its own soul—in redemption."[36]

We have seen previously that, for Rosenzweig, the world is already vitalized by God's creation. By this he meant that the world is ever growing toward life. Redemption is thus already implicit in creation. Creation is the initial ensoulment of the world. Redemption is the complete ensoulment of the world by God.

What is man's role in redemption? The process of redemption is, in part, a reciprocal relation between man and world. Human deeds of love redeem the world. But the world could not be redeemed if it did not already possess *ab initio* a growing tendency to be animated through love.

But in the final act of redemption, the primary, indeed the sole power, is God: "In the redemption of the world by man, of man by means of the world, God redeems himself. Man and world disappear in the redemption, but God perfects himself."[37]

Rosenzweig here appears to have come full circle. He began by inveighing against the tendency of philosophers to assert one monistic all-embracing reality. Now he envisages the ultimate goal of redemption to be the perfection of God alone.

In answer to such a challenge, Rosenzweig would reply that his conception is different from that of the idealistic philosophers in the following way:

> Only in redemption, God becomes the One and All. . . . We had intentionally broken up the All of the philosophers. Here in

the blinding midnight sun of the consummated redemption it has, at last, yea, at the very last, coalesced into the One.[38]

We see, therefore, that Rosenzweig never really abandoned the unifying monistic tendency of idealism. His point of departure is that he envisages unity as the goal of the redemptive process and not as initially given. He has, furthermore, substituted a mystical concept of all-embracing unity for a philosophical one.

The question now arises: How does Rosenzweig view the role of the Jewish people in the redemptive process?

It is to that question which we now turn.

Conception of the Jewish People

Rosenzweig refers to the Jewish people as the eternal people. By this he means that the Jewish people exists beyond history, that "this people is denied a life in time for the sake of life in eternity."[39]

The question thus arises: What does Rosenzweig mean by eternity? And why does he assert this strange thesis of a meta-historical existence of the Jewish people?

These questions are dealt with by Alexander Altmann in an essay entitled "Franz Rosenzweig on History."[40] According to Altmann, Rosenzweig was troubled by the question: What is the role of Judaism in a world where Christianity was the motive force?

Rosenzweig works out his answer to this problem by conceding that Christianity in fact does play the major role in history because its task is to convert the pagan world.

But he affirms Judaism by placing it outside history and by relegating history to a provisional, intermediate, pre-eschatological status. Thus, Rosenzweig maintains that "it is the task of the Jew to sacrifice life in this world for the purpose of testifying to the messianic goal of history. Judaism, he repeatedly declares, lives and has its being in the *eschaton*."[41] Thus, what appeared to be Judaism's weakness is transformed by Rosenzweig into its strength: the significance of Judaism is that it lies outside history and represents the eschatological end or goal beyond history.

Eternity is precisely this dimension beyond history, beyond time. But, paradoxically, eternity is also a present reality for the Jew. Reflecting on the blessing in which God is praised for having implanted eternal life in our midst, Rosenzweig wrote:

"Eternity is a future which, without ceasing to be a future, is nonetheless present."[42] By this he meant that the eschatological end must be expected at any moment; it is a tomorrow that could equally be a today; this is its eternity. And the function of the Jewish people is to live in this dimension, testifying to eternity by its observance of the holidays and the Sabbath as symbolic of eternity, and anticipating the eternal kingdom of God.

We can now understand why Rosenzweig held this peculiar conception of the meta-historical existence of the Jewish people. He was deeply troubled by the fact that Christianity played a more significant role in history than Judaism. Therefore, he aimed to clearly differentiate Judaism from Christianity. Yet, at the same time, he wished to maintain that both Judaism and Christianity are facets of the truth, that both Judaism and Christianity have a significant role to play in *Heilsgeschichte*, in sacred history. And he felt that he could achieve this aim by maintaining that Christianity is the eternal way whereas Judaism represents eternal life.

In other words, whereas the Jew has his being outside of history anticipating redemption, the Christian is forever on the way. The Christian is born a pagan and must become a Christian by baptism. And once having become a Christian, his task is to spread Christianity to the pagan world.

However, Rosenzweig does not consistently maintain the meta-historical character of the Jewish people. Thus he speaks of the Jewish people as a blood-community: "Only a community based on common blood feels the warrant of eternity warm in its veins even now. . . . It does not have to hire the services of the spirit; the natural propagation of the body guarantees its eternity."[43]

This emphasis on a "community of blood" vitiates Rosenzweig's prior stress on the spirituality of Jewish existence. And the "natural propagation of the body" is surely a historical process. This clearly contradicts the assertion of the metahistorical existence of the Jewish people.

And this concept of the nonhistorical character of Jewish existence, taken by itself, fails to do justice to the historical reality of the Jewish people. Here, however, it is important to recognize that Rosenzweig's conception of the metahistorical existence of the Jewish people was also intended as a polemic against Hegel. Rosenzweig's aim was not only to distinguish

Judaism. from Christianity. He also intended to develop a view of Jewish existence as far removed as possible from Hegel's conception of history as the self-realization of God. To accomplish this end, he tried, albeit unsuccessfully, to remove God and the Jewish people from the sphere of history.

In the light of subsequent history (i.e., the Holocaust and the State of Israel), Rosenzweig's conception of the Jewish people may seem to most people to be farfetched, to say the least.

It is, however, unfair to evaluate his view in the light of the subsequent momentous collective tragedy of the Jewish people and its restoration to its land through historical, secular effort. For this reason Rosenzweig has been called the last great theologian of the Diaspora.

Nonetheless, even taken on its own terms, in its own historical context, Rosenzweig's conception of existence as divided primarily between the Jew and the Christian is parochial at best. He also writes about Islam in *The Star of Redemption* but ignores the Far Eastern religions. From the point of view of comparative religion, Rosenzweig's conception of Judaism despite Christianity is myopic. And his conceptions of redemption and eternity in *The Star of Redemption* are castles in the air built by the very flight from experience against which he was struggling.

Attitude Toward Jewish Law

In his later writings, however, Rosenzweig does descend to the plain of pure commonsense experience which was the ultimate goal that he set for himself. We have already noted his polemic against abstract philosophy in *Understanding the Sick and the Healthy,* where the speculative philosopher is compared to a paralytic patient who learns how to walk without the crutches of conceptual constructions.

Significantly, the Hebrew word for Jewish law, *Halacha,* comes from a root meaning to walk. It is therefore no coincidence that Rosenzweig "found his peace in the practice of *Halacha* where the enthusiasm of Divine love is translated into the word of daily prayer, the longing for salvation is resolved in the sober conformation to the *Mitzvot,* and the ecstasy of religious experience is silenced by the commanding word at Sinai and the scrupulous interpretations of the Sages."[44]

Rosenzweig's attitude toward Jewish law is expressed in his essay "The Builders," which was addressed to Martin Buber. Buber denied the authority of Jewish law, arguing that revelation is never a formulation of law. It was Buber's contention that "it is only through man in his self-contradiction that revelation becomes legislation."[45]

In response to Buber, Rosenzweig wrote: "For me, too, God is not a Law-giver, But he commands."[46] The task of the Jew of today, Rosenzweig argued, is to transform law into commandment. Whereas Buber maintained that the Jew addresses God only through a spontaneous I-Thou encounter, Rosenzweig believed that the Jew addresses God in the individual commandment: "Only in the commandment can the voice of him who commands be heard."[47]

Rosenzweig's major concern was to delineate the way back to Judaism for the alienated Jew. For him, this way back necessarily involved the law. In his later writings, he advocated a pragmatic, existential approach to the law—namely, that the law can be experienced as commandment only by practice, by observance. As he states pithily: "For we know it only when we *do*."[48] In other words, we can understand the law only when we enact a religious observance. The test of the law is the feeling of being commanded which it elicits in the individual Jew.

Does Rosenzweig offer any criteria by which the Jew of today can decide which laws are valid for him? Rosenzweig maintained that the original intention of the law ought to be considered in conjunction with the individual's ability or inner power to enact it. Finally, then, for Rosenzweig, observance of the law is a matter of inner personal decision. But this decision must be undertaken in deep seriousness and with a profound sense of responsibility.

Rosenzweig followed this path in his life. He worked toward more and more commitment to Jewish law. It is said that when asked whether or not he put on *tefillin,* he replied, "Not yet." He was striving to ascend to this rung in his "ladder of observance."

We see, therefore, that commitment to Jewish law took on a major importance in Rosenzweig's life. Here he found the way and the path to symbolically walk in the light of his own inner experience of God's command without the crutches of the conceptual constructions of philosophy. This was, for him, the ultimate path of common sense, of pure experience which he had sought throughout his career. Here Franz Rosenzweig finally discovered fulfillment in the temporal and the everyday. Not accidentally, the closing words of *The Star of Redemption* are "into life." Having grappled with eternity, he sought to experience life. That experience of life, he found, in part, in the *Halacha* as a way of life.

Rosenzweig's commitment to Jewish law placed him in marked contrast to Martin Buber. Why didn't Buber share this commitment? How was his attitude to the law shaped by his philosophy? These and other questions we shall examine in the next chapter on Martin Buber.

Critique of Rosenzweig's Thought

Rosenzweig undoubtedly possessed a brilliant and creative mind, a mind exploding with ideas. Unfortunately, his tragic death at a young age prevented him from presenting his thoughts in a clear and precise manner.

This is especially obvious as we turn to our first criterion: consistency. For those who seek to find a virtue in inconsistency, Rosenzweig would qualify as a saint. Even one of his most ardent followers and disciples, Ernst Simon, admits the inconsistency in Rosenzweig's thought:

> Rosenzweig has been called an existentialist, and there does indeed seem to be an inconsistency—shall we say a creative inconsistency?—between his method—of existentialism—and his ultimate aim—of loyalty to traditional Judaism.[49]

Rosenzweig, we have repeatedly noted, aimed to develop an existential Jewish theology as a rationale to help the alienated Jew find his way back to Judaism. This existential approach is clearly evident in Rosenzweig's approach to the law. In his essay "The Builders," we have seen that Rosenzweig advocated an eclectic, existential approach to the commandments resting ultimately on the personal sense of "being commanded" of the individual Jew. Such an approach, it can be readily seen, could lead to religious anarchy. This by no means implies that Orthodoxy is the only alternative. Rather, what is missing in Rosenzweig's discussion are clear criteria of Jewish observance related to the collective historic experience of the Jewish people. And we can well understand why this lacuna exists in Rosenzweig's thought. Although he himself attained, to some degree, the commonsense experience of life he sought, he more than likely continued to espouse the theory of the metahistorical conception of the Jewish people. And eternity, of course, cannot provide criteria in time.

This, however, is not the only inconsistency in Rosenzweig's thought. His goal was an existential Jewish theology "into life." But, as we have seen, because he was so steeped in the conceptual constructions of Germanic philosophy, he never really achieved this goal.

In *The Star of Redemption,* he begins on an existential note with the individual's fear of death. But once he starts to utilize his series of triadic concepts, his thought becomes more and more detached from human experience. In his later writings, he reaches the level of experience he sought; but these writings, insightful as they are, do not, as a whole, develop a sustained argument for an existential theology. Had he been granted life, perhaps Rosenzweig would have accomplished this goal of an existential Jewish theology.

As we turn to our second criterion, empirical reference, we must pause to reflect on those areas where Rosenzweig does illumine human experience. Here it is important to discuss the theory of revelation. Many people have had religious experiences. The nature of such experiences has been described in William James's classic work *Varieties of Religious Experience.* One essential element in such experiences is "a sense of objective presence."

On reading Rosenzweig, one senses that he has had such an experience. In contradistinction to James, Rosenzweig does not describe the experience itself. He insists on its incommunicability to a third party. But there is another reason for his silence. He tells us that he refrains from such descriptions because he does not wish to "run within striking distance of the psychologist's knife."[50] That is, Rosenzweig does not want to allow the psychologist the opportunity to classify (like William James), dissect, or reduce the experience to a psychological rather than a metaphysical reality.

I can understand Rosenzweig's point, but I cannot agree. If one is secure in one's religious experience, one should not be reluctant to communicate it. Furthermore, how can Rosenzweig claim an absolutely empirical approach and at the same time refuse to discuss the experience itself?

Finally, Rosenzweig's insistence on the incommunicability of revelation to a third party is at variance with much of the experience of the Jewish people. What has been the centuries-old experience of the Jewish people if not the ability to communicate "these words" to one's children, to the community at large, and even to the world? By making revelation so private, Rosenzweig vitiates the very possibility of spreading love unless each and every individual Jew directly receives revelations from God.

Nevertheless, his theory of revelation is suggestive and poses some interesting questions. First, can we make any sense out of the assertion that God's love sustains the world and inspires man? One might reason as follows: In order for an infant to survive, he needs love. By analogy, the existence of human life on this planet presupposes a loving, sustaining God who gives life. Individual life cannot exist without Divine love. It is this kind of developed argument that Rosenzweig needed to at least present an existential theology and an existential argument for transcendence—namely, only God can answer man's need for an ultimate object of love.

A counterargument would examine the concept of God's love. What empirical state of affairs would have to exist to support the statement "God loves man"? Is God's love compatible with death by cancer? Is this person under the loving care of God? Or does this state of affairs cause us to endlessly qualify the meaning of God's love to signify His inscrutable will? One wonders if Rosenzweig would have held to the concept of God's love had he lived through the Holocaust.

It is this exchange of argument and counterargument that is missing in Rosenzweig's thought. It is my belief that only by the dialectic of statement and counterstatement, only by the clash of arguments, can a real existential truth be won. After the counterargument, what still remains is the human longing for an ultimate Divine object of love. This need is the existential datum that must be recognized.

The second question posed is whether a theology needs an Archimedean fixed point of absolute truth, affirmed by faith in revelation.

I can understand the need, but I cannot affirm such a fixed point. I believe that the human mind must never be closed to inquiry. It must always remain open to new discovery and insight.

It appears, therefore, that Rosenzweig never entirely abandoned his quest for an absolute truth. Despite his critique of

Hegel, Rosenzweig remained under the spell of the search for absolutes. Thus, Rosenzweig sought to develop a method of absolute empiricism.

We recall that Rosenzweig meant by "absolute empiricism" a pure and complete description of experience without conceptual constructions. Paradoxically, this aim is most unempirical. There is no such thing as a pure and complete description of experience without conceptual constructions. We are forced into them by the very nature of our sense equipment; otherwise we could not distinguish differences in space, depth, or the character of individual objects. Thus, when Rosenzweig says that common sense knows that a chair is a chair, this is not empiricism. An infant looking at a chair would see something but would not know that it's a chair. We can now more readily understand why Rosenzweig never really liberated himself from the conceptual constructions of Hegelian thought. What Rosenzweig sought—namely, an absolute empiricism—is impossible in principle. There is no such thing as pure experience without conceptual construction. Operating with this impossible aim, Rosenzweig had to employ conceptual constructions. Failing to recognize the conceptual elements in ordinary sense experience, he employed Hegelian triads such as God, the world, and man to unify experience. If Rosenzweig had sought merely empiricism, and not "absolute" empiricism, he doubtless would have avoided many unnecessary problems.

What, then, is the pragmatic value of Rosenzweig's thought? It is difficult indeed to assess the pragmatic effect of a concept such as metahistory. As imaginative as this concept is, it must be said that it is hardly consistent with existentialism. The Jewish people as an existential reality apparently did not appeal to Rosenzweig. He does not do justice either to the reality of the Jewish people or to the evolutionary character of Judaism. His inability to accept the Jews as an existential group was probably due to his acquiescence in the submerged state of the Jewish people living in a Christian world. Unable to tolerate the existential Jewish reality, Rosenzweig projects the Jews as an eternal people, beyond time and history. This is eschatology. It is not existential theology. In order to produce an existential Jewish theology, Rosenzweig would have had to apply the same existential categories to the Jewish people as he did to the lonely individual.

The pragmatic value of Rosenzweig's thought lies chiefly in his life, his quest for an existential theology, and in his interpretation of Jewish law. His thought affords some fascinating insights but insufficient illumination. He is most empirical when he writes about the fear of death, most inspiring when he writes on revelation, and most pragmatic when he writes on Jewish law. Yet there is not enough sustained argument to supply the rationale, which the intellectually alienated Jew seeks, to find his way back to Judaism.

In summary, the example of Rosenzweig's life and his own return to Judaism provides a better rationale than his philosophy and theology. The pragmatic value of the thought lies in the man who wrote it. The responsibility for the development of his ideas lies in the hands of his followers. In this chapter, I have tried to show the kind of development that is needed to attain this goal of an existential Jewish theology.

NOTES

1. William Barrett, *Irrational Man* (Garden City, N.Y.: Doubleday and Co., Inc., 1958), p. 3.
2. Editors of Commentary, *The Condition of Jewish Belief* (New York: The Macmillan Co., 1967), p. 4.
3. Letter to Eugen Rosenstock in Nahum Glatzer. *Franz Rosenzweig: His Life and Thought* (New York: Schocken Books, Inc., 1973), p. 135.
4. *Ibid.*, p. xxxvi.
5. Letter of Eugen Rosenstock to Franz Rosenzweig, in Bernard Martin, ed., *Great 20th Century Jewish Philosophers* (New York: The Macmillan Co., 1970), p. 121.
6. *Idem.*
7. *Franz Rosenzweig*, p. xviii.
8. *Ibid.*, p. xix.
9. *Great 20th Century Jewish Philosophers*, p. 122.
10. *Franz Rosenzweig*, p. 179.
11. *Ibid.*, p. 181.
12. *Idem.*
13. *Ibid.*, p. 179.
14. Julius Guttman, *Philosophies of Judaism*, trans. David W. Silverman (New York: Holt, Rinehart and Winston, 1964), pp. 368–369.
15. *Franz Rosenzweig*, p. 191.
16. *Ibid.*, p. 207.
17. *Ibid.*, p. 191.
18. *Ibid.*, pp. 196–197.
19. *Ibid.*, p. 192.
20. N. Rotenstreich, "The Basis of Franz Rosenzweig's Philosophy," *Al Franz*

Rosenzweig, bimlot Shanah li-fetirato (Hebrew) (Hillel, Jerusalem, 5713), p. 83.

21. *Franz Rosenzweig*, p. 193.

22. Franz Rosenzweig, *The Star of Redemption*, trans. William Hallo (New York: Holt, Rinehart and Winston, 1970), p. xiv.

23. Edited and introduced by N. N. Glatzer (New York: The Noonday Press, 1953).

24. *Franz Rosenzweig*, p. 198.

25. *Ibid.*, p. 199.

26. Karl Lowith, "M. Heidegger and F. Rosenzweig: A Postscript to Being and Time," in *Nature, History and Existentialism* (Northwestern University Press, 1966), p. 53.

27. See Glatzer's Introduction to *Understanding the Sick and the Healthy*, p. 9.

28. *Franz Rosenzweig*, p. 198.

29. *The Star of Redemption*, p. 120.

30. *Ibid.*, p. 119.

31. *Franz Rosenzweig*, p. 209.

32. *Ibid.*, p. 243.

33. Franz Rosenzweig, *On Jewish Learning*, ed. N. N. Glatzer (New York: Schocken Books, 1955), p. 118.

34. *The Star of Redemption*, p. 198.

35. Isaiah 43:1.

36. *The Star of Redemption*, p. 239.

37. *Ibid.*, p. 238.

38. *Ibid.*

39. *Ibid.*, p. 304.

40. In *Studies in Religious Philosophy and Mysticism* (Ithaca: Cornell University Press, 1969, pp. 275–291.

41. *Ibid.*, pp. 281, 283.

42. *The Star of Redemption*, p. 224.

43. *Ibid.*, p. 299.

44. *On Jewish Learning*, p. 23.

45. *Ibid.*, p. 111.

46. *Ibid.*, p. 116.

47. *Ibid.*, p. 122.

48. *Idem.*

49. Akiva Ernst Simon, "On Franz Rosenzweig," *PETAHIM*, Bi-Monthly Journal of Jewish Thought, No. 4 (14) September, 1970, p. 8.

50. *Franz Rosenzweig*, p. 243.

4 Martin Buber: Can God Be Encountered?

Among the more popular forms of psychotherapy today are encounter groups. These groups consist of a number of people who meet to ventilate their feelings under the direction of a therapist. Through mutual honesty, self-disclosure, and the revelation of existential truth, they seek to be healed. They have come to the group out of a realization that they cannot be healed alone. They need one another. They seek healing through encounter, through direct, open, personal relationship.

Encounters have thus become fashionable in our time. But encounter is not only a psychological term. It also has a theological significance. And this significance is due in large measure to the philosophy of Martin Buber. Martin Buber's conception of the I-Thou relationship gave rise to a major trend in both Jewish and Christian theology—namely, the theology of encounter.

According to the theology of encounter, we can talk to God but not about God; we can know God through meeting but not through ratiocination. Or, to put it in Buber's graphic terms, God can be addressed but not expressed.

A basic assumption lies behind this theology. This assumption is that a relationship with God is similar to a relationship with another person. There are, according to Buber, two ways of knowing another person.

The first way Buber refers to as an "I-It" relationship. There are many things I may know about a person—his height, his weight, his occupation. This is knowledge by description, knowledge *about* the person. But despite what I may know about the person, I do not know *him*.

I do not know him because, as Buber would say, I have not entered into this relationship with "my whole being." This means that a part of me, let us say my intellect, is all the while evaluating, analyzing, dissecting the other. I do not fully trust him. I am, so to speak, held in reserve. The other person, too, may likewise be held in check. Realizing my restraint, he, too, is reluctant to disclose his true self. The result is that we know certain things about each other but we do not know each other.

The second way Buber refers to as an I-Thou relationship. In such a relationship, I do not merely learn new facts about the other person. I come to know *him* through intimate communication, through close personal relationship, through what Buber calls "dialogue." Buber has written that the essence of dialogue is the fact that "each of the participants really has in mind the other or others in their present and particular being and turns to them with the intention of establishing a living mutual relationship between himself and them."[1] Such a living mutual relationship, the result of dialogue, is what Buber means by an I-Thou relationship.

It is Buber's contention that the knowledge gained in an I-Thou relationship is more profound than any kind of knowledge *about* a person. It is a knowledge by direct acquaintance, an intuition of the real being of another, an authentic meeting between people; in short, an encounter.

I shall not be concerned in this chapter with the question of whether such encounters do in fact happen between people. I believe that most people can look back upon such experiences in their lives.

My concern is rather with the theological implications Buber draws from such experiences. Buber would, of course, have shunned such a term as "theological" because it smacks too much of systematic ratiocination about God. He would even, indeed, have objected to the phrase "about God." If God "may properly only be addressed, not expressed,"[2] we fall short of the mark when we attempt to talk about God. We can only know God through encounter—this is Buber's thesis. And it is this thesis which it is my purpose to examine in this chapter—namely, can God be encountered? It is beyond the scope of this volume to deal with all aspects of Buber's thought. Our concern is with Buber's doctrine of encounter.

First, let us trace the steps whereby Buber came to maintain this position.

Buber's Early Philosophical Development

Philosophy today has become, in large measure, an intellectual game. This is most evident at philosophy conventions. Papers are delivered on abstract topics which bear little or no relationship to the problems people face in their daily lives. Most contemporary philosophers would mock the Medievals for arguing about the number of angels that can dance on the top of a pin. But these same philosophers endlessly discuss such questions as whether or not there can exist a private language. An outsider listening to such a discussion would probably dismiss it as irrelevant and remote from the world of his everyday life.

Martin Buber was diametrically opposed to this kind of philosophizing. For him, philosophy was literally a matter of life and death. For example, at the age of fourteen, the young Buber was everwhelmed by the eternal silence of infinite space and the endlessness of infinite time. This is how he described his perplexity:

> A necessity I could not understand swept over me; I had to try again and again to imagine the edge of space or its edgelessness, time with a beginning and an end, or a time without beginning or end, and both were equally impossible, equally hopeless—yet there seemed to be only the choice between the one or the other absurdity. Under an irresistible compulsion, I reeled from one to the other, at times so closely threatened with the danger of madness that I seriously thought of avoiding it by suicide.[3]

Thus, to Buber, the problems of space and time were not sterile intellectual problems. They gripped his very being. He was tormented by these questions, because, underlying them, "what was at stake was the reality of the world in which one had to live and which had taken on the face of the absurd and the uncanny."[4] Buber could not live in the face of the absurd; he had to make sense out of the world.

To most people, it is hard to imagine how a book could rescue an individual from a personal crisis. But to a philosophical mind seeking ultimate truth, a new idea espoused in a book can quiet the anxieties raised by asking such ultimate questions. This is precisely what happened in Buber's case. Thus he wrote:

> Salvation came to the fifteen year old boy in a book, Kant's *Prolegomena to all Future Metaphysics*. . . . This book showed me that space and time are only the forms in which my human view of what is, necessarily works itself out; that is, they were not attached to the inner nature of the world, but to the nature of my senses.[5]

Kant's insight that space and time were structures of the mind comforted Buber, exercising a quieting effect on him. For now he was able to look at his existence in a different light. "Time", he wrote, "was not a sentence hanging over me; it was mine, for it was ours."[6]

Buber was comforted. He stopped tormenting himself with this particular ultimate question. But he was, of course, not intellectually satisfied for long. If he had been, his philosophical quest would have ceased.

In fact, Kant rescued him from one problem only to pose others: If space and time are forms of human perception, what then is the nature of ultimate reality? And if Being or ultimate reality cannot be understood conceptually, by such concepts as finite and infinite, how can it be comprehended?

These questions concerning the nature of man's relation to ultimate reality are posed by Buber as follows: "But if time is only a form in which we perceive, where *are* we? Are we not in the timeless? Are we not in eternity?"[7]

It is evident that Buber was far more obsessed with the problem of time than with the problem of space. Ever since Augustine asked the question, "What, then, is time?", philosophers have sensed something both mysterious and fascinating about the problem of time. What these philosophers have sensed intuitively is that the riddle of time holds the key to reality. The riddle of time arises when man realizes that ordinary clock time is a human convention and when he then tries to conceive of time as a transhuman reality.

Now Buber was not asking a question of physics—the question to which Einstein's theory of space-time is addressed. In fact, Buber was striving to solve the riddle of time by transcending time. And the vehicle of his transcendence was his attempt to understand the eternal, the timeless.

In the course of grappling with the concept of eternity, Buber was deeply impressed by Nietzsche's *Thus Spake Zarathustra*. Buber was influenced not only by Nietzsche's style but by his thought—especially the conception of eternal recurrence.

The notion of eternal recurrence has been crisply described as the idea that "whatever there is will return again, and that whatever there is, *is* a return of itself, that it has all happened before, and will happen again, exactly in the same way each time, forever."[8] This conception of the eternal return of the same echoes the Greek idea of eternity as a circle. In this view, man transcends time through an endless cycle of repetition.

Buber was fascinated with this idea because of its appeal to the timeless, its transcendence of time. It goaded him to think more deeply about eternity. It acted as a stimulus to his thought. But he could not accept this conception because, to him, it violated "the uniqueness of all happening."[9]

Buber thus was concerned to develop a conception of eternity to which he could relate and which would allow for unique and unrepeatable events. Accordingly, Buber wrote that eternity signified for him "what is incomprehensible in itself, that which sends forth time out of itself and sets us in that relationship to it which we call existence. To him who recognizes this, the reality of the world no longer shows an absurd and uncanny face because eternity is."[10]

Buber's definition of eternity bears an unmistakable Kantian aspect. Like Kant's *Ding an Sich,* it is incomprehensible in itself. Yet it exercises an effect. Here Buber's original conception enters in.

Eternity places us in relation to time. It is, more precisely, the transhuman reality which is the permanent ground of our temporal relationships. And it is this permanent ground which gives reality to man's relation to the world, removing its absurdity.

We can now delineate the direction of Buber's thought. Time, Kant had taught him, is not "out there" but is rather a form of our perception, the way we view the world. But then the question arises: What *is* out there? And what is our relationship to transhuman reality? Buber agreed with Kant that ultimate reality is incomprehensible in itself. We can only know its effect on us. Buber's new concept is that eternity sets us in relationship to time. Eternity can place us in relationship even though we do not comprehend its essential nature. And we can feel at home in the world through this relationship. It is this emphasis on relationship which becomes the dominant motif in Buber's thought.

Before proceeding to trace the development of this motif in Buber's thought, it is important to pause and evaluate his conception of eternity. Let us begin by noting various usages of the term. The term is frequently used in connection with death. The closing words at a funeral typically are: "May he rest in eternity, in peace." Supposed a bereaved person were to inquire: "What is eternity?" What is this person really asking?

The bereaved person is really asking these questions: Is there anything more to life than the processes of birth, growth, maturation, dissolution, and death? Is there something about the deceased that remains eternal, immortal, everlasting? The term "eternity" is thus often connected with such concepts as "immortality" and "soul."

Take another example. A man, recently having suffered the tragic loss of a daughter, says: "You are alive for a short time, but you are dead for an eternity." In this statement, "eternity" is merely used as a synonym for "a very long time." And the implication of this statement is that we ought to appreciate life because of its brevity and also because that is all we really have. To this man, the concept of eternity does not mitigate the absurd. It intensifies it.

These examples show that the meaning and significance of the concept of eternity are contextual: they depend upon the personal life situation of the speaker. Therefore, whether or not Buber's concept of eternity can in fact mitigate the feeling of absurdity depends on the orientation of each particular individual.

It is the present writer's opinion that eternity is both an aesthetic and a metaphysical concept, that one can most readily experience eternity in the beauty of nature and in artistic creations which have an "enduring" quality. And when we consider a human life as a work of art, it takes on a quality of eternity. But these aesthetic conceptions have a metaphysical basis: they are founded on a belief that there is a permanent and enduring structure of value inherent in the universe itself.

Let us now return to Buber's philosophical development. Having reached the point that man can escape absurdity only by affirming a relationship to eternity, Buber sought to develop his conception of this relationship, and of relationship in general.

In this connection, it is important to note the influence upon Buber of another philosopher, whose views also influenced Karl Marx. This thinker was Ludwig Feuerbach.

Buber explained that in his youth, he was given "a decisive impetus"[11] by Feuerbach, especially by this thinker's contention that man's being "is contained only in community, in the unity of man with man—a unity which rests, however, only on the difference between I and Thou."[12]

This statement of Feuerbach epitomizes the direction of Buber's thought—the idea that truth is to be found in relationship. And the very title of Buber's key philosophical work, *I and Thou*, is anticipated in this statement of Feuerbach.

It is important to recognize, however, that the impetus generated by Feuerbach took time to develop and mature in Buber's thought. It was a germ idea that was to come to fruition through Buber's reaction to a decisive life experience.

However, though the influence of Feuerbach is apparent, the use which Buber will make of the I-Thou concept is different in an extremely important respect. Feuerbach confined the I-Thou relationship purely to the human community. To Feuerbach, God was a projection of human need. To Buber, on the other hand, God becomes, most emphatically, the Eternal Thou, existing independently of the human mind. And there is virtually no view to which Buber will object more strenuously than the idea that God is a projection of the human mind.

We have described and evaluated Buber's preoccupation with eternity. And we have noted his interest in Feuerbach's conception of I and Thou. Let us now turn to an examination of how the conceptions of "eternity" and "Thou" became conjoined in

Buber's thought, issuing in his conception of God as the Eternal Thou.

From Mysticism to Existentialism: Buber and the Eternal Thou

"Mysticism" is not a univocal term. It has meant many things to many people. In its widest sense, however, it can be said that a mystic "is a man who has been favored with an immediate, and to him real, experience of the divine, or who at least strives to attain such an experience."[13] The distinguishing feature of the mystic is his claim to have experienced or his quest to experience the Divine directly and unmediated by reason. To the mystic, the Divine is experienced, not inferred. In this wide sense of the term, Buber remained a mystic throughout his career.

In its more technical sense, however, mysticism involves the communion of the soul with God, and even, in some of its forms, a quest for a *unio mystica*—a union of the soul with the Divine. Gershom Scholem points out that the nearest Jewish mysticism came to the idea of union with God was in its idea of *Devekut* or communion with God. Such communion or *Devekut*, Scholem writes, is for the most part "realized only by the paradoxical means of abnegation and denial of the values of this world."[14]

The significant point is that mysticism, in this more technical sense, involves a negation of the world through an experience of ecstasy—a trancelike state in which the mind is fixed on contemplation of the Divine. In this latter sense of the term, mysticism is a stage in the development of Buber's thought which he was to transcend.

The experience of ecstasy is emphasized in Buber's early writings on Hasidism. Take for example, his early essays, *The Life of the Hasidim,* written in 1908. The first of these essays is entitled *"Hitlahavut: Ecstasy."* In this essay, Buber described the Hasidic mystic in a state of ecstasy: "Above nature and above time and above thought—thus is he called who is in ecstasy. . . . The man of ecstasy rules life, and no external happening that penetrates into his realm can disturb his inspiration."[15]

No external happening can disturb his inspiration! In this state of utter negation of the world, no finite event can disturb the mystic's rapture. In this early period of Buber's thought, the "religious" was for him the mystical—a kind of experience that lifted him out of so-called mundane experiences. The "religious" was, to him, an exception from the everyday. At this time in his life and writing, Buber was more concerned with eternity than with the temporal, more with ecstasy than with daily existence, more with what lies beyond the world than the world itself.

But during this period a decisive event occurred in Buber's life, an external happening that disturbed *his* inspiration. Since this event was so decisive for Buber, it is worthwhile to cite his account of it:

> What happened was no more than that one forenoon, after a morning of religious enthusiasm. I had a visit from an unknown man, without being there in spirit. I certainly did not fail to let the meeting be friendly, I did not treat him any more remissly than all his contemporaries who were in the habit of seeking me out about this time of day as an oracle that is ready to listen to reason. I conversed attentively and openly with him—only I omitted to guess the questions which he did not put. Later, not long after, I learned from one of his friends—he himself was no longer alive—the essential content of these questions. I learned that he had come to me not casually but borne by destiny, not for a chat but for a decision.
>
> He had come to me, he had come in this hour. What do we expect when we are in despair and yet go to a man? Surely a presence by means of which we are told that nevertheless there is meaning.
>
> Since then I have given up the religious which is nothing but the exception, extraction, exaltation, ecstasy—or it has given me up. I possess nothing but the everyday out of which I am never taken. . . . I do not know much more. If that is religion, then it is just everything, simply all that is lived in its possibility of dialogue.[16]

There is no doubt that this decisive event was a turning point in Buber's life and thought. Before this event, he sought eternity apart from the everyday. After this event, he sought eternity *in* the everyday, in the temporal flux.

Concerning the event itself, it appears that Buber answered the young man's overt questions but not the hidden, deeper questions that were unasked. Buber chastised himself for not having penetrated beneath the young man's questions to the feelings underlying them. Evidently what was missing in this meeting was empathy—a feeling *with* the other person. And what seared Buber's mind was this realization when he learned that the young man had committed suicide.

Clinically, it might seem naive for Buber to have held himself at all responsible for the personal tragedy of this young man. There are so many factors, tangible and intangible, that converge upon an individual, conspiring in the ultimate act of his self-destruction. Constitutional factors, environmental factors, emotional tendencies—all play a role. Hence, whatever the precipitating cause might be—a disappointment in love, a failure in career—it is the cumulative effect of all the factors in a person's past which are somehow crystallized in the fatal decision.

How, then, can we explain Buber's self-castigation? What could he have done to prevent this tragedy? Buber's reaction, it appears to me, is the reaction not of a psychologist but of an artist. Buber was not seeking clinical causes but the hidden meaning of the event to transmute and refashion through art. It is therefore instructive to compare with this event a similar happening which occurred in the life of another artist. In the case of this artist, however, the person did *not* commit suicide precisely because meaning was conveyed.

The Japanese novelist Soseki Natsume, in his book *Within My Glass Doors,* describes the following incident, doubtless taken from an actual occurrence in his life. A woman, on the verge of suicide, visits a renowned novelist. After their discussion, the novelist begins to escort the woman home. The woman, surprised, says: "It is too great an honor for you to see me home." The novelist replies: "Do you think it an honor?" "I do," she says. The novelist then answers, "If so, you had better live, not die."

This precisely illustrates Buber's point—where he thought he failed the young man and where this novelist reached the woman. The point is that the novelist, by his presence, showed the woman that there was a meaning. More precisely, he showed her that in fact *she* still had a reason to consider life worth living, for she considered his presence meaningful. And this is where Buber felt that he had failed the young man.

To the artist, every life experience is grist for the mill. Thus, in Buber's thought, the pain of this event is deftly woven into the tapestry of his thought. It is this event, he narrates, that gave rise to a decisive transformation in his thought. This transformation was from a preoccupation with mystical ecstasy to an emphasis on life "lived in its possibility of dialogue."

Although Buber eschewed categories, it is nevertheless true to say that this decisive event, and Buber's interpretation of it, signified his shift from mysticism to existentialism. If by existentialism we mean that attitude toward life whereby human existence in the concrete precedes "essence" or abstract theorizing about existence, then it is abundantly clear that Buber's position evolved into an existential orientation to life. Thus, writing about the experience with the young man, Buber reflects: "I know no fullness but each mortal hour's fullness of claim and responsibility."[17] From this point on Buber eschewed all discourse about essence, all attempts to categorize and classify existence. Existence itself, and by this Buber meant his own particular existence in dialogue with others, became the threshold of Buber's thought. What is more, Buber now maintained that any attempt to transcend the here and now is inauthentic. Eternity is not to be found in another world, in another dimension. Eternity is now.

Buber thus did not abandon the quest for eternity. He rather sought eternity in the moment, in "each mortal hour's fullness of claim and responsibility." It is precisely each authentic encounter, be it with another person, with an object of nature or a work of art, which Buber came to view as an opening, a window to the Eternal Thou.

The question now arises: What, for Buber, is an authentic encounter? Buber's thought comes to its full fruition and reaches its decisive clarity in his classic work *I and Thou*. In this work Buber describes the authentic encounter as an I-Thou relationship.

I and Thou is a poetic work. But the poetry belies a precision and rigorousness of thought. With deft strokes, and with poignant clarity, Buber delineates the I-Thou relationship.

The following characteristics differentiate that relationship from all others.

First, an I-Thou relationship involves a person's whole being. In an I-Thou encounter, for example, I am not talking to another person and thinking about something else. My entire being is suffused in relationship. I and Thou denotes an attitude of the whole person. It negates a divided mind.

Second, an I-Thou relationship is exclusive. In Buber's famous example of the tree, he writes: "The tree is no longer *It*. I have been seized by the power of exclusiveness."[18] By this, he means that I encounter only the tree; I am totally absorbed in my relation to the tree itself. The tree stands over against me. It is as if nothing else exists at that moment but my encounter with the tree. I am seized or grasped by the encounter. It is an exclusive relationship.

Third, an I-Thou relationship is direct, free of deception. In an I-Thou relationship with another person, I am not trying to impress him, to "put something over on him." As I am truly myself, so this allows the other person to be truly himself: "As I become I, I say Thou."[19] An I-Thou relationship is thus purely direct, a totally spontaneous meeting. I do not categorize the other. I meet him.

Fourth, an I-Thou relationship is effortless. It is not an act of will. I do not say: "Now I am going to have an I-Thou relationship." Thus, Buber writes: "The Thou meets me through grace —it is not found by seeking."[20] This does not mean that I do not contribute to the relationship. Rather, it signifies that I am responding to the real otherness of the other. An I-Thou relationship is decidedly not a subjective creation.

Fifth, an I-Thou relationship takes place in the present. The notion of the "present" and "presence" is extremely important to Buber. To be sure, the idea of redemption in the future also plays a major role in Buber's thought. But, unlike Martin Heidegger, an existentialist thinker who sees man's being as continually directed to the future, Martin Buber does not view the future as overshadowing the present. Accordingly, Buber would not agree with those philosophers who have held the idea of the "specious present"—that the idea of the present is fiction. In direct antithesis to these philosophers, Buber considers the present to be real and significant.

Sixth, developing out of this notion of presence, Buber emphasizes that an I-Thou relationship takes place *between* people. Buber tries to transcend the subject-object dichotomy by affirming the ontologically prior reality of the "between," the reality of the meeting itself. Consider, for example, two people in a real dialogue. To Buber, something is happening not only to the two participants but between them. It is an organic process whereby the "whole," the interaction and the synergy created thereby, is more than the sum of its parts.

Finally, and most important, an I-Thou relationship is reciprocal or mutual. As Buber writes: "Relation is mutual. My Thou affects me, as I affect it."[21] It is intuitively evident that this should be so in man's relationship to man. It would be nonsensical to consider a relationship between persons as an I-Thou relation if it were not mutual, if both participants were not affected.

The major problem of Buber's thought, however, concerns the element of reciprocity in man's relation to nature and his relationship to God.

Let us consider first man's relationship to nature. We return to Buber's description of an encounter with a tree. How can an encounter with a tree be said to be mutual? Does the tree enter into a relation? If so, is Buber a panpsychist? Does he mean to assert that objects of nature possess consciousness? Buber anticipates these questions by the following elliptical statements:

> Let no attempt be made to sap the strength from the meaning of the relation—relation is mutual. The tree will have a conscious ness, then, similar to our own? Of that I have no experience. But do you wish through seeming to succeed in it with yourself, once again to disintegrate that which cannot be disintegrated? I encounter no soul or dryad of the tree, but the tree itself.[22]

Statements such as these are calculated to try the patience of professional philosophers. And, one is almost inclined to say, deliberately so. Buber again and again resists categorization. He will not go so far as to say that the tree possesses consciousness. For then, philosophers could pigeonhole Buber with the label "panpsychist" and their need to categorize would be sated.

What Buber is saying is that an encounter is *sui generis*—a unique happening. It cannot be analyzed. For to analyze something is to break it up into component parts and therefore to disintegrate it.

Buber is thus affirming the uniqueness of encounter: namely, if one enters into a relationship of one's entire being with *anything,* there will be reciprocity. But the content of this reciprocity cannot be stated in advance. One must simply experience it.

Buber is admirably consistent on this point. It is interesting to note how he stands his ground when questioned by other philosophers.

He is adamant in his refusal to depart from the perspective of encounter. The same firmness, *mutatis mutandis,* animates Buber's discussion of God. The relationship with God, the Eternal Thou, is the consummation of man's particular I-Thou relationships with other persons and with nature. More precisely, these particular I-Thou relationships point to an overarching transcendence which completes, consummates, and grounds these relations. Buber expresses this thought as follows:

> The extended lines of relations meet in the Eternal Thou. Every particular Thou is a glimpse through to the Eternal Thou; by means of every particular Thou the primary word addresses the Eternal Thou . . . the inborn Thou is realized in each relation and consummated in none. It is consummated only in the direct relation with the Thou that by its nature cannot become It.[23]

According to Buber, every I-Thou encounter on the human plane is evanescent and ephemeral—"Every Thou in our world must become an *It*."[24] Every "Thou" in our human world is temporary because it is the nature of the human mind to convert experiences into objects of reflection. Man cannot live forever in the dimension of immediate experience. He is destined always to transform immediacy into reflection. And it is Buber's point that man is, in a sense, *condemned* to transform immediacy into reflection: "Without *It* man cannot live. But he who lives with *It* alone is not a man."[25] Man cannot live without "It" because of his insatiable need to control; but a man who is incapable of a pure, direct, immediate encounter with another is not a man.

Having exalted the I-Thou relation to such a plateau, Buber deems it necessary to ground human encounters in a relation to an Eternal Thou that by its nature cannot become It.

Buber's thought is not regarded as a system. Buber himself would have rigorously denied any systematic tendency on his part. Yet his philosophy is as intricate as a system. For it is evident that what is of supreme value to Buber—the I-Thou encounter—must be somehow given more than transient worth. It must somehow be grounded in eternity. Thus, the necessity for a conception of God as an Eternal Thou follows as rigorously from Buber's aims and objectives as Spinoza's conception of substance followed from his aims.

Now, what precisely does it mean to refer to God as the Eternal Thou? Buber's conception of God, as we have indicated, is entirely consistent with his total orientation to life. Buber's idea of God is concisely expressed in this passage:

God cannot be inferred in anything—in nature, say, as its author, or in history as its master, or in the subject as the self that is thought in it. Something else is not given and God then elicited from it; but God is the Being that is directly, most nearly, and lastingly, over against us, that may properly only be addressed, not expressed.[26]

Here is the heart of Buber's religious message. In essence, we can only really talk to God but not about God. God can only be encountered; He cannot be inferred.

Of course, Buber of necessity has some things to say about God. He does, in fact, talk about God as the Absolute Person, as paradoxically being the unity of unconditional exclusiveness and inclusiveness, and as comprising but not coextensive with the universe and the self. But it would be a mistake either to derive too much theological significance from these statements or to accuse Buber of inconsistency on this point.

Buber has already admitted that in *our* human world, every Thou must become an It.

This holds as well for our conceptions of God, including Buber's own conceptions. But, for Buber, these conceptions of God or God-ideas do not touch the essence of the matter. The essence of the issue is Buber's thesis of a living encounter with God.

In such an encounter, man feels addressed by God. He is, as Buber would put it, given a sign. The sign does not tell man what to do, what to decide. It is not a matter of content. The sign rather establishes that there is a meaning, or, more precisely, that man's meaning in a particular situation is confirmed.

The criteria are thus subjective: the individual may feel a heightened sense of awareness of the Divine or even an inner transformation of his being. It therefore follows that from Buber's particular mode of thought, there can be no objective criteria to determine whether or not one has been addressed.

Rather, it is Buber's thesis that the man "who truly goes out to meet the world goes out also to God."[27] To such a person who meets the world with his whole being, virtually anything can constitute a Divine address. As Buber writes: "The relation with man is the real simile of the relation with God; in it true address receives true response, except that in God's response everything, the universe, is made manifest as language."[28] What Buber is saying is that, to him who has ears to hear, God speaks. True address receives true response.

But what about those who have sought God and not found Him? What about those who have addressed God and not heard His response? Or, to put it another way, what about those who feel that God has never addressed them? How does Buber explain these phenomena?

And further, there is the perennial question on Jewish lips: How can we explain the collective tragedy of the Holocaust?

Was there a response which man did not hear? Or were the gates of Heaven closed? How does Buber deal with these phenomena? It is this question which we now explore.

Buber on Jewish Life After Auschwitz

Before considering Buber's view of Jewish life after Auschwitz, it is important to consider first his mode of approach to Judaism.

Buber's writings on Judaism and the Jewish people reflect his general orientation to life. Thus Buber wrote that "the most deep-seated humanity of our soul and its most deep-seated Judaism mean and desire the same thing."[29] Hence, for Buber, the primally Jewish and what is most deeply human signify the same thing. It is thus impossible to separate Buber's theory of Jewish existence from his theory of human existence. Everything we have seen about Buber up to this point is, for him, as intensely Jewish as it is intensely human. Whereas one thinker once wrote that being Jewish is the least difficult way of being human, Buber would have probably said that being Jewish is the most intense way of being human.

It follows that what Buber emphasized in his general philosophical writings emerged, in part, from his intense study of Judaism, particularly Hasidism; and conversely, what Buber wrote about Judaism is inextricably interwoven with his unique philosophical outlook. In short, Buber's philosophy, unlike that of many others, is an organic whole.

To illustrate: We have noted Buber's preoccupation with the whole person, the unity of man's being. It is therefore not accidental that in his treatment of Judaism, he would emphasize the Jew's passion for unity—the unity of God and man's quest to unify his entire being in *imitatio Dei*.

Furthermore, just as in his general orientation, Buber came

to emphasize the concrete situation, so, too, in his treatment of Judaism, he stressed the deed. Finally, just as in his general orientation Buber stressed the perennial possibility of an individual's redemption in the future, so, too, did he emphasize the messianic ideal in Judaism. Thus Buber wrote:

> The spiritual process of Judaism manifests itself in history as the striving for an ever more perfect realization of three inter-connected ideas: the idea of unity, the idea of the deed, and the idea of the future.[30]

For Buber, the distinctiveness of the Jewish people lies precisely in its unique combination of nationhood and spirituality. Thus, Buber envisages Jewish peoplehood itself as a spiritual process, affirming that there is no other people where "this spiritual process of peoplehood, has become as visible and distinct as in the Jewish people."[31] It is Buber's contention, therefore, that Judaism and the Jewish people are inseparable; both connote this unique spiritual process.

It is important to note, however, that Buber does not view the spiritual process of Judaism in a monolithic manner. This spiritual process has its hills and valleys, its peaks and declines. Buber has a tendency to place the highest value on the primal and the original religious experience. Thus, he finds in the narrative portions of the Bible an authentic account of a real encounter and dialogue between Israel and its God. But he views the evolution of Jewish law as a congealing and hardening of this original, primary experience. Accordingly, he refers to Rabbinism as that "vexatious Talmud,"[32] and he rejects *Halacha* as a way to approach God.

As against the *Halacha,* or Jewish religious law, Buber espouses "the living deed that binds man to God."[33]

By "the living deed," Buber means an effort "to restore to the deed the freedom and sanctity diminished and dimmed by the stern rule of the ritual law, and to release it from the straits of prescriptions that had become meaningless, in order to free it for the holiness of an active relationship with God, for a religiosity of the deed."[34]

Again, Buber's attitude toward Jewish law flows organically from his total philosophy of life. Buber emphasizes the encounter, the concrete life-situation of the individual. For Buber, there are no rules or prescriptions which can prepare an individual for these concrete encounters. Buber offers no formulas for life, no answers in advance. Thus, in his view of Judaism, he also emphasizes the concrete, lived encounters of the people and its God.

Given his view of Judaism as a spiritual process, it is now appropriate to ask: What is the present stage of this spiritual process vis-à-vis the modern Jew? More particularly, what is Buber's conception of Jewish life after Auschwitz? Is dialogue still possible?

The fact that Buber equates the "Jewish" with the intensely human is indicated by the very way Buber phrases the question:

> In this our own time, one asks again and again: how is a Jewish life still possible after Auschwitz? I would like to frame this question more correctly: how is a life with God still possible in a time in which there is an Auschwitz? The estrangement has become too cruel, the hiddenness too deep. One can still believe in the God who allowed these things to happen, but can one still speak to Him? Can one still hear His word? Can one still, as an individual and as a people, enter at all into a dialogic relationship with Him?[35]

From Buber's phrasing of the question, it is clear that the Holocaust calls into question his entire philosophy of encounter between man and God. Indeed, the problem of evil is the test case of a religious philosophy generally. And the Holocaust—unuttterable evil—raises the problem to its highest pitch, shattering our eardrums with its deafening clamor of unrelieved inhumanity of man to man.

Buber's phrasing of the question already sets the tone for his answer. First, he assumes too much when he says that "we can still believe in the God who allowed these things to happen." This statement is simply belied by the fact that there are many people who cannot make even this affirmation. Second, by referring to the idea of God "allowing" these things to happen, he has already severely limited his answer by narrowing the moral dimensions of Deity. Third, he has virtually answered the question already when he speaks of the estrangement as too cruel and the hiddenness too deep.

Buber's response to the Holocaust is embodied in his concept of the eclipse of God, a development of the Biblical concept of the hiding God. Buber's concept of the "eclipse" is not free from ambiguity .

First, he writes that the term "eclipse" refers to something that happens *between* man and God. This would be a negative parallel to his positive ontological concept of the dimension "between" man and God. Accordingly, Buber says that just as an eclipse of the sun is something that happens "between the sun and our eyes, not in the sun itself,"[36] so the eclipse of God represents the character of the "historic hour through which the world is passing."[37]

But later on he writes that in our age the I-It relationship has usurped the I-Thou relationship.

In this version, it is the "omnipotent 'I' " that "steps in between and shuts off from us the light of heaven."[38]

It thus seems to be unclear whether, for Buber, the eclipse of God is a nonsubjective reality or a human psychic reality.

What, then, is man to do during this period of eclipse? He is to await the appearance of the "hiding one."[39] And, Buber adds, when He comes again, "though His coming appearance resemble no earlier one, we shall recognize again our cruel and merciful Lord."[40]

It would appear from this passage that the eclipse of God is a nonsubjective reality. To be sure, human evil, human intransigence, is partially responsible for this barrier. But the Divine, as it were, is nonresponsive to the victims of evil.

It therefore follows, and Buber is not averse to drawing this conclusion, that the Divine allows itself to be eclipsed. And it follows in turn from this, as Buber unflinchingly writes, that the God we await is the cruel and merciful Lord.

This is indeed a difficult conclusion with which to acquiesce.

But, though we may not agree with it on moral grounds,[41] it is significant to note that Buber is consistent in drawing this conclusion.

With this in mind, it is now time to critically evaluate Buber's thought.

Critique of Buber

Throughout our discussion of Buber's thought, we have noted that Buber's philosophy is distinguished by its consistency. From the time he first arrived at his doctrine of encounter, Buber consistently held the position that God can only be encountered and not inferred. The only note of inconsistency in Buber's thought is the ambiguity in his concept of the eclipse of God.

Otherwise, his mature philosophy is an organic whole emerging out of his affirmation of a living encounter of man with the Eternal Thou.

When we examine Buber's thought from the point of view of empirical reference, however, we traverse more difficult ground. The difficulty is that, while Buber writes deeply out of his own experience, it is not at all self-evident that the experience he is at pains to communicate is available for all. We are not referring here to the I-Thou relationship between man and man but rather to the idea of an encounter between man and God.

It would follow from Buber's thought that an atheist would be insensitive, deaf, or blind. He simply does not see the signs. Thus, Buber criticizes Jean Paul Sartre for starting with the silence of the transcendent without asking himself what part our not hearing has played in that silence.[42] One could just as easily criticize Buber for starting with the efficacy of transcendence without asking himself what part his hearing has played in the voice—whether, in fact, Buber *thought* he heard the voice.

One must reckon seriously, however, with Buber's contention that one who really, with his whole being, goes out to meet the world will meet God. This was true in Buber's case, but it is decidedly not a universal human experience.

In fact, more common to human experience is the slow but decisive erosion of faith and disillusionment with the world encountered by many people with the same ardor and passion of Buber. It is the present writer's opinion that Buber does not give sufficient weight to the kind of experience described in *Of Human Bondage* by Somerset Maugham. This is the experience of Philip Carey, a young man with a clubfoot, who sincerely and *with his whole being* prays to God to be healed of his infirmity.

In utter self-abasement he kneels down beside his bed, removes his clothes, and in utter nakedness prays to be healed. Anticipating his redemption, he goes to sleep. He awakens in joy, but as soon as he confronts again the reality of his clubfoot, his joy sours. And in the introduction to *Of Human Bondage*, it states: "The touching incident of Philip's prayer to be healed of his infirmity is taken directly from the author's experience. When

Maugham's stammer did not disappear in spite of his complete and passionate faith, he suffered his first religious disillusion."[43]

To this, Buber would doubtless reply that this prayer was not truly an I-Thou relationship, for Philip (and Maugham) expected something of God. But the question turns back on Buber when we ask: If the person feels no confirmation of meaning, what then is the sign of God's response? Through which question, we would ultimately be led to Buber's doctrine of the eclipse of God.

The eclipse of God is, in this writer's opinion, the weakest point in Buber's thought. Let us evaluate it according to our third criterion, pragmatic value.

What are the consequences of asserting that our time is one of eclipse of God? It follows, according to Buber, that our time is one of waiting for God.

One is reminded immediately of Samuel Beckett's play *Waiting for Godot*. The trouble is that Godot never comes.

Despite the sublime character of much of Buber's thought, his doctrine of the hiding God and man's waiting for His appearance is all too reminiscent of a children's game of hide and seek. Surely we are entitled to a nobler conception of God at this point from a man of Buber's stature.

Not only is Buber's concept of the eclipse of God deficient from a moral point of view. It is aesthetically unappealing. Buber, we have noted, is a great artist. From an artistic, aesthetic point of view, the silence of God would be far more appropriate for "the historic hour" Buber describes.

Some years ago, another great artist, Ingmar Bergman, made a film called *The Silence,* depicting this very theme. This would have been a far more aesthetic response on Buber's part. The fact is that our historic hour calls for a different concept of God than the one adumbrated by Buber. I agree with Buber that God must be at least personal. But "personal" must be defined in a different way, so that God can not only be addressed but expressed.

This is not to deny the power of Buber's thought, the grandeur of its organic development, and the compelling discussion of the I-Thou relationship between man and man. And the consistency with which Buber maintains his position of encounter is an admirable illustration of a man standing his ground. But ultimately, for those interested in the theoretical dimension, Buber's emphasis on encounter is simply not enough. Encounter may constitute a legitimate beginning, but it reaches its true fruition and fulfillment in man's efforts to conceive of God.

Surely a God worthy of worship is a God we can also talk about —and talk about with clarity, conceptual rigor, and aesthetic refinement.

NOTES

1. Maurice Friedman, *Martin Buber: The Life of Dialogue* (New York: Harper Torchbooks, 1955), p. 87.
2. Martin Buber, *I and Thou*, trans. Ronald Gregor Smith (New York: Charles Scribner's Sons, 1958), pp. 80–81.
3. Martin Buber, *Between Man and Man*, trans. Ronald Gregor Smith (Boston: Beacon Press, 1961), p. 136.
4. Maurice Friedman and Paul Schilpp, eds., *The Philosophy of Martin Buber* (La Salle, Ill.: Open Court, 1967), p. 12.
5. *Between Man and Man*, p. 136.
6. *The Philosophy of Martin Buber*, p. 12.
7. *Ibid*.
8. Arthur C. Danto, *Nietzsche as Philosopher* (New York: The Macmillan Co.), pp. 201–202.
9. *The Philosophy of Martin Buber*, p. 13.
10. *Idem*.
11. *Between Man and Man*, p. 148.
12. *Ibid*., p. 147.
13. Gershom Scholem, *On The Kabbalah and Its Symbolism*, trans. Ralph Manheim (New York: Schocken Books, 1969), p. 5.
14. Gershom Scholem, *The Messianic Idea in Judaism* (New York: Schocken Books, 1971), p. 203.
15. Martin Buber, *Hasidism and Modern Man*, ed. and trans. by Maurice Friedman (New York: Harper Torchbooks, 1958), p. 77.
16. *Between Man and Man*, pp, 13, 14.
17. *Ibid*., p. 14.
18. *I and Thou*, p. 7.
19. *Ibid*., p. 11.
20. *Idem*.
21. *Ibid*., p. 15.
22. *Ibid*., p. 8.
23. *Ibid*., p. 75.
24. *Ibid*., p. 16.
25. *Ibid*., p. 34.
26. *Ibid*., pp. 80–81.
27. *Ibid*., p. 95.
28. *Ibid*., p. 103.
29. Martin Buber, *On Judaism*, p. 55.

30. *Ibid.*, p. 40.

31. *Ibid.*, pp. 40–41.

32. Martin Buber, *Israel and the World*, trans. Maurice Friedman *et al.* (New York: Schocken Books, 1963), p. 23.

33. *On Judaism*, p. 45.

34. *Ibid.*, p. 46.

35. *Ibid.*, p. 224.

36. Martin Buber, *Eclipse of God* (New York: Harper Torchbooks, 1952). p. 23.

37. *Idem.*

38. *Ibid.*, p. 129.

39. *On Judaism*, p. 225.

40. *Idem.*

41. See, for example, Harold Schulweis, "Buber's Broken Dialogue," *Reconstructionist*, December 1972.

42. *Eclipse of God*, p. 69.

43. W. Somerset Maugham, *Of Human Bondage*, introd. by Richard A. Cordell, p. xvii.

5 Richard L. Rubenstein:
The Encounter with Nothingness

In our examination of the thought of Martin Buber, we have noted that its chief inadequacy was his response to the Holocaust. We found his concept of the eclipse of God to be problematic both empirically and pragmatically.

A more radical response to the Holocaust is presented in the theology of Richard Rubenstein. From the unutterable evil of the Holocaust, Rubenstein draws the conclusion that the traditional Jewish conception of the God of history is no longer tenable.

The uniqueness of Rubenstein's approach lies in his application of psychoanalytic concepts to Jewish theology. We shall first examine the key events in Rubenstein's life which led him to formulate his unique psychoanalytic response to the Holocaust.

Richard Rubenstein is presently Professor of Religion at

Florida State University. He was ordained as Rabbi at the Jewish
Theological Seminary and received the degrees of S.T.M. and
Ph.D. from Harvard University. It is to his life and work that
we now turn.

The World of Richard Rubenstein

To understand the work of a thinker requires an act of intellectual sympathy: one must try to enter his world, to view the
world temporarily from his point of view. This effort quite often
reveals a recurrent theme, a dominant image, and, at times, an
obsession.

The philosophy of Richard Rubenstein revolves around his
own personal obsession with death. As a child, he relates,[1] he
hoped that science would invent a cure for death. When he
realized the futility of this hope, he nevertheless still nourished
a yearning for immortality, on the unconscious level. This yearning for immortality, he writes retrospectively, was his underlying
motivation for religious observance: "Yet the yearning for immortality was the most compelling reason for my life of religious
discipline. At the most primitive level of my being I simply
refused to accept the fact that, like all men, I was inevitably
fated to perish."[2]

Also significant in the formation of Rubenstein's attitude
toward religious observance was the fact that he did not have a
Bar Mitzvah. Bar Mitzvah is a religious ceremony symbolic of
the attainment of religious "manhood" at the age of thirteen.
Rubenstein's parents refused him this rite. Because of that refusal, Rubenstein felt that he had not been confirmed in his
identity as a man or as a Jew at the crucial turning point of
adolescence.

Consequently, Rubenstein adopted an attitude toward religious ritual in marked contrast to that of his parents. Unlike
his parents, he maintained that he could never again regard
religious ritual as without significance. Eventually, he came to
regard ritual as a historically and psychologically authenticated
way of dealing with the crises of life.

Another critical event in Rubenstein's life was the death of
his infant son, Nathaniel, on the morning before the Day of
Atonement, in 1950.[3] His illusions about immortality were
shattered. He began to realize that he could deceive himself no
longer. Furthermore, through psychoanalysis, he became aware

that much of his inner life had been a denial of his own mortality. His wish to be an obedient son, his eagerness to please his elders, associated with his desire to "perform" in the academic world—all these aspects of his behavior he began to view as a futile attempt to escape the realization that he, Richard Rubenstein, was getting older and would die.

But the road to this realization was a slow and painful route— the way of psychoanalysis. Along this way Rubenstein was plagued with feelings of nameless rage which aroused in him intense anxiety.[4] It was this inner unexplainable rage that accounted, in part, for the effect of the Nazi Holocaust on his thinking:

> Perhaps no event in contemporary history had so searing an effect upon me both intellectually and emotionally as the Nazi extermination of the Jews. The Nazis frightened me far more by my realization of how like them most men, including myself, could be, than by any feeling of how different they were. At the time, my greatest fear was my own nameless rage. Beneath the surface, my predominant emotion was objectless anger.[5]

In his writing, however, the object of Rubenstein's anger is identified, the focus of his rebellion is crystallized. Psychoanalytically, the target of his unconscious rage may have been the very authority figures he was consciously trying to please.

Theologically, however, the object of his anger was the supreme authority figure: the idea of an omnipotent Lord of history, supreme over life and death. It is this conception of God, Rubenstein contends, that is no longer valid after Auschwitz.

Auschwitz and the God of History

One may wonder why this particular thinker should have been selected for consideration at this juncture. The reason is that Rubenstein's thought constitutes a challenge that must be faced. This challenge is both to theology in general and to Jewish theology in particular.

Rubenstein projects into bold relief some of the most crucial general theological problems.

First, the problem of evil. This problem is usually posed in the following way: If God is a Being both all-powerful and all-good, why is evil so rife in the world? To Rubenstein, this problem is not merely academic. It has been personally devastating to him.

Second, the problem of psychology and religion—namely, can theological issues such as the existence of God be reduced to problems of a psychoanalytic nature? Is God merely a universal father figure and religion the obsessional neurosis of mankind, as Freud argued?

Third, death-of-God theology. The idea of this theology is that we are living in a cultural milieu where, for all intents and purposes, God is dead—in the sense that the problem of God is not a live issue. In other words, modern man is so blatantly secular that, in the words of the Frenchman Pierre Laplace, God is merely a hypothesis that man can do without. These are the general theological issues posed by Rubenstein.

And they are all bound together with what is considered by many to be the crucial problem in contemporary Jewish theology—namely, how can a Jew believe in God after Auschwitz? What concept of God can a Jew hold after Auschwitz?

The presupposition of the problem is that it is self-evident that Auschwitz forces us to change, or at least reexamine, our theological categories. What are these theological categories?

It has been a perennial Jewish belief that God is supreme and active in history. Furthermore, traditional Jews have believed that there is a special relationship between God and the Jewish people. By virtue of this relationship, the Jews are God's chosen people. Jewish apologists have vigorously argued that no assertion of superiority is intended. Rather "noblesse oblige"— Israel's chosenness bespeaks obligation and responsibility. If Israel fulfills its obligations to God, the Jews will flourish as a people. But if they reject God and His covenant[6]—the contractual relationship He imposes—they must suffer the consequences of their disobedience.

Now, if this traditional theological scheme is accepted, how is Auschwitz to be explained? Rubenstein believes that he takes the traditional position to its logical, inevitable, and unspeakable conclusion:

> If I believed in God as the omnipotent author of the historical drama and Israel as His chosen people, I had to accept Dean Gruber's conclusion that it was God's will that Hitler committed six million Jews to slaughter. I could not possibly believe in such a God nor could I believe in Israel as the chosen people of God after Auschwitz.[7]

Rubenstein here has loaded the dice by presenting the traditional scheme in the worst possible light.

Even according to the traditional view, God's omnipotence is a highly qualified omnipotence—qualified, that is, by human freedom and human behavior. There is virtually no idea that is stressed more in the Bible than human freedom of choice. Man is called upon to choose life itself: "I call heaven and earth to witness against you this day, that I have set before thee life and death, the blessing and the curse; therefore choose life" (Deuteronomy 30:19). According to this conception in Jewish theology, it was man who chose death at Auschwitz, not God.

Rubenstein's rejoinder at this point would probably be along the following lines: Yes, man chose death, but God allowed it to happen. After all, if we accept the view that God is omnipotent, then God has the power to control events. Why, then, did God allow the Holocaust?

In effect, Rubenstein's rejoinder applies not only to the Holocaust but to all human suffering. Rubenstein says this in the following paragraph, which, incidentally, contradicts his own insistence about the uniqueness of the Holocaust as an example of human suffering:

> In *The Brothers Karamazov,* Dostoevsky puts into the mouth of the atheist Ivan the final, irrefutable, and unanswerable objection to a personal or theistic conception of God. In the chapter on Rebellion, Ivan first offers example after example of the cruelty of man to man and of God's *implication in that cruelty if He has the power to control it.* . . . A God who tolerates the suffering of even one innocent child is either infinitely cruel or hopelessly indifferent.[8]

Rubenstein here is tacitly admitting that, theologically, the suffering of one innocent child is as problematic as the death of millions. The mass murder in our time is in part a function of technology, which the poet William Butler Yeats profoundly prophesied at the turn of this century to be the savage god of the modern age.[9]

And our reaction to tragedies in terms of numbers is itself a product of technological thinking—that is, thinking of human beings in terms of statistics or in other impersonal ways.

For Rubenstein, then, Auschwitz is the collective Jewish analogue in our time for the universal problem of human suffering. And, for him, it is human suffering that is "the final, irrefutable and irrevocable objection to a personal or theistic conception of God."

Again, it must be stressed that Rubenstein does not take human freedom seriously enough. This is especially odd for an existentialist. Despite his existentialist leanings, the following recurring refrain persists in Rubenstein's diatribe against a personal God: "God would not allow, God would not tolerate, God would not permit. . . ."

This seems to me to be the height of inauthenticity. If God grants freedom to man, then the responsibility rests squarely on man's shoulders. And man must take the good with the bad. He must be willing to suffer the consequences of his freedom.

A far more consistent approach than Rubenstein's is that of the German Protestant theologian Dietrich Bonhoeffer. Bonhoeffer was born in Breslau in 1906. The son of a famous German psychiatrist, he studied in Berlin and New York. His political activities in the Resistance during the early years of the war led to his arrest by the Nazis in 1943. He was hanged in April 1945.

Bonhoeffer pointed out the inauthenticity of implicating God in human evil. In a very paradoxical yet extremely meaningful way, Bonhoeffer underscored man's freedom. It is God's will, Bonhoeffer argued, for man to live without Him. It is God's will for man to stand on his own feet. And in his most celebrated phrase, "Man has come of age," Bonhoeffer argued for a new theology of human freedom and responsibility: "So our coming of age forces us to a true recognition of our situation vis-à-vis God. God is teaching us that we must live as men who can get along very well without Him."[10]

Can we apply this theology to a post-Auschwitz Jewish philosophy of history? Or must we accept Rubenstein's verdict of the death of the God of history?

At this point, some further observations are necessary concerning Rubenstein's verdict. We have seen his reliance on Dostoevsky in the passage about the suffering of an innocent child. Even more heavily does Rubenstein rely upon the statement Dostoevsky puts in the mouth of Ivan Karamazov: "If God does not exist, all things are permitted." Commenting on this passage Rubenstein writes:

> In both Judaism and Christianity, all moral restraints are ultimately derivative of God's lordship over the created world. The wish to murder God is the terminal mythic expression of

mankind's ineradicable temptation to moral anarchy. . . . The death camps are one possibility in a world devoid of God.[11]

Let us analyze Dostoevsky's statement and Rubenstein's comment. In the first place, Dostoevsky's statement is by no means self-evident. One is compelled to ask: permitted by whom? Is God the only sanction for ethics? What about society? What about conscience?

Far more interesting, for our purposes, is Rubenstein's interpretation of Dostoevsky's statement. Closer inspection reveals that Rubenstein's comment is based on a logical fallacy—the fallacy of affirming the consequent. Rubenstein is actually arguing as follows: "All things were permitted in Nazi Germany. Therefore, God does not exist."

Psychological factors, however, are more important than logical considerations in evaluating Rubenstein's theology. One cannot help but feel Rubenstein's wish to murder God.

In this connection, it is apposite to repeat Rubenstein's later reflections on the impact of the Nazi Holocaust on his thinking: "The Nazis frightened me far more by my realization of how like them most men, including myself, could be, than by any feeling of how different they were."[12]

The following conclusion, I believe, can be drawn. For Rubenstein, the God who is dead is the omnipotent authoritarian God. Psychoanalytically, Rubenstein has acted out his wish to murder this God. But he has illicitly identified this conception of God with all conceptions of a God of history. Therefore, he has concluded that the God of history is dead.

This conclusion I believe to be premature, and for this reason. The phrase "God of history" is by no means univocal; it is in fact highly ambiguous. There is absolutely no *a priori* reason to identify the God of history with an omnipotent Being pulling the strings of reward and punishment.

I have suggested an alternative conception of the phrase "God of history." God can be conceived of as that power that goads man as an individual and men as nations to freedom, self-determination, and righteousness. We are living at a time when man must learn to shoulder ethical responsibility himself. The function of God is not to relieve man of that responsibility but to encourage him to accept it.

Let us now apply this conception to the particular relationship of God and the Jewish people. It should be clear at the outset that it is *supremely* applicable here.

Auschwitz taught the Jewish people once and for all that they must stand on their own feet. This is the theological meaning of the State of Israel in our time: the principle of Jewish self-determination.

We can, perhaps, give the much abused concept of "covenant" a contemporary interpretation.[13] It is no longer a master-servant or overlord-vassal relationship. God is manifested in the will to self-determination, and Israel is the embodiment of this will. The principle of the covenant, we might say, is that the present age is precisely the time to stop asking: "Why did God allow these things to happen?" It is rather the time to start asking: "How can we enact God's will—the will to freedom and self-determination of peoples in history?"

I therefore do not agree with Rubenstein that the God of history is dead. Rather, I believe that the phrase "God of history" must be reinterpreted in our time, and I have suggested such a reinterpretation.

It is singularly unfortunate that Rubenstein has decided to abandon any attempt to reinterpret the conception of a "God of history." For Rubenstein's conception of the Jewish people after Auschwitz would in fact be reinforced by the kind of reinterpretation I have suggested. It is to Rubenstein's conception of the Jewish people that we now turn.

Rubenstein's Conception of the Jewish People

One of the dominant influences on the thought of Richard Rubenstein was the nineteenth-century German philosopher Friedrich Nietzsche. Three of Nietzsche's doctrines have been adopted by Rubenstein.

First, he has accepted Nietzsche's doctrine of the death of God as a cultural fact. In this connection it is important to recall that Nietzsche emphasized that man has killed God. William Barrett has cogently suggested a reason for Nietzsche's strange assertion: "Man killed God, he says, because he could not bear to have anyone looking at his ugliest side. Man must cease to feel guilt, he goes on, and yet one senses an enormous hidden guilt and feeling of inferiority behind his own frantic boasts."[14]

Rubenstein's motives for espousing a death-of-God philosophy are astonishingly similar. Rubenstein maintains that the Jewish people in exile (from the Roman defeat in 70 C.E. to the founding of the State of Israel in 1948) were a compliant, powerless, and guilt-ridden or self-repressed community. The rigorous religious discipline the Jews imposed on themselves during this time Rubenstein explains as a strategy for survival of a repressed minority:

> Lacking effective power over their own destiny, Jews were compelled to control their counteraggressive hostilities. . . . Surrender, appeasement, and withdrawal were the classic modes of Jewish relation to the non-Jewish world. Nevertheless, Jewish anger had to be controlled. The need to control the community against the possibility of futile explosions of aggression was undoubtedly one of the reasons for the extraordinary measure of self-repression that Rabbinic Judaism placed upon the Jew in so many areas of life. Religious Jews were convinced for almost two thousand years that the system of self-repression was divinely ordained.[15]

Rubenstein then goes on to argue that the Holocaust decisively showed the futility of this strategy for survival. The strategy of compliance and appeasement simply did not work. This was the lesson of Auschwitz to the modern Israeli: no longer compliance, no longer appeasement, no longer powerlessness. The Israelis, Rubenstein claims, have adopted a different strategy for survival—the will to power.

The doctrine of the will to power is the second of Nietzsche's ideas that Rubenstein has espoused. Nietzsche (and also, incidentally, the psychologist Alfred Adler) maintained that people were motivated primarily by the will to power, or to self-assertion. By employing this concept, Rubenstein's aim is to change the image of the Jew from one of powerlessness to one of power. And the modern Israeli is his prototype.

It is at this point that Rubenstein's realism changes in tone to an apocalyptic vision. So enamored is he of Israel and the Israelis that he advocates a return to a paganism of the land:

> Jewish history has written the final chapter in the terrible story of the God of history. The straight line of Jewish history has become the circle of eternal return. The people who gave the world the dread illusion of the angry sky-god recants its folly. The joy of Israel's Jews at the Western Wall was the joy of homecoming. After nineteen hundred years, Jews have begun to

return home, to the only home they ever knew. Archaic man
has reappeared in the midst of the children of Abraham the
wanderer. So, too, have the archaic gods.[16]

Here Rubenstein displays the influence of Nietzsche's third
doctrine: the myth of the eternal return. The myth of the eternal
return is an attempt to annul the irreversibility of time and the
linear conception of history. In this view, history is not conceived of as moving in a straight line (linear), but as an eternal
repetition in an endless cycle.

Rubenstein here, like Nietzsche, aligns himself with the ancient
Greek cyclical view of history rather than the Hebraic Biblical
linear conception.

Rubenstein's espousal of paganism is perhaps the most problematic aspect of his thought. And it is aggravated by a sloppiness
in description and an exaggeration that virtually nullifies his
realism in the treatment of the Jewish self-image. In the first
place, to speak of a "final" chapter in the terrible story of the
God of history is to leave the realm of disciplined thought to
make unverifiable and virtually meaningless assertions. For a
thinker who seems to be so sensitive to the cultural climate, talk
of a "final" chapter is bizarre indeed.

In the second place, Rubenstein paints an especially repugnant,
one-sided, and Christian picture of the God of the Old Testament
as "an angry sky-god." And with what conception does he replace
it? In his own words, ". . . the only God I believe in is the cannibal Mother Goddess of Earth who brings forth her children only
to consume them and take them back unto herself."[17]

This is hardly more appealing than the angry sky-god. In fact,
the mixture of paganism and psychoanalysis (rebellion against
the father-god and return to the mother) is surely not the kind
of theology which makes for coping with reality.

For this purpose, a theology in which God is conceived of as a
power making for self-determination is far more apposite. Take,
for example, Rubenstein's statement: "Israelis are convinced that
they can trust nothing save their own determination to fight to
the last man should an enemy seek to annihilate them."[18] How
much more satisfying would a positive theology be in reinforcing
this view of the Jewish people? Why, then, does Rubenstein
advocate such a negative theology? It is this question which we
now examine.

Rubenstein's Post-Auschwitz Theology: God as Holy Nothingness

As a writer, Rubenstein evokes many moods. When he attempts to shock, he waxes pagan and speaks of God as a cannibal mother-goddess. In his more sophisticated essays, he waxes philosophical and speaks of God as Holy Nothingness.

This forbidding phrase is really not difficult to understand. Rubenstein simply means that God is no thing—that is, God cannot be identified with anything. This is admittedly a mystical conception, and Rubenstein explains it as follows:

> When God is thus designated, he is conceived of as the ground and source of all existence. To speak of God as the Holy Nothingness is not to suggest that he is a void. On the contrary, he is an indivisible plenum so rich that all existence derives from his essence. God as the Nothing is not absence of being but a superfluity of being.
>
> Why then use the term Nothingness? Use of the term rests in part upon a very ancient observation that all definition of finite entities involves negation. The infinite God, the ground of all finite beings, cannot be defined. The infinite God is therefore in no sense a thing bearing any resemblance to the finite beings of the empirical world. The infinite God is nothing.[19]

Close analysis reveals this conception to be self-contradictory. The point of speaking about God as Holy Nothingness, we are led to believe, is a function of the indefinability of God. But Rubenstein proceeds to do just that—namely, to suggest that God is the ground and source of all existence.

What Rubenstein has done is transparent. He has taken Paul Tillich's conception of God as the Ground of Being,[20] and entitled it Holy Nothingness in order to incorporate it into his pessimistic and death-centered conception of reality. Rubenstein himself explains his conception of Holy Nothingness in this manner:

> This affirmation acknowledges the ultimacy of God. Nevertheless, it reflects the conviction that human existence cannot be based on any hope which transcends the terms and limitations of the body and its timetable. He who speaks of God as the Holy Nothingness abandons all ultimate hope.[21]

What does Rubenstein mean by ultimate hope? To answer this question, we must return to the all-pervasive theme and obsession of his thought—namely, death. Indeed, Rubenstein goes so far as to identify the Messiah with the Angel of Death.

> I have been compelled to assert that if there is a Messiah, he can only be the Angel of Death. Understandably, this paradoxical idea has been the subject of some confusion. To refer to the Angel of Death as the Messiah is another way of saying that the dilemmas and ironies of personal existence can only be terminated by death, that life necessarily involves the limitations and the harsh ambiguities of *unredeemed existence*.[22]

Here, I believe, we find the crux of the issue. Redeemed existence, for Rubenstein, connotes redemption from death. Therefore, life is ultimately absurd or meaningless. There is no ultimate hope. Our only recourse, Rubenstein holds, is to accept our mortality and to endure our earthly existence as best we can.

What, then, is the purpose of Judaism? For Rubenstein, Judaism represents primarily a way of sharing by ritual the fundamental crises of existence: birth, puberty (Bar Mitzvah), marriage, and death. Rubenstein contends that these rituals are meaningful even without belief in God. He provides as an illustration the Bar Mitzvah ceremony:

> Primitive man never left the individual to face the crises of life unaided by meaningful myths and rituals as we do. The Bar Mitzvah ceremony is significant because it confirms the young man in his growing identity at a most appropriate time and in a setting of the greatest possible significance. Even without God, this ritual would remain emotionally indispensable for Jews.[23]

The function of Judaism, then, is a communal one. The purpose of the synagogue is to be a Jewish communal institution which enables the Jewish people to share the existential crises of life and death together. And its most important function, as we would expect Rubenstein to say, is to enable the Jew to face the primary existential crisis—the crisis of death.

Rubenstein's philosophy, then, begins and ends as an effort to come to terms with death. Rubenstein himself came to terms with death by the slow and painful realization, through analysis, that there is no redemption from death. But is redemption from death the only kind of redemption? And is the encounter with death or the encounter with nothingness the root psychoanalytical problem?

These are some of the questions we now raise in our critique.

Critique of Rubenstein's Thought

At first blush, it might seem that Rubenstein is particularly vulnerable to criticism. In fact, in some circles he has even been cavalierly dismissed because of his psychological problems. This, I believe, is extremely unfair and violates the canons of decent discourse. But since he relies so heavily on psychoanalysis, he is open to criticism along theoretical psychoanalytical lines. First, however, let us examine his thought on purely philosophic grounds, using our first criterion: inner consistency.

In a number of ways, it must be said, Rubenstein is an extremely consistent thinker. He is absolutely unremitting in his tragic, pessimistic vision of man. He offers man no hope. He is stark and bold in his modes of expression.

Nevertheless, Rubenstein is not consistent in his thinking about God. He would be far more consistent if he adopted the outright atheism of a Bertrand Russell and the outright secularism of many of the modern Israelis he so admires.

Instead, after announcing the death of God as a cultural fact, he informs us that it is only the "God of history" that is dead. It is only the "patriarchal" God that is dead. Rubenstein then proceeds to introduce a concept of God as Holy Nothingness, a "maternal" ground and source of our being to which we return at death—in harsher terms, an earth goddess which devours us at death.

Now just what is the point of introducing this concept of God? Rubenstein is at pains to indicate that this God offers no hope. Nor does belief in this God lead to any kind of improvement of man and his world. What purpose, then, does it serve?

It seems to me that Rubenstein is engaged in a salvage operation. People need religion. Jews need Judaism. Therefore, let the synagogue serve as a means of meeting this need; i.e., sharing the crises of life. Judaism presupposes a belief in God. Therefore, Rubenstein engages in a dubious effort to construct a concept of God so that there will be some ultimate foundation for religion.

But Judaism also presupposes that belief in God adds meaning and significance to human life. It therefore seems that Rubenstein's concept of God is really a *deus ex machina* invoked to legitimize his theology as a *theo-logy,* or discourse about God.

We now examine Rubenstein's thought in terms of our second criterion: empirical reference. Rubenstein's philosophy is based on his own personal experiences. He considers his experiences to be prior to abstract and objective thought. In this respect, he is an existentialist. And the vehicle of his self-discovery was psychoanalysis.

Now the central theme of Rubenstein's thought, we have seen, is his own personal encounter with death. And he has repeatedly asserted that this awareness is fundamental to psychoanalysis.

It is at this point that Rubenstein makes a fundamental mistake—but a mistake that is not uncommon to existentialists. The mistake is to generalize or universalize one's own experience. Reading Rubenstein's thought would lead one to believe that the fundamental problem of human beings, and the major issue of psychoanalysis, is the fear of death. To be sure, Rubenstein does inform us periodically that he is speaking from his experience. But he writes with such authority and vehemence that one is lead to believe that his psychological problem is universal.

In fact, however, Rubenstein, like many other existentialists, fails to take seriously the very concept of the movement—namely, that each individual's experience is unique. One man may fear death. Another person may fear rejection or failure. Yet another may fear crowds. In fact, many people are more afraid of life than of death. Otherwise, why would suicide exist?

Empirically and psychoanalytically, Rubenstein has overstated his case. Neurosis is a product of childhood anxieties. And no two people have had identical childhoods. In short, each person's experience is unique. Therefore, Rubenstein's thought is applicable to *his* experience but not necessarily to the experience of others.

Let us consider, for example, the experience of two people. The first, Benjamin Wolstein, is a prominent psychiatrist. It is his contention that philosophies such as Rubenstein's exaggerate the psychoanalytic importance of the fear of death: "Other philosophies also come to terms with the unalterable fact of death, without, however, making it the primary principle of life."[24]

The other, A. J. Ayer, is a leading British philosopher. Ayer criticizes the tendency of many existential philosophers to dwell on the fact of one's own death. He, personally, sees absolutely no virtue in living *sub specie mortis*—under the aspect of death. Ironically and rhetorically, Ayer asks: "But granting that most of us do not live *sub specie mortis,* is it at all clear that we should?"[25]

In short, Rubenstein's theology may be true for his own experience. But this by no means implies that it has genuine empirical reference to the experience of others.

In terms of the criterion of pragmatic value, our evaluation of Rubenstein's thought should be clear from the preceding remarks. I believe Rubenstein's thought to be singularly deficient in not offering man a principle or a belief that would generate a will to improvement, a will to fulfillment, a will to redemption in this life.

For this reason, I have criticized his dismissal of the "God of history" and suggested the need for a reinterpretation of this phrase in terms of the power that makes for self-determination.

Rubenstein might rejoin by saying that "the truth hurts"— that in robbing man of his illusions he has performed a valuable service. This claim would have merit if there were sustained arguments or attempted justification on Rubenstein's part for the truth of his position.

For the most part, however, Rubenstein engages in *ex cathedra* pronouncements. His authorities are Nietzsche, Camus, Sartre, Heidegger, and Tillich.

Rubenstein epitomizes the weakness of contemporary Jewish theology in general—namely, the lack of argumentation. What, one might ask, is Rubenstein's theory of knowledge? On what basis does he claim to know the truth of what he asserts? What are his criteria? Are there any, besides his personal experience? It is clear that there are none.

These, then, are the problems raised by an examination of this contemporary Jewish theologian. And these are problems, we shall see, that will persist throughout contemporary Jewish thought.

NOTES

1. Richard Rubenstein, *My Brother Paul* (New York: Harper and Row, 1972), p. 14.
2. *Ibid.*, p. 15.
3. *Idem.*
4. *Ibid.*, p. 8.
5. *Idem.*
6. This term will be explicated in more detail in connection with the theology of Eugene Borowitz.
7. Richard Rubenstein, *After Auschwitz: Essays in Contemporary Judaism* (New York: The Bobbs-Merrill Company, Inc., 1966), p. 46.

8. *After Auschwitz,* pp. 86–87.

9. See A. Alvarez, *The Savage God* (New York: Random House, Inc., 1971), pp. 236–262.

10. Dietrich Bonhoeffer, *Letters and Papers from Prison* (New York: The Macmillan Co., 1972), letter of July 16, 1944.

11. *After Auschwitz,* pp. 12–13.

12. *My Brother Paul,* p. 8.

13. As I shall note in more detail later, this is precisely what Jewish "covenant" theologians (e.g., Eugene Borowitz) fail to spell out.

14. William Barrett, *Irrational Man* (Garden City, N.Y.: Doubleday and Co., Inc., 1958) p. 162.

15. Richard Rubenstein, "Homeland and Holocaust," in *The Religious Situation 1968,* ed. Donald R. Cutler (Boston: Beacon Press, 1968), pp. 47–48.

16. *Ibid.,* p. 61.

17. *Ibid.,* p. 56.

18. *Ibid.,* p. 50.

19. Richard Rubenstein, *Morality and Eros* (New York: McGraw-Hill Book Co., 1970), pp. 185–186.

20. See *Ibid.,* p. 190.

21. *Ibid.,* p. 193.

22. *Ibid.,* pp. 195–196. Italics added.

23. *After Auschwitz,* p. 235.

24. Benjamin Wolstein, *Irrational Despair: An Examination of Existential Analysis* (New York: The Free Press of Glencoe), p. 41.

25. A. J. Ayer, *Metaphysics and Common Sense* (Freeman, Cooper and Co. 1969), p. 211.

6   Eugene B. Borowitz and Emil L. Fackenheim: From Covenant Theology to Commanding Voice

Richard Rubenstein's radical response to the Holocaust is not shared by most contemporary Jewish theologians. Eugene Borowitz, for example, maintains that the Jew can still affirm a belief in the covenant after Auschwitz. Emil Fackenheim agrees with Rubenstein that the Holocaust forces the Jew to restructure his theological categories. But he differs decisively from Rubenstein in his heroic attempt to extract a positive theological commitment from the ashes of Auschwitz.

Borowitz and Fackenheim both share the emphasis which Martin Buber placed on a living encounter between man and God. We turn now to the thought of these two theologians who espouse Buber's doctrine of encounter and attempt to apply it to the relationship between the Jewish people and God. Thus, the question to which we address ourselves in this chapter is:

How shall we conceive of the relationship between the Jewish people and God?

Traditionally, the relationship between the Jewish people and God has been denoted by the term "covenant." A covenant is a spiritual contract or agreement which the Jewish people entered into when they accepted the Torah at Mount Sinai. According to Jewish tradition, the Jewish people were constituted as a people by the event at Sinai. This event refers to that unique occurrence in history when God revealed His will to a people and chose that people as the instrument of His purposes in history. The Jewish people, in this view, are the elect people of God, through whom the Divine kingdom will be realized on earth. The task of the Jewish people is to be "a kingdom of priests and a holy nation" and to thereby be a "light unto the nations." By accepting this role of God's covenant people, they received God's protection and promise. God was to protect them from their enemies and fulfill His promise to bring them into the Holy Land. But this Divine protection and promise were conditional upon Israel's capacity to remain faithful to its terms of the covenant.

Conceived in this manner, the Bible can be read as *Heilsgeschichte*—sacred history.

In the Bible, there is a constant dialectic and tension between the will of God and the people of Israel. When the people act in accordance with God's will, they prosper. But when they rebel against God and fall prey to idolatry, they are severely punished for their apostasy.

The question before us is this: Can the relationship between the Jewish people and God still be conceived of in this manner? The events of the twentieth century are a supreme test case for this view. During the Nazi Holocaust, six million Jews perished. Can this unparalleled tragedy of a people. be related in any way to the will of God? Were the Jewish people being punished for their sins? Were they performing the role of God's suffering servant? Or was this a time of the eclipse of God?

The problem becomes more complicated when we consider that this century also witnessed the return of the Jewish people to their land after nearly two thousand years of exile. The establishment of the State of Israel in 1948 was the light after the darkness of the Holocaust. It is tempting to regard Israel, and especially its victory against overwhelming odds in the 1967 Six-

Day War, as a miracle. But if Israel is regarded as a miracle, as the will of God, then so, too, Auschwitz must be conceived of as somehow within the arena of sacred history.

Thus, our question becomes more precise: Can we still conceive of Jewish history as sacred history? Is God acting and somehow superintending the events of Israel's history?

How shall we *now* conceive of the relationship between the Jewish people and God? This is the question to which we now address ourselves. First, let us examine the views of Eugene Borowitz.

Eugene Borowitz: His Aim and Method

Eugene Borowitz is Professor of Education and Jewish Religious Thought at Hebrew Union College—Jewish Institute of Religion in New York. He is an articulate spokesman of Judaism and a lucid writer. His aim is to discover a mode of theology which he feels is congenial to the uniqueness of Judaism and the Jewish people.

First and foremost, Borowitz is a fideist. That is to say, Borowitz considers faith in God to be the *sine qua non* of Jewish existence. His major aim is to underscore the importance of faith in the spectrum of modern Judaism.

It follows that Borowitz is radically opposed to any conception of Judaism and the Jewish people which minimizes the role of faith. Thus, he excoriates proponents of secularism in Jewish life, especially when such people are found within the "sacred" precincts of the synagogue. Accordingly, Borowitz writes:

> Those, then, who consciously or unconsciously are turning the synagogue into an effectively secular institution are blaspheming a sacred history of millennia, indeed, all the history the Jewish people has ever cared to remember until recent years.[1]

Borowitz is thus a proponent of *Heilsgeschichte,* of sacred history —more precisely, he wishes to maintain that this view of history still holds, and unequivocally so, for the modern age. Those members of synagogues who do not view Jewish history through these eyes of faith—and these are the majority—are simply guilty of blasphemy. What is to be done with these people? To this, Borowitz answers:

> No one wishes to lose Jews for Judaism, but the time has come when the synagogue must be saved for the religious Jew,

when it must be prepared to let some Jews opt out so that those who remain in, or who come in, will not be diverted from their duty to God.[2]

It can therefore be seen that Borowitz's aim is to clarify what he considers to be the nature of Jewish faith for the saving remnant, for the perpetual minority. Thereby, through clarification of the issues, we will presumably be able to separate the chaff from the wheat, and the synagogue will be the home of true believers alone. Although Borowitz's view is singularly uncharitable to the nonbeliever, as a Rabbi I can understand why he proposes it. It is one of the major frustrations of the American Rabbi that he is forced to deal with a majority who are supremely indifferent to and uninterested in theology. It would surely be easier for the modern American Rabbi if he did not have to deal with these "secularists."

But, then again, instead of regarding the secularists as blasphemers, it would perhaps be the better part of wisdom to take them seriously—at least, more seriously than Borowitz takes them. Their very secularism is the index of the collapse of the sense of transcendence in the minds of many modern men. This is *the* religious problem of our time. And it must be faced. One cannot simply run roughshod over it. However, from the perspective of faith, which is the view of Borowitz, it is clear why he considers secularists in the light which he does.

Since Borowitz is a fideist, the next question to ask is: What kind of faith does he seek? Borowitz has as his aim to develop a conception of faith which reflects authentic Judaism but at the same time is intensely personal. For this reason, Borowitz for the most part argues that existentialism is the proper method of Jewish theology. It is important to emphasize the qualifying phrase "for the most part," because Borowitz comes to realize that a full existentialist stance leads to problems.

What, then, does Borowitz mean by existentialism? For Borowitz, existentialism constitutes a defense of the person, of the individual in our mass society and technological age. To Borowitz, it is absolutely clear, beyond a shadow of a doubt, that existentialism is a view that is congenial to human personhood, whereas scientific naturalism is a stance that is inimical to the survival of man in the twentieth century.

If there is one virtue in Borowitz's work, it is that one can have no doubt about where his sympathies lie. One can tell by the very chapter headings of his *A New Jewish Theology in the Making*. Thus Chapter 5 is entitled "The Limits of Naturalism" and Chapter 6, "The Lure of Religious Existentialism." Wherein lies the lure? According to Borowitz, it is only "the existential, not the scientific"[3] mode of thinking that can speak to the fundamental problem of our age—namely, how "to be and stay a person."[4]

This dichotomy that Borowitz draws between "existential" and "scientific" thinking cannot stand the test of scrutiny. Let us take, for example, two atheists: the existentialist Jean-Paul Sartre and the scientific philosopher Bertrand Russell. To Jean-Paul Sartre, man is a "useless passion," whereas Russell's essay "A Free Man's Worship" is a testament to the nobility of the human mind.

Furthermore, in adducing arguments to support his point, Borowitz displays a lack of familiarity with modern philosophy. For instance, in referring to Whitehead and Hartshorne and their "process" metaphysics, Borowitz charges them with "impersonalism and abstraction."[5]

Whitehead, he seems to forget, argued against the fallacy of misplaced concreteness, and Hartshorne is one of the most vigorous proponents of the idea of a personal God in modern philosophy. In fact, it is Hartshorne's chief contention that a personal God is more a logical than an impersonal force. Hence, instead of using these thinkers as support for his personalism, Borowitz makes the egregious error of classifying their metaphysics as "impersonal" when in fact they are supremely personal. What, for example, could be more "personal" than Whitehead's conception of God as a "constant companion?"

Notwithstanding these inaccuracies, Borowitz's intention is clear: he is seeking a personalistic philosophy of religion. Thus Borowitz, writing about Buber, seeks God in "the everyday, in the immediate, in the simple, even as the grace we are expected to say before we bite into our hamburger in some greasy diner should testify."[6] Like Buber, Borowitz seeks God in the concrete, lived relationship between persons and in the occurrences of everyday life, as his mundane example of the diner aptly illustrates.

To summarize: Borowitz is a fideist and an existentialist. The problem is now methodological. Can existentialism serve as a method for explicating Judaism to the faithful minority?

Borowitz struggles admirably with the problem of whether any philosophy at all can be used to explicate Judaism.

After all, in using a philosophy as a hermeneutical tool, are we not introducing an alien factor to explain the indigeneous phenomenon of Judaism? Why can't Judaism be expounded in its own terms?

These questions lead Borowitz to the conclusion that the Jewish tradition should take precedence over any philosophy which is used to interpret it. Nevertheless, he is reluctant to abandon existentialism because it is so congenial to the personal stance he seeks. The outcome of this dialectical tension can be seen in the following statement of Borowitz's position:

> In this new approach to Jewish thought it is the tradition openly held, which is the most important criterion of the philosophy used to interpret it. Which of the modern options is most congenial to its content, not which is the most widely held or persuasively represented on campus this decade, determines the mode of doing theology in an open traditionalism. In terms of my Jewish affirmations, religious existentialism is the most complementary philosophic style available. It supplies the hermeneutic instrument for interpreting Judaism in modern terms but may not usurp that role as a means to replace the primacy of traditional Jewish faith for me. That is what this self-conscious commitment to open traditionalism clarifies. Now when the religious existentialist insights contradict what study shows is classic Jewish faith, as is true in the areas of society, history, and law, I do not automatically judge Judaism to be wrong. Rather, I investigate to see what it is that I truly affirm. Perhaps I believe as the existentialists do and thereby discover a principle to my dissent and thus a higher faith which I affirm. Perhaps here I do autonomously uphold traditional belief and am thus led to criticize and correct religious existentialism. In the case of society and history it seems to me the existentialists are wrong and need the interpersonal, time-oriented vision which Jewish faith provides. In the case of law, I dissent from both positions. That leads me to a Jewish sense that all authentic existence must be structured, an understanding foreign to existentialism. Yet I am also moved to an existentialist reworking of Jewish law in personalist terms it could not traditionally tolerate.[7]

From this statement of his position, it is clear that Borowitz is wrestling with the tension, as he sees it, between the authority of Jewish tradition and an existentialist approach. The view that

Borowitz is advocating is an open traditionalism—one which respects tradition but at the same time is open to the possibility of dissent from it.

The problem with this position is that Borowitz fails to see the variety either in tradition or in existentialism. It is important to ask: What does Borowitz mean by "tradition?" Does he mean the tradition according to the Bible, the Talmud, or the Codes? Or does he mean the tradition sung about in *Fiddler on the Roof?* In short, when Borowitz refers to "the tradition," we must ask: the tradition according to whom?

The problem here is that the term "tradition" is used here in a monolithic sense—and it is assumed that this sense of the term is self-explanatory. The term Judaism is employed here in a similar monolithic sense. However, the fact is that neither "Judaism" nor "tradition" is a univocal term. There are many "Judaisms" and many "traditions" within these varieties. The real question is: What gives organic unity to them all?

The same problem is involved in Borowitz's treatment of the second pole of the tension—existentialism. Borowitz writes of *the* religious existentialist, as if to imply that, as a group, they all contradict "Judaism" in the areas of society, history, and law. Furthermore, existentialists are said to need the interpersonal, time-oriented vision of Judaism, and, moreover, they fail to see that authentic existence must be structured.

This view simply overlooks the variety of existentialist postures. Take, for example, the philosophy of the existentialist Martin Heidegger. Heidegger's thought, to put it mildly, is time-oriented. Man is thoroughly enmeshed in temporal existence. Thus, Heidegger's major work is *Being and Time*. Furthermore, Heidegger views existence as *ab initio* structured.

The human life-world is structured according to various patterns: temporality, anxiety, and being-toward-death. This one example shows that Borowitz cannot include all existentialists within the categories he employs.

But the major difficulty of Borowitz's position, as adumbrated here, is that it turns out to be self-contradictory. First, we are told that the tradition, openly held, is the most important criterion of the philosophy used to interpret it. But then we are told that, in case of dissent from tradition, one may discover a "higher faith" as a principle for one's dissent.

Now if the tradition is the criterion, there can be no higher faith. But if, in principle, a higher faith can be discovered, the tradition is not the criterion. Borowitz cannot have it both ways.

Evidently, Borowitz is aware of this problem. Hence, in his succeeding volume, he writes: "Thus in Jewish theology I object to using a Neo-Kantian or naturalist or existentialist approach because the resulting interpretations of Judaism seem to me have distorted my continuing faith in the people of Israel, the God of Israel, and the Torah of Israel respectively."[8] What is the nature of Borowitz's faith? To answer this question we now turn to his covenant theology.

Covenant Theology

Covenant theology, as described by Borowitz, emphasizes the relationship between God and the Jewish people. The term "covenant" designates the nature of this relationship. And it is defined by Borowitz to signify that throughout the ages "the one God of the universe was using the Jews in a unique way to carry out His purpose in history. The Covenant exists to bring the Messianic Era, to create and await the Kingdom of God."[9]

The first feature of covenant theology, then, is that it involves what has been called "the scandal of particularity." What does this phrase mean? It means that the idea of the universal and timeless God selecting a *particular* people as the instrument of His salvation of mankind is a scandal to the philosophical mind. To the philosophical mind, truth is universal and timeless. It is scandalous to the philosophical mind to assert that one particular people is the embodiment of truth, that one particular people is God's chosen vehicle of mankind's redemption. It can therefore only be understood from within.

What are the terms of the Covenant, according to Borowitz? Borowitz writes: "God's responsibility in that relationship is, among other things, to save his people."[10] By this, Borowitz does not, of course, mean that God will save His people from particular catastrophes. Rather he is asserting that God will always preserve the Jewish people and will ultimately vindicate their cause.

Now God's activity in the Covenant does not absolve man of responsibility. But, significantly, Borowitz interprets the Covenant to mean that the human side of it is far less than the Divine. Thus, Borowitz says:

The human side of the Covenant dialectic of action is, as befits man's stature to God's, far more limited. For man simply to act on his own, that is to say, without regard for his Covenant partner, is always wrong. It may seem to lead to success but is nonetheless sin and will be met with punishment. Man's action is truly significant only when it takes place in accordance with God's will. Since He is sovereign in history such acts can endure and bring blessing. More, when a man does them, he knows he does them with God's help, for that is the direction in which God Himself is moving history. The act is now quite precisely a Covenant act in which man and God join together to do a deed, yet each remains himself in his own integrity.[11]

It is especially important to note that Borowitz writes quite easily about such difficult theological concepts as "sin," "punishment," "God's will," and, most amazingly, "God's responsibility." Unfortunately, Borowitz does not take the trouble to explicate precisely what he means by these terms. But, then again, how could he? How can man really say *anything* meaningful about God's responsibility? And how is man to know *when* God is helping him? How, in short, is man to understand God's will?

Borowitz would be on much firmer ground if he simply adopted an Orthodox framework and was fully committed to the practice of *Halacha*. He admits that he is under the Covenant: "The Covenant did not begin with me. I came into it when I was born. It was, so to speak, there waiting for me."[12] But he also writes that he interprets the Covenant "in personal rather than in legal terms."[13] Thus, he has not abandoned existentialism, despite his contention to the contrary. Nevertheless, he feels that he and the Orthodox Jew stand as part of "the same Jewish people united in the same basic relationship with the same God."[14] His only point of difference with the Orthodox Jew is on the nature of the "required action"[15] under the Covenant.

Thus, the same difficulty which confronted Borowitz before rears its head again. Once we admit a *personal, existential* dimension to the concept of Covenant—namely, that the individual somehow decides what is important and what is not, how is it possible to speak of being *bound* by the Covenant? In fact, one is bound by the Covenant only if he accepts it in legal terms as a real obligatory contract with the Divine. Thus, Borowitz does not and cannot spell out what "required action" means other than referring to action in accordance with God's will, as if this mode of expression were self-explanatory.

A further difficulty is how the Holocaust can be incorporated in Borowitz's scheme of sin and punishment. Here Borowitz admits an exception, for "the social suffering was too great to be seen as any sort of Divine punishment or instruction."[16] Was God then active at all in history at this time? Borowitz's answer is that although God did not act then, subsequent history, especially the Six-Day War, gives rise to a renewed faith in or openness to the possibility of God's action in history. It would thus appear that Borowitz would not disagree with Buber's theory of the eclipse of God.

However, Borowitz differs from many other Jewish thinkers of our time in the fact that he does not place much theological weight on the Holocaust. Accordingly, he writes: "I only know that for me, and I believe for the Jewish people as a whole, the Holocaust was shattering but not determinative. It was not the Sinai of our time."[17] Therefore, it should not become "our paradigm for future history."[18] Borowitz rather sees the importance of the Holocaust not in itself but in the fact that the Holocaust did not give rise to a mass desertion of Judaism. Borowitz views the moral indignation and moral protest of the Jew and his commitment to Jewish survival after the Holocaust as indicative of a refusal "not to believe."[19]

In this respect, Borowitz differs especially from the thinker to be discussed next: Emil Fackenheim. Borowitz maintains that the terms of the Covenant remain the same after Auschwitz. Fackenheim, like Borowitz, refuses to give up the idea of God acting in history. But, unlike Borowitz, Fackenheim is unwilling to divorce the Holocaust from the Divine.

Hence, in addition to the concept of the Covenant, he will emphasize the idea of God's commanding voice. After summarizing our evaluation of the thought of Eugene Borowitz, we shall turn to an examination of Fackenheim's theology.

Critique of Borowitz

First, let us examine the thought of Eugene Borowitz from the standpoint of our first criterion—inner consistency.

It should be evident from our discussion that there is a basic conflict inherent in Borowitz's theology. On the one hand, Borowitz is sympathetic with existentialism, emphasizing the elements of personal faith and individual choice. On the other hand, Borowitz is seeking a faith which is in consonance with what he considers to be the authenticity of Jewish tradition. This gives rise to a tension between individual autonomy and the authority of tradition.

Borowitz attempts to utilize the concept of Covenant to mediate this tension. But we have seen that this effort does not resolve the tension since Borowitz interprets the Covenant in personal rather than legal terms.

Thus, it must be pointed out that Borowitz cannot have it both ways. Once the individual becomes the arbiter of what is significant and required in Jewish life today, he becomes his own authority and is not acting under the authority of Jewish tradition. Furthermore, as I have pointed out, the concept of "tradition" is too vague in Borowitz's thought. Borowitz fails to clarify this term sufficiently. Hence, Borowitz's thought is marred by internal conflict rather than inner consistency.

In terms of empirical reference, it should also be clear from our discussion that Borowitz does not adequately define or clarify his terms. He uses such expressions as "God's will," "God's responsibility," "sin," and "punishment" as if they are indubitable deliverances of human experience.

Furthermore, rather than attempting to understand the "secular" way of experience characteristic of so many Jews today, Borowitz chastises such Jews for blasphemy and berates them for their lack of interest in theology.

The empirical reference of Borowitz's thought is for those who already have faith and are seeking to clarify its nature.

Again, the pragmatic value of Borowitz's theology is that it may help to strengthen those who already possess the faith he urges. Those who can readily experience the reality of God's will, without difficulties of interpretation, will find Borowitz's theology of practical value for them. Moreover, those who share Borowitz's antipathy toward scientific naturalism will also find Borowitz's thought congenial.

But those who seek precision of terminology and a theology which takes into consideration the difficulty modern man experiences in the struggle for faith will see little understanding of their problem and, hence, sparse pragmatic value in the theology of Eugene Borowitz.

Emil Fackenheim: The Odyssey of a Jewish Theologian

There are various characteristics of a thinker which command our respect. Not the least of these is the capacity of a philosopher to adapt and revise his views. This is a distinguishing feature of the thought of Emil Fackenheim, Professor of Philosophy at the University of Toronto.

Professor Fackenheim was ordained as a Rabbi in Berlin in 1939. After three months' internment in a Nazi concentration camp, he went first to Scotland and then to Canada, where he is now a citizen.

However, it is important, initially, to note those theses that remain constant throughout Fackenheim's thought. First, like Borowitz, Fackenheim is a fideist; he emphasizes the importance of "faith," which he defines as "total commitment."[20] For the Jew, this commitment is "to an all-consuming experience in the present, or else to memories of such experiences which had taken place in the past."[21] From this stress on "experience," one can note immediately Fackenheim's existentialist orientation. His concern is not the concept of God. Rather, the experience of God's presence (existence) takes precedence over any human attempt to define or demarcate the meaning (essence) of the term God. Existence, for Fackenheim, is decidedly prior to essence.

This existentialist orientation of Fackenheim gives rise to the second constant element in his thought—the primacy of encounter. Thus, Fackenheim writes that a theological affirmation to which he has been committed throughout his career is that "Judaism is a history of encounters between God and Israel of which the evolution of ideas is a mere human reflection."[22] Here the influence of Buber is evident. What is of primary significance, for Fackenheim, is the living, existential encounter between man and God. This encounter, Fackenheim contends, is irreducible to essentialist, ideational, and psychological terms. As he has said, "The evolution of ideas is a *mere* human reflection." It follows that Fackenheim is a firm believer in revelation, which for him differs "qualitatively"[23] from human inspiration and is "an event of Divine incursion shot through with human interpretation."[24]

Hence, a significant problem recurring in Fackenheim's thought is: How do we distinguish the Divine from the human in an encounter? Or, what are the criteria for discovering God's presence in history, in human life?

We can note already that Fackenheim does not hold an Orthodox view of revelation. Revelation, for him, was not a "once
and for all" occurrence at Sinai. Rather, if revelation was real
in Biblical times, it must also be available for modern man.
Why, then, is it not? This gives rise to the third constant element in Fackenheim's thought.

Throughout his career, Fackenheim has argued that revelation is not available to modern man because he has shut his ears
to it. Illustrative of this tendency of modern man is the oft-
quoted remark of the eighteenth-century astronomer Laplace
about God: "Sire, I do not require that hypothesis." This tendency Fackenheim calls "subjectivist reductionism."[25] The scientist reduces God to a hypothesis; the psychologist reduces
God to a projection of feeling; many modern philosophers reduce God to an idea. Perhaps the most important recurring
theme in Fackenheim's thought is that God is a reality and not
merely an idea, and furthermore, that there is no *a priori* reason for not assuming that the reality of God is prior to our ideas
of Him.

To summarize: the three constant elements in Fackenheim's
thought are his emphases on faith, encounter, and openness to
the *reality* of the presence of God.

We now turn to those areas where Fackenheim has seen fit
to revise his thoughts. Like Eugene Borowitz, Fackenheim was,
in the early stages of his thought, quite unsympathetic with
secularism and humanism. In fact, his early writings[26] were largely polemics against secularist humanism. Fackenheim writes:

> I then stood, as it were, between an apologetic, compromising
> liberalism which I saw as dissipating into humanism, and the
> convenantal reaffirmation of revelation, largely understood in
> the terms of Buber and Rosenzweig; my thought, therefore, was
> essentially polemical. Had I then stood *within* the covenantal
> affirmation I would have been freer to take modern life and its
> problems into it.[27]

What Fackenheim is saying is that in his early thought, he
was writing as a polemical philosopher, attempting to show the
weaknesses of liberalism and secular humanism and the consequent existential need for a "leap into faith"[28] to a supernatural God. More precisely, because of the contradictory tensions
of human existence, because of the uneasy combination of the
animal and the spiritual in man, because every effort of man

to pull himself up by his own bootstraps is doomed to failure, man, for his own self-realization, needs God. Man is simply incomplete and doomed to a Sisyphus-like existence without faith in a supernatural God. This was Fackenheim's contention in his early essays.[29] Now he rejects such a categorical dichotomy of faith versus despair as spurious: "There is both despair within faith and serene confidence without it."[30]

This is an interesting admission. As a philosopher, writing *about* faith, Fackenheim had a tendency to idealize it as a panacea to man's sense of alienation. Now, standing *within* the circle of faith, that is, within the covenantal affirmation, Fackenheim is realistic enough to admit that there is despair within faith. Doubtless, his confrontation with the Holocaust made this despair within faith quite real and palpable.

Furthermore, confronting the Holocaust gave rise to a different attitude, on Fackenheim's part, to Jewish secular humanists committed to Jewish group survival. In his early writings, Fackenheim did not see religious value in Jewish survival as such. More precisely, Jewish survival as a *duty* was only intelligible to Fackenheim within the scope of religious faith. Thus, at that time, Fackenheim asserted that "the Jew of today who persists in regarding Jewish survival as a duty, either persists in something unintelligible, or else he postulates, however unconsciously, the possibility of a return to faith in a living God."[31] Even more emphatically, Fackenheim further stated that it is possible to reaffirm the ancient duty of Jewish survival only if the modern Jew has "accepted as authentic the ancient encounter of his people with the living God."[32]

Now, however, Fackenheim sees religious value in Jewish survival as such. Fackenheim made this change in stance as a result of his initial response to the Holocaust. In an interview with the present writer, Fackenheim referred to the psychic pain elicited by his first confrontation with the Holocaust in his writing. This confrontation was a symposium for *Judaism* in 1967 on "Jewish Values in the Post-Holocaust Future."[33]

Fackenheim related that, as a result of having to deal with the Holocaust in his writing, he felt that an authentic response to the Holocaust is the realization that survival as such is a Jewish duty. Thus, Fackenheim radically reversed his earlier position with respect to Jewish survival. Subsequent to that symposium, Fackenheim has elaborated on his conception of Jewish survival as a religious duty. He has referred to it as the 614th commandment and as a holy duty. Thus he has written: "Jewish survival, were it even for no more than survival's sake, is a holy duty as well."[34]

Fackenheim now maintains that the secular Jew who is interested in survival only for survival's sake is performing a holy duty. He furthermore looks back and admits that in his earlier writings in the fifties he did not understand "the religious significance"[35] of the secularist's commitment to Jewish survival.

Why did confrontation with the Holocaust elicit this change of stance on Fackenheim's part? It is to this question that we now turn.

The Commanding Voice of Auschwitz

If there is one salient feature that emerges from Fackenheim's works, it is that of unflinching, stubborn faith in a God of history. By the term "God of history," Fackenheim refers not only to God's providence over history but also to His presence in history. In this respect, Fackenheim believes that he differs from other Jewish and Christian theologians. Thus, he writes:

> And the modern Jewish and Christian theologian cannot affirm God's *presence in* history but at most only *His providence* over it—a providence caused by a God who may somehow use nature and man in history, but who is Himself absent from history.[36]

Fackenheim distinguishes between two conceptions of Divine providence—the older, externally superintending kind and the newer, immanent kind. The older doctrine refers to the idea that God is using and controlling history for His purposes. The newer doctrine is that Divine providence is immanent in human freedom. Both of these doctrines, Fackenheim maintains, are called into question by the tragic events of the twentieth century:

> Indeed, Hiroshima and Auschwitz seem to have destroyed any kind of Providence—the newer, immanent kind no less than the older, externally superintending kind. After these dread events, occurring in the heart of the modern, enlightened, technological world, can one still believe in the God who is necessary Progress any more than in the God who manifests His Power in the form of a superintending Providence?[37]

Fackenheim does not do justice to the subtleties of immanent conceptions of Divine providence. In the more sophisticated versions of this conception, human cooperation is necessary in order for the immanent ideal to be realized. What Fackenheim is criticizing are views of necessary progress such as that advocated by the French enlightenment thinker Condorcet.

Fackenheim is primarily concerned with the supernaturalist view of a superintending Providence over history. He sees this view as radically challenged by the tragic events of the twentieth century, especially by the Holocaust. And the tragedy of the Jewish people, in particular, constitutes the test for this doctrine.

The uniqueness of the Jewish people, in this regard, lies in a most tragic irony. The Jews, Fackenheim writes, were the "first to affirm the God of history."[38] Moreover, he contends that their collective survival throughout the ages was bound up with this doctrine. But at Auschwitz, Jews were singled out for destruction, "not because they had disobeyed the God of history, but rather because their great-grandparents had obeyed him."[39]

The uniqueness of the Jewish tragedy in the Holocaust is that Jews were murdered not because of their own faith but because of the faith affirmed by their ancestors. What faith, for example, could have been affirmed by a child cruelly and viciously cast into the flames of Auschwitz? This child was murdered because of the Jewish faith affirmed by one of his ancestors. The uniqueness of the tragedy of Auschwitz, then, is that the Jews who died there by and large did not choose martyrdom.

There was no escape possible through conversion or apostasy, as in other collective Jewish tragedies. Jews there were singled out because of the faith affirmed by their ancestors. And, irony of ironies, the faith was in many cases faith in a God of history. Thus, it would appear that today Jews are morally bound to reject the God of history.

Having argued such a persuasive case *against* the applicability of a God of history to contemporary Jewish life, Fackenheim refuses to draw the logical conclusion of rejection of this concept. He writes, dramatically, that before taking such a step the Jewish believer "must pause, and pause at length."[40] He must pause because this belief has been a constant throughout Jewish history and, moreover, because this belief has helped the Jewish people to sustain their faith in previous periods of national suffering and catastrophe. The burden of Fackenheim's argument now becomes a defense of the God of history—more precisely, a refusal to disconnect God from history. How does Fackenheim set forth this argument?

It is important to note that Fackenheim does not deal in a straightforward manner with this problem. He is far too sophisticated a theologian to opt for a crude supernaturalism by stating that God was somehow in control of events and hence responsible for the Holocaust. Rather, Fackenheim's defense of the concept of a God of history takes an oblique route. His argument is that God's *presence* was manifested at Auschwitz. Whether or not God can still be conceived of as an external power that controls and is responsible for Jewish destiny is a question left open by Fackenheim.

In short, Fackenheim phrases the theological question in terms of God's providence over history but works out the answer in terms of God's presence in history.

However, since Fackenheim, as we have seen, considers God's presence in history to be a stronger belief than God's providence over it, one might infer that if an argument can be sustained for the former, a belief in the latter follows as a logical consequence. According to Fackenheim, one can believe in God's providence over history and yet deny God's presence in history. To affirm God's presence in history, therefore, would imply that one believes as well in the doctrine of God's providence over it, *unless* one believes in a finite God who is present with man in his suffering but powerless to do anything about it. Since Fackenheim rejects this latter doctrine,[41] it follows according to the logic of his case, that if he can somehow affirm God's presence in history, belief in God's providence is also implied.

Because of moral and emotional reasons that are readily comprehensible, Fackenheim cannot state unequivocally that he still believes in God's providence after Auschwitz. The most he can do is to argue for God's presence at Auschwitz and leave the inference of God's providence to be implied.

With this preliminary consideration in mind, the first question to be raised is: What does Fackenheim mean by God's presence in history? Here Fackenheim relies heavily on Buber's doctrine of encounter. He quotes approvingly a passage from Buber's *Moses* regarding the miracle at the Red Sea:

> What is decisive with respect to the inner history of mankind . . . is that the children of Israel understood this as an act

of their God, as a miracle, which does not mean that they interpreted it as a miracle, but that they experienced it as such,
that as such they perceived it.

The concept of miracle which is permissible from the historical approach can be defined at its starting point as an abiding
astonishment. . . . The real miracle means that in the astonish-
ing experience of the event the current system of cause and effect becomes, as it were, transparent and permits a glimpse of
the sphere in which a sole power, not restricted by any other, is
at work.[42]

According to this interpretation of miracle, the important
factor is not a supernaturalist conception in which the laws of
nature are superseded. Rather, the essence of a miracle is a perception of abiding astonishment, of wonder, which permits a
glimpse of the unitary power of God at work. The Divine presence, according to this interpretation, is directly manifested in
a natural, historical event. What is of special significance is Buber's contention, which Fackenheim adopts, that God's presence
is directly and immediately experienced in the event. Both Buber
and Fackenheim are at pains to deny that any inference has
taken place here. The Divine presence is not inferred as an explanation for the event. It is directly experienced. It is an encounter.

Since Fackenheim relies so heavily upon this passage from Buber, it is important to pause and reflect on it. Notice that Buber
has said that the Israelites did not interpret the event at the
Red Sea as a miracle but rather that they experienced it or
perceived it as such. This is quite simply a contradiction in
terms. Perception involves, by its very nature, an element of interpretation. I see a brown patch against a white background. I
perceive a table against the background of the white wallpaper.
Fackenheim's doctrine of immediate Divine presence, based on
Buber's conception of an immediate experience of Divine power, rests on a blurring of the distinction between sensation and
perception. It was precisely because the ancient Israelites inhabited a universe of discourse where what *we* call natural-historical events were *interpreted,* quite often, as incursions of the
Divine, that they were able to perceive the events of the Red
Sea as a miracle (in Buber's sense of the term).

The miracle at the Red Sea constitutes, for Fackenheim, a
root experience in Jewish history.[43] A root experience has three

characteristics. First, it is a past event which makes a present claim—namely, that God is present in history. Second, it has a public, historical character. Third, and most important, this past event is still presently accessible.

The third condition is clearly the most important, since, for Fackenheim, these past events or root experiences have no power for the believer unless they are accessible in the present:

> Thus the pious Jew remembering the Exodus and the salvation at the Red Sea does not call to mind events now dead and gone. He reenacts these events as a present reality; only thus is he assured that the past saving God saves still, and that He will finally bring ultimate salvation.[44]

It is clear that Fackenheim has set for himself a formidable task. It would have been far easier for him to assert that we must take the event at the Red Sea as a miracle by virtue of faith in the Scriptural account. Not being an Orthodox fundamentalist, however, Fackenheim attempts to defend the thesis that it is not enough to reflect on God's presence in the past. Rather, Fackenheim's retrospective reading of Jewish faith rests its case on the accessibility of past to present, on the capacity of the believer to experience God's presence in the here and now. Thus, like Buber, belief in an encounter in the past is predicated on the possibility of encounters in the present.

Now the events at the Red Sea constitute an example of God's *saving* presence. On reenacting the events at the Red Sea, the modern Jew reenacts the abiding astonishment felt by the ancient Israelites and appropriates this experience for himself in the present.

Thus, Fackenheim maintains, the past experience becomes present and memory turns into hope and faith.

The events at Sinai, on the other hand, constitute a different kind of root experience—namely, God's commanding presence. The phenomenology of a commanding Divine presence differs from that of a saving presence, and in the following manner:

> Because it is a *commanding* rather than a saving Presence, however, the abiding astonishment turns into deadly terror. . . . As sole Power, the Divine commanding Presence destroys human freedom; as gracious Power, it restores that freedom, and indeed exalts it, for human freedom is made part of a covenant with Divinity itself. And the human astonishment, which is terror, at a Presence at once Divine and commanding, turns into

a second astonishment, which is *joy,* at a Grace which restores and exalts human freedom by its commanding Presence.[45]

A problem is manifested in Fackenheim's phenomenological description of God's commanding presence. If God is sole Power, what difference does human obedience make? Add to this the Midrash which Fackenheim cites: "When the Israelites do God's will, they add to the power of God on high. When the Israelites do not do God's will, they, as it were, weaken the power of God."[46] We are thus led to a contradiction between Divine power and human freedom. If God is sole Power, how can He be weakened by human intransigence?

At this point, Fackenheim holds fast to what he calls "the logic of Midrashic stubbornness,"[47] by which he means the tendency of the Midrash to "hold fast to the truth of these contradicting affirmations even as it expresses their contradictoriness."[48]

This is exemplified by the phrase *K'b'yakol* "as it were," which signifies "on the one hand, that the affirmation is not literally true but only a human way of speaking; and on the other hand, that it is a truth which cannot be humanly transcended."[49]

This leads to an affirmation of the reality of history in the sight of God. By this, Fackenheim means a rejection of the view that men are pawns in a cosmic chess game and that what is real for man is but an insignificant shadow for God. Rather, human obedience makes a difference vis-à-vis God! This is Fackenheim's contention. Fackenheim then moves from the logic of Midrashic stubbornness to the stubbornness of God and man in Judaism: "Thus God and man in Judaism pay each their price for the stubbornness with which they hold fast to actual—not 'spiritual'—history."[50] History is not transformed or transfigured by the Divine gaze. Actual history is the arena where God and man meet, if they are to meet at all.

It is with this stubbornness, a stubbornness which refuses to abandon the Midrashic framework and *its* stubbornness, that Fackenheim confronts the Holocaust. The Holocaust is, for Fackenheim, an epoch-making event. An epoch-making event occurs when the old faith is tested in the light of contemporary experience. The Holocaust, however, towers over previous epoch-making events in Jewish history, such as the destruction of the second Temple.

For Fackenheim, the Holocaust has no precedent within Jewish history. The uniqueness of the Holocaust, he contends, lies neither in the numbers of the people killed nor in the monstrous use of technological efficiency. Rather, the uniqueness lies in these aspects:

First, no rational end was served by the Nazi annihilation of the Jews: "It was annihilation for the sake of annihilation; murder for the sake of murder; evil for the sake of evil."[51]

Second, even more unique than the crime was the situation of the victims. This Fackenheim illustrates by the more than one million Jewish children murdered in the Nazi Holocaust: "Since Nazi law defined a Jew as one having a Jewish grandparent, they were murdered because of the Jewish faith of their great-grandparents."[52] Thus there follows the monstrous irony that had their great-grandparents abandoned their faith, these children might have lived.

Should one then cease to be a Jew because of the possibility of such a tragedy happening to his children? This option is renounced by Fackenheim. For the Jew to cease to be a Jew is, in effect, to credit Hitler with the destruction of Jewish faith as well as Jewish lives. And for Jews to cease being Jews is to abandon their past, "as witnesses to the God of history."[53] But how can the Jew, *after* Auschwitz, still be a witness to the God of history?

Fackenheim's answer to this question is radical indeed. It is interesting that, with respect to the Holocaust, he rejects Buber's doctrine of the eclipse of God. Having accepted many of Buber's other concepts, why does he reject this one? Fackenheim cogently argues that if all *present* access to the God of history is lost, the God of history is Himself lost.[54] A Divine eclipse which is total in the present cuts off both past and future. Here Fackenheim is surely correct. Either one believes in a God of history or he does not. Either God is present or He is not. Fackenheim rightly perceives that the concept of the eclipse of God, even though elaborated by his renowned mentor Martin Buber, is an evasive concept.

Fackenheim also rejects other modes of "saving the phenomenon" of faith. He rejects, of course, the notion that Auschwitz was punishment for the sins of Israel. Of what sins were innocent children guilty?

He rejects, as well, any equation of the Holocaust with martyrdom. He rightly points out that the Nazi extermination machine was designed to murder martyrdom itself, to stifle the

Shema Yisrael on Jewish lips before it murdered Jews themselves.

Moreover, as we have noted, Fackenheim rejects the notion of a finite God, that God was powerless, because he considers this concept perilously close to the Christian concept of the death of God.

What, then, is the position which Fackenheim takes?

Fackenheim argues that a commanding Voice speaks from Auschwitz to both the Jewish secularist and the religionist. What does this Voice of Auschwitz command?

> Jews are forbidden to hand Hitler posthumous victories. They are commanded to survive as Jews, lest the Jewish people perish. They are commanded to remember the victims of Auschwitz lest their memory perish. They are forbidden to despair of man and his world, and to escape into either cynicism or otherworldliness, lest they co-operate in delivering the world over to the forces of Auschwitz. Finally, they are forbidden to despair of the God of Israel, lest Judaism perish. A secularist Jew cannot make himself believe by an act of will, nor can he be commanded to do so. . . . And a religious Jew who has stayed with his God may be forced into new, possibly revolutionary relationships with Him. One possibility, however, is wholly unthinkable. A Jew may not respond to Hitler's attempt to destroy Judaism by himself co-operating in its destruction. In ancient times, the unthinkable Jewish sin was idolatry. Today, it is to respond to Hitler by doing his work.[55]

Now there is a studied ambiguity in Fackenheim's treatment of the secularist Jew. He writes that a secularist Jew cannot make himself believe by an act of will. Nor can he be commanded to believe. Yet the secularist Jew who fights for his own survival and the survival of the Jewish people testifies to the fact that he is commanded! Thus, Fackenheim writes:

> Jewish opposition to Auschwitz cannot be grasped in terms of humanly created ideals but only as an *imposed commandment*. And the Jewish secularist, no less than the believer, is absolutely *singled out by a Voice* as truly *other* than man made ideals—an imperative as truly given—as was the Voice of Sinai.[56]

Now what if the secularist says that he hears no such voice? This does not matter. "After Auschwitz even the most secularist of Jews bears witness by the mere affirmation of his Jewishness, against the devil."[57] Fackenheim's point is quite simply that there is no logical human reason why someone would want to remain a Jew and expose himself and his children to the perils of another Auschwitz. Hence the secularist, even though he may be unconscious of it, is acting under a supernatural command. Jewish survival, as such, is a *holy* duty. It is a commandment which brooks no compromise. And it was this Voice to which the Israelis responded in the 1967 war.

This argument has much emotional appeal. Furthermore, one cannot help but admire the stubbornness with which Fackenheim clings to the God of history.

Yet it must be said that Fackenheim exceeds the domains of propriety when he compares his "Voice of Auschwitz" to the Voice of Sinai. Many an Orthodox Jew would be horified by the attempt of Fackenheim to place his words in any context comparable to Sinai.

And I daresay that many a secularist would consider it a grave affront to his dignity to be told that he was acting, however unconsciously, in accord with the command of a supernatural Voice. To be sure, Fackenheim is to be commended for his effort to bridge the gap between the secularist and the religionist. But he goes too far when he makes of the secularist a bearer of a revelation which he may not hear.

Furthermore, the suspicion cannot be ignored that Fackenheim is playing upon the guilt feelings of those who did not experience the Holocaust in order to evoke from them a quasi-religious sentiment.

To lean so heavily upon the memory of Hitler to evoke Jewish commitment may smack, in the minds of many Jews, of inauthenticity.

Nevertheless, in the present writer's opinion, Fackenheim emerges as a sincere and honest proponent of Jewish faith. And the distinguishing feature of his thought is the stubbornness with which he clings to faith in the God of history.

Critique of Fackenheim

Since Fackenheim relies so heavily on Buber's doctrine of encounter, the same comment made about Buber would hold as well in Fackenheim's case. Steadfastly, Fackenheim holds to this doctrine. And unlike Buber, he maintains it even in the face of the Holocaust, for he rejects as untenable Buber's concept of the eclipse of God.

Once one is ready and willing to adopt the standpoint of encounter, one can note and admire the inner consistency of Fackenheim's thought.

It is another matter when we come to the question of empirical reference. Here a difficulty emerges because Fackenheim questions the empiricist criterion itself.

> To affirm even the possibility of an immediate Divine Presence is already to stand within the circle of faith; to begin with mere felt experiences is already to have stepped outside that circle and to rule out by initial fiat any possible immediate Divine Presence.[58]

How then can a stalemate between believing openness and subjectivist reductionism be avoided? Fackenheim's answer is that the question must be broadened, as follows:

> Is an immediate Divine Presence compatible with experience as modern thought understands it? If compatible, on what grounds is it claimed, and what is its content? Any one of these questions exceeds the grasp of empiricism.[59]

Fackenheim here is protesting against what he considers to be the narrowness of some contemporary British analytic philosophers. He is arguing for an honest encounter between the "believing openness" of Judaism and the skepticism of many of these philosophers.

Again Fackenheim's stubbornness manifests itself, this time in an attempt to defend what he considers to be the essential Jewish concept of believing openness against empirical criteria.

Fackenheim's point and challenge are well taken, but they do not take us very far. For it is precisely the point that an immediate Divine Presence is *not* compatible with experience as understood by modern thought. Modern thought teaches that an element of interpretation is involved in *any* experience—an experience of a table, let alone experience of the Divine. Try and wrestle as he does, Fackenheim does not succeed and cannot succeed in transporting two universes of discourse, the ancient and the modern, to the same plane.

For example, he argues against those who consider the idea of God to be a hypothesis to account for the facts. The basis of his argument is that Biblical man did not consider "God" to be a hypothesis but a reality. He then argues that those who consider God as hypothesis have not understood the fact that, to Biblical man, God was a reality and that, furthermore, the Biblical position should be a live option in an encounter with modern philosophy.

But this attempt fails to reckon with the fact that atheism was not a live option in the ancient world. Ancient man simply inhabited a universe of discourse saturated with the Divine. And Biblical man lived in a universe of discourse where the will of the One God was the dominant reality.

Modern man does not live in such a universe of discourse. His social reality is different. God is not an immediate but an inferred reality to most moderns. And it simply makes little sense to argue for an encounter between Biblical (or Rabbinic) openness to the Divine and modern empirical philosophy. As one critic of Fackenheim has stated:

> Unfortunately, modern man cannot be in the sixteenth and the twentieth century at one and the same time . . . unless we define either term in such a Pickwickian sense that we are no longer speaking of the world in which we live.[60]

What is the pragmatic value of Fackenheim's thought? It cannot be denied that there is a powerful emotional appeal in his stubborn effort to wrest theological conclusions from the survivalist instinct of the twentieth-century Jew. Furthermore, his effort to bridge the gap between secularist and religious Jew is laudable.

But he goes too far in this attempt. To be sure, there is a studied ambiguity in the concept of the commanding Voice. Perhaps some secularists, viewing it as a metaphor, might be responsive to it. But most secularists, especially the defiant among the Israelis, would most assuredly resist it and resent it. A personal "encounter" will illustrate why this is so.

In Israel, I remember a conversation I had with a young Israeli who fought in the Six-Day War. He said that he believed firmly in what he called "Masoret"—that is, Jewish tradition as culture. But, because of his war experiences, he could not connect this belief with any religious view. He then told of his decisive experience. His best friend, standing next to him, was blown up by a grenade during the war. "How," he asked, "could I believe in the Divine will? I would then have to say that my life was worth more than my friend's. This I refuse to do."

Doubtless, this Israeli would be singularly unresponsive to any talk of a commanding Voice from Auschwitz.

Finally, one further point must be made. The major weakness in Fackenheim's thought is the lack of an articulate concept of God. This arises from his existentialist orientation which places the center of gravity on man's relationship to God rather than a concept of God. Yet Fackenheim's writing itself shows the need for a concept. Take, for example, Fackenheim's assertion that "we are here, exist, survive, endure, witnesses to God and man even if abandoned by God and man."[61]

The only way this statement could make any sense is if the first mention of God refers to some kind of God-concept. What does it *mean* to be a witness to God? And why should one witness to a God who has abandoned him?

This passage shows the inadequacy of existentialist emphasis on a relationship between the Jewish people and God, or between man and God, without some clarification of what we mean by the term God. The existentialists, generally, are reluctant to undertake such attempts at clarification because they feel that such attempts undermine the relationship.

I disagree with this tendency of Jewish existentialists. To try to frame an intelligible *concept* of something does *not* mean that I am degrading what I am talking about. Thus, to return to the question with which this chapter began: How shall we conceive of the relationship between the Jewish people and God? We find that the attempts to understand this relationship in terms of covenant and commanding voices are inadequate without clarification of what is meant by the term "God."

Therefore, in the next section, we must face this question: How shall we conceive of transcendence? It is to this task that we now turn, as we seek a viable conception of transcendence for our time.

NOTES

1. Eugene Borowitz, *A New Jewish Theology in the Making* (Philadelphia: The Westminster Press, 1968), p. 49.
2. *Ibid.*, p. 53.
3. *Ibid.*, p. 119.
4. *Ibid.*
5. *Ibid.*, p. 113.
6. *Ibid.*, p. 131.

7. *Ibid.*, pp. 208–209.

8. Eugene Borowitz, *How Can a Jew Speak of Faith Today?* (Philadelphia: The Westminster Press, 1969), p. 7.

9. *A New Jewish Theology in the Making*, p. 41.

10. *How Can a Jew Speak of Faith Today?*, p. 43.

11. *Ibid.*, pp. 43–44.

12. *Ibid.*, p. 67.

13. *Ibid.*, p. 68.

14. *Idem.*

15. *Idem.*

16. *Ibid.*, p. 52.

17. *Idem.*

18. On this point, see also Borowitz, *The Masks Jews Wear* (New York: Simon and Schuster, 1973), p. 202.

19. *Ibid.*, p. 54.

20. Emil Fackenheim, *Quest for Past and Future: Essays in Jewish Theology* (Boston: Beacon Press, 1970), p. 114.

21. *Idem.*

22. *Ibid.*, p. 8.

23. *Idem.*

24. *Idem.*

25. Emil Fackenheim, *God's Presence in History: Jewish Affirmations and Philosophical Reflections* (New York: New York University Press, 1970), p. 41.

26. See, for example, the essays in *Quest for Past and Future.*

27. *Quest for Past and Future*, p. 8.

28. *Ibid.*, p. 101.

29. See, for example, "Self-Realization and the Search for God," *Ibid.*, pp. 27–51.

30. *Ibid.*, p. 9.

31. *Ibid.*, p. 125.

32. *Ibid.*, p. 129.

33. Emil Fackenheim, "Jewish Values in the Post-Holocaust Future: A Symposium," *Judaism* (Summer, 1967), pp. 266–299.

34. *God's Presence in History*, p. 86.

35. *Quest for Past and Future*, p. 7

36. *God's Presence in History*, p. 5.

37. *Ibid.*, p. 6.

38. *Idem.*

39. *Idem.*

40. *Idem.*

41. *Ibid.*, pp. 77 ff.

42. *Ibid.*, pp. 12–13.

43. *Ibid.*, pp. 9–11.

44. *Ibid.*, p. 11.

45. *Ibid.*, pp. 15–16.

46. *Ibid.*, p. 23 (*Midrash Raba*, Lamentations on Lam. 1:6).

47. *Ibid.*, p. 21.

48. *Ibid.*, p. 24.

49. *Idem.*
50. *Ibid.,* p. 25.
51. *Ibid.,* p. 70.
52. *Idem.*
53. *Ibid.,* p. 71.
54. *Ibid.,* p. 79.
55. *Ibid.,* p. 84.
56. *Ibid.,* p. 83.
57. *Ibid.,* p. 82.
58. Emil Fackenheim, *Encounters Between Judaism and Modern Philosophy,* p. 28.
59. *Idem.*
60. *Reconstructionist,* Vol. XXVII, Nov. 19, 1971, p. 10.
61. *God's Presence in History,* p. 97.

Part 3 Toward a Conception of Transcendence

7 Leo Baeck:
The Far Yet Near God

The concept of Divine transcendence can be understood best by a reflection on human self-transcendence. The capacity of man to transcend his present life-situation is the image of the Divine in man. And the life of Leo Baeck (1873–1956) is a moving example of this self-transcendence.

Baeck was born in Lissa, Posen (at that time a part of Prussia), on May 23, 1873. He studied in Breslau, Silesia and Berlin. He received his Ph.D. from the University of Berlin and his Rabbinical diploma from the *Lehranstalt für die Wissenschaft des Judentums.*

Baeck's first pulpit was in Oppeln, in Upper Silesia. There he served for ten years, from 1897 to 1907. It has been said that Baeck was "a completely modern Rabbi: pastor and preacher, scholar and teacher, as much at home in the secular as in the

religious disciplines of learning."[1] His first and most widely
known book, *The Essence of Judaism,* was published during this
period, in 1905.

In 1912 he was called to Berlin, where he served until 1942.
Baeck became the acknowledged leader of German Jewry. When
Hitler came to power in 1933, a small committee was formed to
represent the Jews of Germany vis-à-vis the government. Baeck
was elected president of this representative body which was
called the *Reichsvertretung der Juden in Deutschland.* The main
work of the *Reichsvertretung* which Baeck headed was "the task
of slowing down the inevitable; of fighting for time, fighting
for the rights of children to leave their parents and settle in
foreign lands, fighting to keep brutality at bay as long as possible."[2]

In 1939 the *Reichsvertretung,* which was founded by the members of the Jewish community themselves, was abolished. In its
place the Germans set up a successor organization—the *Reichs-
vereinigung*—and insisted that Baeck be its head. Baeck's acceptance of this position has been the subject of controversy.[3]
In defense of Baeck, it has been argued that

> the unwilling officers of the *Reichsvereinigung* saw themselves as
> the equivalent of an officers' council in a prisoner of war camp,
> where it is a function of such a council to transmit the orders of
> the jailers. . . . These men and women continued their work in
> welfare, education, and general maintenance of the Jewish com-
> munity until all of them had been transported to concentration
> camps, where most of them died.[4]

The important point is that Baeck refused to leave Germany.
In 1943, Baeck himself was deported to the concentration camp
Theresienstadt. There he became a number—187,894—but he refused to remain a number. Remarkably, he led his fellow in-
mates in moral resistance. He taught philosophy as well as religious subjects within the concentration camp. "From seven to
eight hundred persons would press into a small barracks in order to listen to his lectures on Plato and Kant."[5] What a stirring
example of human self-transcendence!

The camp was liberated in May of 1945. Baeck had lived
through the darkness and had survived. He was then in his sev-
enties. For the next ten years, he traveled between London, New
York, and Cincinnati. At the Hebrew Union College in Cin-

cinnati, Baeck taught Midrash. On October 29, 1956, Baeck signed his name to the proof sheets of *This People Israel,* which he had written in the concentration camp. He was stricken that afternoon and died on November 2, 1956, in London.

There is a strange irony in Leo Baeck's capacity for self-transcendence, exemplified by his book written in the concentration camp. I have already discussed the implications Richard Rubenstein has drawn from the concentration camps—the utter collapse of transcendence and the encounter with nothingness. But Rubenstein himself was not a victim of these camps. I have also discussed the thought of Emil Fackenheim, who *was* interned in a concentration camp for three months. Fackenheim, we have seen, also recognized the fact that Jewish theology after Auschwitz must be different. But he refused to despair. He urged both religious and secular Jews to bear witness, by their very survival, to a commanding Voice of Auschwitz. Nevertheless, both Rubenstein's and Fackenheim's response have one thing in common: they are existential; they confront the particularity of the Holocaust in all its evil and absurdity. The strange irony is that Leo Baeck, from within the concentration camp, could still write *sub specie aeternitatis,* under the aspect of eternity—emphasizing the idea of rebirth and a forward movement of the Jewish people to transcendence. This irony is sharpened when we compare Baeck to Rubenstein in particular.

> A Richard Rubenstein, standing outside the death camps, defines man within its limits. For him, to the extent that Auschwitz, the *anus mundi,* fills the world, man is excrement. A Leo Baeck, being in the inner circle of that hell, can contemplate man's nature as it transcends this evil. But in Baeck there is a forward movement characteristic of Jewish life: Rebirth takes place, man can transcend the past and it is not destroyed while he atones.[6]

We are thus presented with a strange phenomenon. Viewing the Holocaust from the outside, Rubenstein gives an existentialist response. From within the concentration camp, Baeck reaches out for a global, cosmic, transcendent perspective.

There is one conclusion to be drawn from this irony: One's response to the Holocaust stems from one's own personal stance, life-style, and orientation. The nihilist, Rubenstein, views the Holocaust as the epitome of the absurd and as the consummation of the collapse of transcendence. The fideist, Fackenheim,

strives to maintain his faith in a God of history despite Auschwitz. And Baeck, the seeker after transcendence, seeks hope and
rebirth.

Let us therefore examine the thought of Leo Baeck to determine the various facets of his concept of Divine transcendence
and human self-transcendence which gave rise to his particular
response.

Baeck's Approach to Judaism

Baeck's approach to Judaism is, first of all, polemical in nature. In 1900, Adolf Harnack, the Protestant theologian, published *The Essence of Christianity*. In this exposition of liberal
Protestantism, Harnack claimed that "the essence of Christianity was contained in two teachings of Jesus: the fatherhood of
God and the brotherhood of man. The Gospels were taken out
of the flux of time, isolated from the Jewish tradition of earlier
times and the Christian thought of later times."[7]

In 1905, Leo Baeck published *The Essence of Judaism*. Even
though no direct reference is made in the text to Harnack's
work, the title of Baeck's book indicates its polemical nature.
And one does not have to read very far to get to Baeck's polemical thrust against Christianity.

Thus, in the very first chapter, Baeck contrasts the high value
which Judaism places on the good deed as one of the "strong-
est possible checks against dogmatism. A precise, conceptual determination of creed arises in the Church, where the creed is
regarded as knowledge which, on the other hand, is presented
to the people as creed."[8]

Throughout *The Essence of Judaism*, such polemical thrusts
appear. The apologetic nature of this book, unfortunately, dis-
tracts our attention from some of the brilliant insights unfolded
there.

Second, Baeck's approach is typological. Again, by the very
title of Baeck's major work, we can begin to understand this
method. It is the search for an inner essence or type of the phenomenon in question. Here Leo Baeck was influenced by the
philosopher Wilhelm Dilthey, who in 1907 published a book entitled, as befits the Zeitgeist, *The Essence of Philosophy*. Dilthey
distinguished between *Naturwissenschaften*—natural sciences,
and *Geisteswissenschaften*, spiritual sciences. He maintained that
there are spiritual forms or types with their own structure and

laws just as there exist natural laws in the universe. Hence, in *The Essence of Judaism,* Baeck sought the inner spiritual core or typology which distinguished Judaism.

Third, Baeck stresses the primacy of ethics in Judaism. Here the influence of the nineteenth-century Jewish neo-Kantian philosopher Hermann Cohen is manifest. But Baeck departs from Cohen in an important respect. Although he stresses ethical monotheism, "God," for Baeck, does not become merely an idea which guarantees ethics.

This point of departure from the Neo-Kantian approach of Hermann Cohen is epitomized in this statement about Judaism: "Ethics constitute its essence. Monotheism is the result of the absolute character of the moral law; moral consciousness teaches about God."[9]

This subtle difference gives rise to the fourth characteristic of Baeck's approach—the emphasis on a unique religiomoral consciousness or feeling. In this respect Baeck took cognizance of Friedrich Schleiermacher's definition of religion as a feeling of absolute dependence on God. But Baeck did not fully agree with Schleiermacher. Although he agrees with Schleiermacher on the importance of a distinctive kind of religious consciousness, he differs from him in that he sees a feeling of dependence as one aspect of the consciousness which must be balanced by the quest for freedom and autonomy.

One can already see that Baeck did not align himself totally within any one system of thought. This gives rise to the fifth, and most important, aspect of Baeck's method—his concept of polarity.

One of the most frequent idioms of Baeck's thought is: "It is something twofold." Baeck views many of the beliefs of Judaism in terms of a tension between opposites that are held together in a dynamic unity. This creative tension, for Baeck, is one of the factors that gives rise to the distinctive features of Judaism.

Baeck's Conception of the Uniqueness of Judaism

The Essence of Judaism is a testament to the uniqueness of Judaism. Baeck locates an aspect of the uniqueness of Judaism in the profound spiritual consciousness of the Jewish people, which he defines as a "consciousness of possessing a world of their own."[10]

What is the nature of this life-world of the Jewish people? What are the unique spiritual forms which constitute the essence of Judaism? First, Baeck emphasizes the intellectual character of Judaism:

> The Jews have always been a minority. But a minority is compelled to think; that is the blessing of its fate. It must always persist in a mental struggle for that consciousness of truth which success and power comfortingly assure to rulers and their supporting multitudes.[11]

This collective quest for the truth was the product of the Jewish people's struggle for self-perpetuation. Baeck's point here is an important one. Because the Jews were a minority and could not survive the evolutionary struggle for existence by the attainment of political power, they evolved a unique intellectual, moral, and spiritual self-consciousness. This self-consciousness was instrumental in effecting the survival of the Jewish people.

What characterizes this self-consciousness of the Jewish people, according to Baeck? Baeck emphasizes the unique capacity of Judaism for historical development throughout the ages. It has been the particularity of Jewish genius to constantly renew itself by absorbing various elements of other civilizations and at the same time adapting these elements to its unique individuality. This adaptability of the Jewish people Baeck attributes to the absence of a congealing creed and a fixed system. Thus, to Baeck, the "dominant form of Judaism always remained that of a religious philosophy of inquiry, a philosophy which produced method rather than system."[12]

This emphasis on inquiry gave rise to the unique capacity in Judaism for renewal and rebirth precisely because Judaism never became a fixed totality. This is poignantly expressed by Baeck:

> The Bible remained the Bible, the Talmud came after it, and after the Talmud came religious philosophy, and after that came mysticism, and so it went on and on. Judaism never became a completed entity; no period of its development could become its totality. The old revelation ever becomes a new revelation: Judaism experiences a continuous renaissance.[13]

As I have remarked before, the term "Judaism," strictly speaking, is a misnomer if it gives rise to the mistaken notion that Judaism is a monolithic phenomenon. The preceding statement by Baeck explains why this is so. The greatness of Judaism is that it is always in the making. It is a dynamic, unending, and unfinished process. Nevertheless, despite this fluid character of Judaism, something must remain constant. And this constant factor must give an organic unity to the changing developments. What, to Baeck, is the constant factor in Judaism?

To Baeck, the constant factor in Judaism is that which can be extracted from the highest levels of its development: "What is most characteristic of a people is best found in the highest levels of its history, so long as these levels are reached again and again."[14]

Furthermore, just as the essence of art is best grasped through a study of great artists, so the nature of religion is best grasped through "a study of the geniuses of religion."[15]

The archetypal genius, for Baeck, is the prophet. The prophet is overwhelmed by an irresistible inner compulsion. The profound inner experience of the prophet transcends analysis. It cannot be dissected or defined. "Genius, the divine, cannot be defined. This daimonic power, this conviction of revelation, is the spiritual peculiarity of the prophets' work."[16]

We see from this that Baeck's thought is not a sterile rationalism. The nonrational, the "mystery," has a place in his thought. But, wisely, Baeck does not attempt to penetrate the mystery. What, to Baeck, is the prophetic message? He writes: "The prophets speak not so much of what God is in himself, but what he means to man, what he means to the world."[17]

This is an important statement. Here we find the essence of Baeck's liberalism. To the liberal mind, the emphasis is on *what God means to man*. In the next chapter we will consider the thought of A. J. Heschel, who reverses this liberal emphasis, stressing *what man means to God*. This contrast between Baeck and Heschel on this issue is a very significant highlight in contemporary Jewish thought. What then does God mean to man? Baeck writes that the prophetic knowledge of God "becomes the synonym for the morality by which every soul can mold its existence. . . . To know God and to do right have thus become synonymous in prophetic speech; each has become commandment."[18]

To Baeck, then, ethics—and the paradigmatic exponents of ethics are the prophets—constitute the constant factor, the essence of Judaism. Thus, he writes: "Ethics constitute its essence.

Monotheism is the result of a realization of the absolute character of the moral law; moral consciousness teaches about God."[19] The essence of Judaism, to Baeck, consists of ethical monotheism and ethical optimism.

Baeck considers ethical monotheism, viewed as a unique creation of the Jewish genius, to be the embodiment of revelation: "In so far as this form of religion is a creation, embodying an entirely new and fruitful principle, we are entitled to call it historically, quite apart from supernatural conceptions—a revelation."[20] Here Baeck brackets the supernatural concept of revelation. Like Geiger, who defined revelation as "the peculiar Jewish genius for religion,"[21] Baeck views revelation as the unique and original creation of ethical monotheism by the Jewish people.

Ethical monotheism, the belief in the One God who is the source of the moral law, leads to Baeck's conception of ethical optimism. Ethical optimism, for Baeck, involves his belief that existence has transcendent value: "Only an existence which is not content with the mere fact of existence can have any value."[22]

For Baeck, human finite existence has value only insofar as it reflects the unconditional character of the good. And the unconditional character of the good has its source "only in the One God, the outcome of whose nature is the moral law. In him the good finds the certainty of its eternal reality."[23]

God, for Baeck, is not only the source of the good. In addition, the One God

> is the answer to all mystery; he is the source of all that is eternal and ethical, creative and ordered, hidden and definite. From this allegiance between the secret and the commandment issues all existence and all significance. Thereby their unity is apprehended. Commandment is linked to secret and secret to commandment.[24]

Here we find the first stirrings of one of Baeck's major concepts: the polarity of mystery and commandment. By polarity is meant the tension and contrast between opposite qualities. Whereas the mystery is infinite, indefinite, boundless, unknowable, and unfathomable, commandment is definite, limited, knowable—a task to be realized.

And the concept of God, in this view, is the *coincidentia oppositorum*—the unity of opposites.

Why are both mystery and commandment necessary? Mystery alone yields a religion which evaporates in the vagaries of mysticism. Commandment, or the ethical alone, yields a world-view which is indistinguishable from the secularism of ethical culture societies. Therefore, Baeck emphasizes the polarity of mystery and commandment in Judaism and their unity in the One God.

It is, finally, the belief in One God which generates the ethical optimism that Baeck envisages at the core of Judaism. By ethical optimism, Baeck means the ethical affirmation of the world, epitomized in the Biblical statement: "And God saw that it was good."

In direct contrast to Buddhism, which negates the world, Judaism is a world-affirming doctrine. But Judaism has no superficial optimism. The history of the Jewish people has been too replete with sorrow for such a facile, polyanna attitude. Rather the optimism of Judaism lies in its tenacious awareness of the ideal. The world is faced not in resignation but with "the will to change it and with the commandment to realize the good in it."[25] That the good is somehow endorsed by God, that the commandment is related to the mystery of the ultimate, that there is a power beyond man that somehow fortifies man and signifies that what *ought* to be realized *can* be realized—this is the essence of Baeck's ethical optimism.

Specifically, Baeck sees the optimism of Judaism consisting, first, in the belief in God. This belief gives rise, secondly, to a belief in man, "who is able to realize in himself the good which first finds its reality in God."[26] And this belief in man includes belief in oneself, belief in one's neighbor, and belief in the spiritual possibilities of mankind.

One of the outstanding features of Baeck's ethical optimism is his emphasis on faith in man. All too often religion loses itself in speculations about faith in God. Nevertheless, as Baeck has stated, faith in man is a necessary but not a sufficient condition for the uniqueness of Judaism. The commandment must be grounded in the mystery. Thus arises the crucial question to be raised about Baeck's understanding of Judaism: Does he convincingly show *why* and *how* the commandment requires the mystery as its ground? Does his ethics *follow from* his conception of transcendence? It is to this question that we now turn.

Mystery and Commandment: The Far Yet Near God

One of Baeck's most celebrated essays is entitled "Mystery and Commandment." Here he develops the germ idea of polarity adumbrated in *The Essence of Judaism.*

It is to Baeck's credit that he defines what he means by the term "mystery." Hence he cannot be accused of a mystery-mongering approach. By the experience of the mystery, Baeck refers to the feeling of or consciousness of "the presence of something lasting, of some reality beneath the surface."[27] It is, furthermore, the consciousness of man that "he was created," that "his life is framed by infinity and eternity, by that which transcends all human knowledge and apprehension and surpasses all that is natural and existent."[28]

Baeck's emphasis here is on what Rudolf Otto has called "creature-feeling"—namely, man's consciousness that he is a creature of God. Unlike Otto, however, Baeck does not rest at this point. Religious experience, or, more precisely, the Judaic religious experience, according to Baeck, is not only creature-feeling. It is, in Baeck's characteristic terms, a twofold experience. The experience of the mystery is complemented by the commandment, the task which man is to realize.

But how are mystery and commandment *connected?* What gives this twofold experience its unity? Baeck writes: "The twofold experience can also be intimated in this way: the consciousness that we have been created versus the consciousness that we are expected to create."[29] And again: "All consciousness that we have been created means and suggests the demand to create, and every demand to create means and suggests the consciousness that we have been created."[30]

But why is this so? Why does it follow that because I have been created I am obligated to create? Baeck simply seems to state that, in Judaism, these two experiences are experienced "as one, in a perfect unity."[31] It is not explained why and how this unity is brought about. We therefore look for clarification in his conception of God. Here again, however, Baeck relies on the doctrine of polarity: "Judaism lacks any foundation for the conflict between transcendence and immanence. Jewish piety lives in the paradox, in the polarity with all its tension and compactness."[32] The analogue to the polarity of *mystery* and *commandment* is the paradox of the transcendent yet immanent Deity, the far yet near God!

Paradox is a term frequently used in religious discourse. A paradox is what *appears* to be a contradiction which arises when the human mind attempts to deal with an object that is too great for its comprehension. To be sure, even the scientist at times must live with contradictions. For example, the phenomenon of light has been studied in this century by reference to two seemingly incompatible models—wave movements and particle movements. Why did the scientist hold to both models?

The reason is that had he renounced either, he would have lost a hypothesis with immense explanatory power. Can the same be said of religious statements? With this question in mind, we return to Baeck, who writes:

> In man's religious knowledge of having been created there is a paradox which welds into a unity the feelings of separation and belonging, of the here and the beyond, the exalted and the intimate, the mystery and the revealed, the miracle and the law.[33]

Notice, first, that Baeck speaks of religious knowledge—namely, he knows that he has been created. There is an unfortunate vagueness here. Is Baeck advocating a doctrine of creation or is he merely stating the fact that man is born into a world not of his own making? Second, Baeck speaks of feelings of separation and belonging. Here Baeck is making a valid point. It is psychoanalytically true that contradictory feelings can exist simultaneously within the human mind. Love and hate, for example, can be obverse sides of the same coin. By the same token, man can experience the Divine, sometimes as far, other times as near. Baeck, however, overstates his point when he writes:

> Since Judaism equally emphasizes both the near and the far, it is often filled with a feeling of tension. . . . Judaism is filled with an anxiety because of the remoteness of God and with a longing for his proximity; but at the same time it is certain in the possession of him.[34]

Baeck here is referring to the fact that in Jewish sources, God is experienced not only as exalted, as "the dweller on high," but also as near, as dwelling with the man of "contrite and humble spirit." But, although certain of God's existence, it is doubtful whether Biblical man was certain of the possession of God. Here the thought of Buber is an appropriate corrective: Woe unto him who feels that he can possess God.

It is clear, then, that Baeck believed firmly in a personal God, in the unity of God's exaltedness and intimacy with man, and in "the paradox that man's life possesses its personal God in the Infinite, the Unfathomable One."[35]

Baeck, then, believed in the far yet near God, realizing full well the paradoxical nature of this belief. Baeck does not argue; he expresses his feelings about what the essence of Judaism means to him.

Mystery and commandment are not demonstrated to be organically related. They are simply stated to be the elements of man's twofold experiences.

Nevertheless, there is a grandeur in Baeck's approach. And this grandeur is nowhere more evident than in his treatment of this people Israel. Here Baeck's idea of the far yet near God gains power.

This People Israel: The Idea of Rebirth

The distinctive feature of Leo Baeck's conception of the Jewish people is the unique sense of perspective he attributes to this people. This perspective is indicated by the old Biblical term for history—*Toldot,* literally meaning generations. Baeck's interpretation of this term is truly instructive:

> This people had a sense of history . . . it acquired the ability to think in generations and to live in generations. It was now able to look backward into the far reaches and to look forward into the great distances. Through history, this people came to be what it is: the people of the great memory and the great expectation.[36]

Baeck here is emphasizing the unique, collective self-consciousness of the Jewish people. And he sees as an essential aspect of this self-consciousness the unique capacity of the Jewish people to take a long look, to view events in a larger perspective, to possess patience and a vision of the future.

Out of this vision of the future there emerges the unique capacity of the Jewish people for rebirth. This people Israel, Baeck wrote, "always carries its future within it."[37] The Jewish people, like a phoenix, can rise out of its own ashes. This ability of the Jewish people, which is most dramatically epitomized in our time by the creation of the State of Israel after the darkness of Auschwitz, stems from its unique inner form or spirit of rebirth:

> The rebirth arises only out of that which is its own, out of what are its characteristic beginnings—out of nothing else, whether from within or without. Only the self is reborn. Only that which dwells in the foundation of the particular returns. This individuality one day arises again. The beginning, and with it the great belief, commences anew, the belief that it is always revolutionary, always born out of genius.[38]

Just as the monotheism of Biblical Israel was a new intuition, a stamp of original genius, a new beginning, so the Jewish people throughout history has had, latent within its soul, its characteristic genius, a capacity to make new beginnings, a will to be reborn. And this will to be reborn is rooted in the original Jewish genius. Thus, Baeck quotes approvingly the words of Isaiah (37:31) : "[it] shall again take root downward, and bear fruit upward."

The capacity of the Jewish people for rebirth is manifested as hope. True hope, for Baeck, is not a puerile optimism. It is rather the "expression of a strength that has its origin in the certainty of the way. Hope and strength therefore became practically one word in the Bible."[39]

Jewish thinkers tend to see in the people of Israel those qualities they themselves most prize. Leo Baeck exemplified and idealized inner strength. So he sees the essence of the Jewish people in its inner strength.

It can be seen that in this later book, written in the concentration camp, Baeck is more concerned with the existence of the Jewish people. This is manifested by its title: *This People Israel: The Meaning of Jewish Existence.* However, it would be a mistake to consider this book to mark a major shift from essence to existence. Baeck's major preoccupation is still *essence*—that is, the *meaning* of Jewish existence. And this meaning is still viewed largely in terms of the unique spiritual form, genius, or essence of the Jewish people. Thus when Baeck writes about Jewish existence, it is an existence inseparable from essence.

It is precisely because he still stresses *essence* that Baeck's writing transcends the particularity of the horrors of the concentration camp. It is surely remarkable that in *This People Israel,* written in the concentration camp, Baeck can write about rebirth and hope.

The reason for this uncanny self-transcendence of Baeck lies in the fact that his conception of hope was a long-range phenomenon. It has been said that nature does not leap. To this Baeck added that history also does not leap.[40] An idea needs a long time to develop and bear fruit. Thus, it has been correctly observed that Baeck's approach is that of "millennial messianism. There is no short-term hope here . . . Baeck looks into the vast reaches of the millenniums."[41]

Clearly, then, Baeck retained a broad philosophical approach, in the sense of a tendency to view reality *sub specie aeternitatis* —under the aspect of eternity. It is no accident that he taught Plato and Kant in the concentration camp. Essence, the *idea,* remains supreme in his thought.

Herein, as we shall now see, lie both the strength and weakness of his thought.

Critique of Leo Baeck

Despite his recourse to mystery, polarity, and paradox, Baeck's thought contains an inner consistency. Like the man himself, who was said to combine both adamantine strength and gentleness in his personality, Baeck's polarities of mystery and commandment and the far yet near God are held together by an inner unity and coherence. This inner unity is Baeck's firm and unswerving faith in the One God.

If there is an inconsistency in Baeck's thought, it lies in the fact that his theology is not totally one of liberalism. Although he stresses man's quest for God, there is no doubt that he firmly believed that the commandment derives from God. His liberalism lies not in an effort to reinterpret what to him was the fact of God's commandment. Rather his liberalism lies in his emphasis on the ongoing, unfinished character of Israel's response to this commandment. Thus Baeck writes:

> By the fulfillment of God's commandment a people must truly become itself. It must make itself into a people. . . . The knowledge of God and the knowledge of self became a unity that remains indivisible in this people. Whether Israel lived through bright or dark days, it always knew who was above it and who was before it.[42]

God remains at the center of Baeck's thought, God not as an idea but a reality, and God not merely as an abstraction but as a living, personal Creator and Redeemer in history.

The strength of Baeck's thought lies in its dignity. Although he devoutly believed in a God of history, he wisely does not attempt to connect God with specific historic particularities.

Baeck does not say: God was here and not there or God was there and not here. Audacity and definite statements about God are not, in my opinion, a sign of strength. Theological tentativeness requires patience. The strength of Baeck's thought is his theological humility:

> Baeck cannot permit the existential breakthrough of faith that would carry him into the secure knowledge of the heart of the mystery, the leap of faith that finds the true knowledge of the Beyond in the moment of encounter.[43]

To be sure, Baeck possessed great faith. But this faith was based not on a momentary incursion but a longtime process. Accordingly, the following comment about Baeck's thought is apposite:

> Revelation, for Baeck, is placed into the continuous experience of the Jewish people. It is not the special content of a special moment in the past which must be mediated for changing groups. It is a constant of Jewish life: *The Jewish people itself is a revelation.* What there is of mediation is bound up with the mission of Israel to bring this to the rest of the world.[44]

For Baeck, revelation, election, and mission became interchangeable terms, as in the following passage:

> Only in Israel did an ethical monotheism exist, and wherever else it is found later, it has been derived directly or indirectly from Israel. The nature of this religion was conditioned by the existence of the people of Israel, and so it became one of the nations that have a mission to fulfill. That is what is meant by the *election* of Israel. Hence the word primarily expresses an historical fact: there was assigned to this people a peculiar position in the world by which it is distinguished from all other peoples.[45]

This passage typifies the weakness of Baeck's thought. Let us analyze these weaknesses in terms of our second criterion: empirical reference.

The weakness of Baeck's position is that he maintains the traditional terminology but invests it with a meaning that is too vague to yield empirical reference. The Jewish people, Baeck contends, was assigned a particular task. By whom? The implication is clear: by God. Israel is therefore elected or chosen. Its

mission is to exemplify and spread the doctrine of ethical monotheism to the world.

The usual criticism of this doctrine is that mankind does not
need the existence of the people Israel to learn this doctrine.
The doctrine is there. It has been taught. The world can read
the literature of the Jews. Why is the continued existence of
the people necessary?

The fact is, however, that the world has not learned this
lesson. The Watergate tragedy is ample evidence that the so-
called Judeo-Christian tradition has not penetrated to the minds
and hearts of America's leaders. The idea of the Jewish people
as an exemplar of ethical monotheism cannot be so easily dismissed.

The real and important question, however, is not adequately
answered by Baeck—namely, how can the Jewish people function as an exemplar of ethical monotheism? How is the particular genius of the Jewish people to be made manifest today?
Baeck's answer would obviously involve a renewed commitment,
on the part of the American Jew, to the commandments. For
Baeck, let us recall, the greatness of Judaism lies in its classical
character. Unlike Christianity, which Baeck considered romantic
and otherworldly, Judaism, he maintained, has its feet on the
ground and expresses itself in a series of specific duties and responsibilities. But why should the modern Jew commit himself
to these duties and responsibilities? Baeck's inspiring and edify-
ing writings will provide the believing Jew with added impetus
and motivation. But this appeal to the mystery and his emphasis on a return to the commandments will have little empirical
value for the Jew who has not experienced the mystery and the
sense of being commanded.

Pragmatically, the moral courage and heroism of Baeck's life
offer a stirring example of the Jew's capacity for self-transcendence. In the hard and stubborn political realities of our time,
Baeck's strength and gentleness, his moral courage and his optimism, stand as a testimony to the human spirit. And his idea
of rebirth is concretized in the State of Israel.

The task for world Jewry is how to transform the rebirth of
the Jewish people in Israel into a moral and spiritual rebirth
for all Jews everywhere. The Jewish people must elevate itself
first and rediscover its own identity before it can even consider
its mission to mankind.

NOTES

1. Leo Baeck, *This People Israel*, intro. Albert H. Friedlander, p. xi.
2. Albert H. Friedlander, *Leo Baeck: Teacher of Theresienstadt* (New York: Holt, Rinehart, and Winston, 1968), p. 40.
3. *Ibid.*, pp. 44 ff.
4. *Ibid.*, pp. 44–45.
5. *Ibid.*, p. 46.
6. *Ibid.*, p. 10.
7. *Ibid.*, p. 50.
8. Leo Baeck, *The Essence of Judaism* (New York: Schocken Books, 1961), p. 14.
9. *Ibid.*, p. 59.
10. *Ibid.*, p. 9.
11. *Ibid.*, p. 11.
12. *Ibid.*, p. 16.
13. *Ibid.*, p. 29.
14. *Ibid.*, p. 9.
15. *Ibid.*, p. 31.
16. *Ibid.*, p. 32.
17. *Ibid.*, p. 35.
18. *Ibid.*, p. 36–37.
19. *Ibid.*, p. 59.
20. *Ibid.*, p. 60.
21. *Leo Baeck*, p. 159.
22. *The Essence of Judaism;* p. 83.
23. *Ibid.*, p. 84.
24. *Idem.*
25. *Ibid.*, p. 85.
26. *Ibid.*, p. 87.
27. "Mystery and Commandment," in *Judaism and Christianity: Essays*, trans. Walter Kaufmann (New York: Atheneum, 1970), p. 171.
28. *Idem.*
29. *Ibid.*, pp. 172–173.
30. *Ibid.*, pp. 173–174.
31. *Ibid.*, p. 173.
32. *Ibid.*, p. 174.
33. *The Essence of Judaism*, p. 100.
34. *Ibid.*, p. 103.
35. *Ibid.*, p. 106.
36. *This People Israel*, p. 150.
37. *Ibid.*, p. 153.
38. *Ibid.*, pp. 153–154.
39. *This People Israel*, pp. 160–161.
40. *Ibid.*, p. 319.
41. *Leo Baeck*, p. 255.
42. *This People Israel*, pp. 8–9.
43. *Leo Baeck*, p. 173.
44. *Ibid.*, p. 9.
45. *The Essence of Judaism*, p. 61.

8 Abraham J. Heschel: The Meaning Beyond Mystery

On Saturday, December 24, 1972, Rabbi Abraham Joshua Heschel, Jewish philosopher, theologian and leader, died at the age of 65. Dr. Heschel had been Professor of Jewish Ethics and Mysticism at the Jewish Theological Seminary, where he had taught for the last twenty-seven years of his life.

Shortly before his death, Heschel was interviewed on television by Carl Stern. During the course of the interview Heschel was asked: "What is the meaning of God?" He answered, "The certainty that there is a meaning beyond mystery."[1] What did Heschel mean by "certainty" and how did he arrive at it? What did he mean by "mystery" and why did he stress this concept in his writings? How is the meaning beyond mystery to be conveyed to finite, fallible man? And what are the implications of these concepts for the contemporary man?

These are the questions we shall examine in this chapter.

Heschel's Life and Major Works

Born in Warsaw, Poland, in 1907, Abraham Joshua Heschel was the descendant of a long line of outstanding leaders of Hasidism. It has been said that Heschel's life and works can be conceived of as "an attempt to achieve a creative viable synthesis between the traditional piety and learning of Eastern European Jewry and the philosophy and scholarship of Western civilization."[2]

At the age of twenty, Heschel enrolled as a student at the University of Berlin and the *Hochschule für die Wissenschaft des Judentums*. His study on Hebrew prophetic consciousness, *Die Prophetie,* earned him a Ph.D. degree in 1933.

At the University of Berlin, Heschel learned the phenomenological method, originated by Edmund Husserl, which was the dominant philosophical viewpoint espoused by the faculty at that time. It was this method that he employed, but with certain reservations, in his study of the prophetic consciousness.

In 1937, Heschel entered the field of adult education. He was selected as the successor to Martin Buber at the *Jüdische Lehrhaus* in Frankfurt. There were many similarities in the philosophical orientations of Heschel and Buber. The Hasidic emphasis on the living presence of the Divine and the joy of living a life compatible with that presence, the belief that the eternal can be present in the temporal, and the emphasis on religious experience were ideas shared in common by Buber and Heschel. But whereas Buber sought the primal religious encounter, unencumbered by the Rabbinic tradition, Heschel worked within the framework of that tradition, seeking to make its teachings vital to the contemporary Jew.

Sadly, the German-Jewish cultural renaissance came to a sudden end with the pogrom of November 1938. In October 1938, Heschel was forced to return to Warsaw, where he taught briefly at a Rabbinical seminary. In 1939 he departed for London where he established the Institute for Jewish Learning. In 1940 he received a call from the Hebrew Union College in Cincinnati, where he was Associate Professor of Philosophy and Rabbinics for five years. In 1945 he joined the faculty of the Jewish Theological Seminary of America, where he taught until his untimely passing.

One of Heschel's most moving books is *The Earth is the*

Lord's: The Inner World of the Jew in East Europe. This work, published in 1950, was a memorial to the destroyed faith and culture of East European Jewry.

Perhaps the most perfect literary masterpiece by Heschel, *The Sabbath: Its Meaning for Modern Man,* was published in 1951. In this work, he elaborated one of the themes that was to become a major motif of his thought—the idea of holiness in time. In contrast to modern technological civilization and its emphasis on space, Judaism, Heschel taught, constitutes an architecture of time. Its sacred times, its Sabbath and holidays, are its cathedrals. And the Sabbath is the symbol of eternity *par excellence.*

The first of Heschel's two major theological works, *Man Is Not Alone: A Philosophy of Religion,* was published in 1951. Four years later, its sequel, *God in Search of Man: A Philosophy of Judaism,* appeared. Heschel's philosophy is not systematic. To systematize Heschel's work, his disciple Fritz Rothschild prepared an anthology of Heschel's writings entitled *Between God and Man: An Interpretation of Judaism from the Writings of Abraham J. Heschel.* This work was published in 1959.

The topic of Heschel's doctoral dissertation, it has been noted, was the prophetic consciousness. His major work on this theme, *The Prophets,* was published in 1962. Here he contrasts Aristotle's conception of God as the unmoved Mover with the prophetic concept of the Divine pathos wherein God is conceived of as "the most moved" Mover.

Heschel's most profound book, in the present writer's opinion, is *Who Is Man?,* published in 1965. This is Heschel's major defense of human dignity against philosophies which reduce man to a set of behaviors rather than emphasizing man's capacity for self-transcendence.

There is hardly an aspect of Jewish life that Heschel did not touch upon in his writings. Thus the Six-Day War moved him to write *Israel: An Echo of Eternity,* published in 1969.

Heschel was a master of languages, and these included not only English, but German, Hebrew, and Yiddish. Among works in other languages are his biography of Maimonides, published in Germany in 1935, and his study of types of Rabbinic theology (*Torah Min Ha-Shamayim*), two volumes of which were published in 1962 and 1965.

Heschel, however, was not only a master of words. He was

also a man of action. The study of the prophets was no mere academic matter to Heschel. He exemplified and represented their teachings. He represented prophetic involvement when he marched with Martin Luther King in defense of civil rights. About this event he was reputed to have said: "I felt that my legs were praying." One of the earliest opponents of American involvement in the Vietnam War, he was co-chairman of Clergy Concerned About Vietnam. In 1964, Heschel met with Pope Paul VI, with whom he discussed the need for a strong declaration on the Jews by the Vatican Council II. Ultimately, the council passed a resolution denying Jewish guilt in the crucifixion.

Testifying to Heschel's ecumenical efforts was his appointment to the faculty of the Protestant Union Theological Seminary in New York. He was the first Rabbi ever to become appointed to this faculty.

In the light of Heschel's prodigious achievements, it is difficult to assess his work purely as philosopher and theologian. A further impediment to an impartial assessment is his style of writing.

Aphoristic and poetic in form, evocative and emotive in style, Heschel's books are inspiring. Yet the inspiration one receives can blur an objective appraisal of content. It is singularly difficult to deal in a detached manner with a writer of such aesthetic and emotional sensitivity. Yet Heschel was a philosopher and a theologian. As philosophy and as theology, his work deserves impartial analysis and assessment. It is to this task which we now turn.

Beyond Phenomenology

To be a philosopher, it would seem, requires a degree of detachment. Yet, if there is one quality which Heschel's writings do not display, it is detachment. On the contrary, Heschel's writings are suffused with passion, emotion, and involvement. Why this lack of detachment?

To answer this question, it is important to remember that Heschel studied phenomenology at the University of Berlin. Moreover, he utilized the phenomenological method, in part, in his study of the prophetic consciousness—the topic of his doctoral dissertation.

Now the phenomenological method is the epitome of detachment. Originated by Edmund Husserl, its purpose is to study the structure (*logos*) of human experience (*phenomena*) without making any judgment about the existence of the objects of consciousness. For example, as a phenomenologist, one could study the belief of primitive man in spirits without making any judgment as to whether such spirits actually *exist*. The existence of spirits is thus bracketed, that is, put in parentheses or placed in abeyance. One studies the *consciousness* of primitive man.

This is precisely what Heschel undertook to do in his original study of the prophetic consciousness in his dissertation. Having studied phenomenology at the University of Berlin, he attempted to utilize this method for an understanding of the prophetic consciousness. The employment of this method requires a suspension of belief on the part of the investigator. The alleged *referent* or reality of the prophetic experience was to be bracketed, or suspended. Only the experience itself was to be analyzed.

The phenomenological method is the epitome of philosophical elegance. Furthermore, it makes possible a dispassionate study of the consciousness of ancient man. Dogmatic judgments are ruled out. One cannot say the belief in spirits is nonsense. Rather, one must say: "This is how the world appeared to primitive man. Let us respect his consciousness as a datum."

Can such a method be applied to the study of the prophetic consciousness? Let us turn to Heschel's observations on this question. In his introduction to *The Prophets*, he writes:

> What I have aimed at is an understanding of what it means to think, feel, respond, and act as a prophet. . . . The procedure employed in an inquiry for gaining such insight was the method of pure reflection. . . . Such an inquiry must suspend personal beliefs or even any intent to inquire—e.g., whether the event happened in fact as it did to their minds. It is my claim that, regardless of whether or not their experience was of the real, it is possible to analyze the form and content of that experience. The process and result of such an inquiry represent the essential part of this book as composed a good many years ago.[3]

From these words, we see that originally Heschel employed the phenomenological method in his study of the prophets. He attempted to analyze the form and content of the prophetic experience without making any judgment as to whether or not the event happened in fact as it *appeared* to the prophets. He-schel's original study of the prophets was published in 1936.

Why, then, did Heschel eventually abandon this method? He explains:

> While I still maintain the soundness of the method described above, which in important aspects reflects the method of phenom-enology, I have long since become wary of impartiality, which is itself a way of being partial. The prophet's existence is either ir-relevant or relevant. If irrelevant, I cannot truly be involved in it; if relevant, then my impartiality is but a pretense. Reflection may succeed in isolating an object; reflection itself cannot be isolated. Reflection is part of a situation.[4]

Here we have the starting point of Heschel's philosophy. Re-flection alone is an insufficient pathway to reality. Conceptual thinking, taken by itself, is inadequate. It must be complemented by situational thinking. Accordingly, Heschel asserts: "The religious situation precedes the religious conception and it would be a false abstraction, for example, to deal with the idea of God regardless of the situation in which such an idea occurs."[5]

The aim of Heschel's work is precisely to evoke in man an awareness of the religious situation. To accomplish this end, he strives to sensitize the reader to the primary feelings which en-gender this situation. We turn now to an analysis of the method.

Heschel's Method: The Evocation of the Religious Situation

One of the most significant aspects of religion today is the study of religious language. The purpose of this type of inves-tigation is to determine the function of religious language.

This study yields the insight that the purpose of religious lan-guage is not only to describe features of our experience, but to evoke feelings. And these feelings, it is maintained by Heschel, allude to or point to a transsubjective reality.

Heschel's aim, therefore, is to evoke the feelings that he deems necessary for an appreciation of the religious situation. But this is only the first step. His second step is to show that these feel-ings have cognitive import—that is, they point to or indicate a spiritual reality. Thus, for Heschel, religious language is both evocative or emotive and indicative—that is, evocative of feel-ings and indicative of reality.

In order to evoke an awareness of the religious situation, Heschel first attempts to activate in the mind an impulse to raise the questions to which religion is an answer.

Here, as in many instances, there is a similarity between Heschel's approach and that of the Protestant theologian Paul Tillich. Tillich defined religion as ultimate concern—that is, concern about ultimate questions. By ultimate questions are meant such questions as: "Why does the world exist?" or "What is my purpose in this world?" For Heschel, religion is not *only* ultimate concern. "Religion is an answer to man's ultimate questions."[6] This is Heschel's contention. Like Tillich, Heschel seeks to instill ultimate concern. Unlike Tillich, ultimate concern, for Heschel, is the necessary but not the sufficient condition for defining religion. But it is clear that Heschel must first evoke a feeling for the questions before he can suggest answers.

This task which Heschel sets for himself is by no means easy. Contemporary secular man tends to be one-dimensional. He is concerned with tangible, palpable realities: money, security, power. He is not prone to ask about his place in the universe *unless* he is confronted with tragedy or death. Modern man, in short, needs to be shocked out of his complacency.

This is precisely what Heschel attempts to do. Thus, he writes: "The beginning of situational thinking is not doubt, detachment, but amazement, awe, involvement."[7] It should not take a tragedy to stir man out of his complacency. Rather, the wonder of life itself should instill in a man a sense of radical amazement. Characterizing such a state of mind, Heschel explains: "We are amazed at seeing anything at all; amazed not only at particular values and things, but at the unexpectedness of being as such, at the fact that there is being at all."[8]

Heschel is trying to instill an attitude of wonder. Wonder, so both Plato and Aristotle taught, is the beginning of philosophy.

It has been said that a philosopher is one who is astounded by the obvious. This attitude was not confined to Plato and Aristotle. Even the modern father of analytical philosophy, Ludwig Wittgenstein, had his mystical moments.

Thus, the following comment made about Wittgenstein in a memoir by Norman Malcolm is apposite:

> Wittgenstein says in the *Tractatus*: "Not *how* the world is, is the mystical, but *that* it is" (6:44). I believe that a certain feeling of amazement that *anything should exist at all,* was

sometimes experienced by Wittgenstein, not only during the *Tractatus* period, but also when I knew him.[9]

It is precisely this feeling of amazement that Heschel is striving to convey.

What is the objective referent of this feeling of radical amazement? This Heschel calls "the ineffable." Since this term looms so large in Heschel's writing, it is important to provide a dictionary definition:

1. Too overpowering to be expressed in words.
2. Too lofty or sacred to be uttered.
3. Indescribable, indefinable.[10]

The ineffable, then, refers to a dimension of reality that is inexpressible, unutterable, and indefinable. We cannot convey its significance in words. But this is precisely what Heschel proceeds to do.

Now it is patently obvious that talking about the ineffable *seems to be* a self-contradictory enterprise. Yet this is exactly what mystics have done throughout the ages. Thus, such a criticism would be too hasty and unwarranted, for it is also clear that mystics are surely aware that they are open to this objection. Yet this does *not* deter them.

Heschel's way out of this dilemma involves his conception of religious language. To Heschel, religious language is not only evocative but indicative, by which he means that "while we are unable either to define or to describe the ineffable, it is given to us to point to it. By means of *indicative* rather than descriptive terms, we are able to convey to others those features of our perception which are known to all men."[11]

These features of our perception are those conveyed by the diversity of human efforts to depict reality, manifested in the manifold philosophies, poetic visions, and artistic representations created by the human mind. By virtue of the diversity of these conceptions, Heschel infers that reality is far richer than any human representation can convey. To apply this to the Divine, this suggests that anything we say about God is an understatement. This is Heschel's fundamental thesis. It follows that what we cannot say, what we are unable to convey in words, supports the notion that what we do say is an understatement.

It is important to note that Heschel is a philosophical realist. A realist, simply stated, is one who believes that our perception of reality is revelatory, at least in part, of objective reality and that we can refer to this reality without being caught in the egocentric predicament.

Testifying to Heschel's philosophical realism is this statement:

> Subjective is the *manner*, not the *matter*, of our perception. What we perceive is objective in the sense of being independent of and corresponding to our perception. Our radical amazement responds to the mystery, but does not produce it. You and I have not invented the grandeur of the sky nor endowed man with the mystery of birth and death. We do not create the ineffable, we encounter it.[12]

The ineffable, then, is not merely a subjective state. It is a dimension of reality, existing independent of our knowledge of it. We do not create it; we discover it, we encounter it.

But *what* exactly do we encounter? Heschel writes: "What we encounter in our perception of the sublime, in our radical amazement, is a spiritual suggestiveness of reality, an allusiveness to transcendent meaning."[13]

Heschel's view of reality now becomes manifest: Things point beyond themselves to further meaning. An act of vision is not a self-enclosed datum. What we see intimates transcendence—it points beyond itself to a deeper meaning. Transcendence, for Heschel, is a dimension of meaning pointed to or alluded to by our sense of the ineffable. This meaning beyond mystery, or transcendence, is the Divine.

On what grounds does Heschel assert that transcendence is a dimension of meaning? He writes: "That the sense of the ineffable is an awareness of meaning is indicated by the fact that the inner response it evokes is that of awe or reverence."[14]

Heschel's argument here is more subtle than is generally recognized. The mystery is not the conclusion of Heschel's argument. Rather, the conclusion Heschel seeks to establish is that there is a transcendent meaning beyond mystery *because* a feeling of awe is elicited by perception of the ineffable. In the following section we shall appraise this argument.

Heschel has, I believe, succeeded in evoking the religious situation. His major task is now to show that this religious situation corresponds to a transsubjective reality.

The Meaning Beyond Mystery

neely

The term "mystery" is ambiguous. One usage of the term denotes what is in principle inexplicable. The word "mystery" also refers to an unanswered but not necessarily unanswerable question. According to yet another usage, mystery means "secret." This usage stems from cultural phenomena in various primitive societies, consisting of practices associated with ceremonies of initiation. Participants in this ceremony were called *mystai;* and they were enforced by vows of secrecy not to disclose the contents of these rites. Etymologically, this gives rise to the following definition of the term mystery:

> The term mystery derives from the Greek verb *mouein,* meaning to initiate, and this, in turn, is derived from the verb *muein,* to close the eyes or mouth. The latter term has a double appropriateness in this context; first, because at a crucial stage in the ceremonies, the initiate was asked to close his eyes, so that upon opening them he might experience the revelation or display of the sacred objects that were shown to him in the bright light that accompanied the final, culminating stage of the ceremony. Second, the closing of the initiate's eyes represents a going into darkness, just as was his being led, at one stage of the ceremonies, through cavernous, underground passages. Also, of course, the closing of the mouth is appropriately descriptive of the fact that the initiate was obliged to hold in secret, and was not, under any circumstances, to disclose the contents of what he had seen.[15]

From this historical background of the etymology of the term "mystery," we can readily see that "mystery" and "ineffable" are virtually interchangeable terms: both convey the idea of a dimension of reality whose contents are not easily disclosed and about which one ought to close the mouth.

Now Heschel, of course, does not use the term "mystery" to refer to something that can be revealed only to the initiated. Rather, for Heschel, mystery is an ontological category; it refers to the inexplicable character of being as being. There is not one particular esoteric quality or one particular secret. Rather, everything holds the secret. Thus, Heschel writes:

> The mystery is an ontological category . . . it is a dimension of all existence and may be experienced everywhere and at all times. In using the term mystery we do not mean any particular esoteric quality that may be revealed to the initiated, but the

essential mystery of being, the nature of being as God's creation out of nothing, and therefore, something which stands beyond the scope of human comprehension. . . . Everything holds the great secret. . . . The world is something *we apprehend but cannot comprehend.*[16]

We see from this passage that Heschel is thoroughly acquainted with all the meanings of the term "mystery." He wishes immediately to dissociate his use of the term from any particular quality to be revealed to the initiated. Rather, for Heschel, "mystery" refers to the inexplicable nature of being *qua being;* it is not one thing but everything that holds the great *secret.* Heschel, therefore, does use 'mystery' also in the sense of *secret;* but he is not referring to any particular secret but the secret allegedly contained by "being" as such.

Heschel's approach bears some similarity to that of the German philosopher Martin Heidegger. Heidegger begins one of his studies on metaphysics with the question: "Why is there something rather than nothing?" This question suffers from various difficulties. First, to ask why anything exists is to ask an unanswerable question unless one has in mind a theistic answer. Second, the question presupposes that we can conceive of absolute nothingness. The fact is that we cannot.

Heidegger's question is unanswerable because he does not propose a theistic answer. Heschel's question is answerable precisely because he does. But the problem is that the way Heschel frames his query begs the question when he describes the essential mystery of being as God's creation out of nothing. Heschel here has answered the question in his very raising of the question.

The issue is therefore joined. Either the question "Why does the world exist?" is an unintelligible, unanswerable question or it is intelligible and presupposes that the reason for the world's existence lies in the will of God. More precisely, to ask the question the way Heschel raises it presupposes that the answer is already *known.*

This is the fundamental difficulty in Heschel's philosophy which will continue to arise—namely, one will not find a spirit of free, untrammeled inquiry. *The answer is already implicit in the question.* In this respect, there is a similarity with Tillich's method of correlation. According to Tillich, the problematics of human existence are correlated with theological doctrines which resolve and fulfill the deficiencies of human finite existence.

The question thus arises: On what basis is the answer already known to Heschel? Three answers suggest themselves. First, we have already noted that, for Heschel, there is a meaning beyond mystery because of the feelings of awe and reverence elicited. Heschel correctly observes that an objection can be raised, namely, that a psychological reaction, i.e., awe, is no evidence for an ontological fact, that we can never infer an object from a feeling. The subtlety of Heschel's position is manifested in this passage:

> That objection is, of course, valid. Yet what we infer from is not the actual feeling of awe but the intellectual certainty that in the face of nature's grandeur and mystery we must respond with awe; what we infer from is not a psychological state but a fundamental norm of human consciousness, a *categorical imperative.*[17]

The argument rests on moral and aesthetic grounds. Heschel is appealing to these tendencies in human nature. What he is implying is that only an arrogant individual, bereft of spirituality, would respond to nature's grandeur without awe. He is further suggesting that there is a categorical imperative, according to which an individual *must* respond with awe to nature's grandeur. And this response points to a transsubjective reality to which we are responding. This transsubjective reality is the meaning beyond mystery—the Divine. As Heschel explains: "God is a mystery but the mystery is not God. . . . The certainty that there is a meaning beyond mystery is the reason for ultimate rejoicing."[18]

A possible objection to this argument lies in the fact that there are morally and aesthetically sensitive individuals who do not see a categorical imperative manifested in this situation. It is precisely nature's grandeur and man's finitude in contrast to this grandeur, that generates, for Albert Camus, the sense of the absurd. A more fundamental objection is now implicit— namely, how can feelings be legislated? This intellectual certainty, argued by Heschel, that in the face of nature's grandeur we *must* respond with awe, is not a certainty shared by all intellectuals. Therefore, we must conclude that Heschel's argument, though subtle, is not necessarily convincing.

The second reason that the answer is already known to Heschel involves his constant use of the word certainty. The following passage is instructive:

> Proofs for the existence of God may add strength to our belief; they do not generate it. Human existence implies the realness of God. There is a certainty without knowledge in the depth of our being that accounts for our asking the ultimate question, a preconceptual certainty that lies beyond all formulation or verbalization.[19]

What is a certainty without knowledge? One commentator has referred to this expression as an example of purposeful obscurity.[20] This is both too severe and erroneous, for it ignores Heschel's conception of knowledge. Heschel follows Plato in conceiving of knowledge as a set of reminiscences.[21] Accordingly, he writes: "We always deal in our thoughts with posthumous objects."[22] Obviously, therefore, by a certainty without knowledge Heschel means an immediate apprehension which we feel or intuit to be a faithful index of reality. Here there is an important similarity to Bergson's idea of *intuition* and Buber's idea of *presence*. Heschel's idea of certainty is an existential conception; it is a subjective experience of the present and cannot be communicated to others. Yet, Heschel claims, it is an experience *of* the real. In short, it is an encounter. Thus Heschel writes that "We have a *certainty without knowledge,* it is real without being expressible. It cannot be communicated to others; every man has to find it by himself."[23]

If we were to take this passage by itself, we would consider Heschel an existentialist, relying, like Buber, on the doctrine of encounter. We would interpret him to be saying: I have an existential certainty of the Divine. I cannot communicate it to you. I can only allude to it. You have to experience it yourself.

Yet such a judgment would be premature. There are, to be sure, existentialist overtones in Heschel's thought, as in the above passage. But Heschel is concerned not only with existence but with essence.

Accordingly, he is not content with a mere preconceptual certainty. Rather, from this *feeling* of certainty Heschel moves to the certainty of the realness of God, a movement which is "a transition from an immediate apprehension to a thought, from a preconceptual awareness to a definite assurance, from being overwhelmed by the presence of God to an awareness of His existence."[24]

What is the thought to which Heschel moves? It is the idea that belief in God is not a transition from idea to reality but rather an ontological presupposition. By this ponderous expression, Heschel is merely applying the philosophical doctrine of realism to the idea of God—namely, that God as a reality is prior in being (ontologically) to our idea of God. More precisely, the premise of the real existence of God external to the mind presupposes or underlies all our thinking about God. And whatever we say about God alludes to but does not capture the reality. Thus, Heschel writes: "The statement 'God is' is an understatement."[25]

It is a familiar scholastic doctrine that, ontologically, the reality of God is prior to our idea of God. But this does not take us very far. The scholastic realists knew this, and they therefore added to the ontological doctrine the epistemological concept that in the intellect our idea of God precedes the reality of God. What is Heschel's idea of God?

Bearing in mind the caveat that whatever we say about God is an understatement, it is still interesting to note that Heschel does attempt to define God. Thus he writes: "God means: no one is ever alone; the essence of the temporal is the eternal; the moment is an image of eternity in an infinite mosaic. God means: *Togetherness of all beings in holy otherness.*"[26]

This statement decisively shows that, despite existentialist overtones, Heschel cannot be classified as an existentialist. He is quite definitely concerned with *essence*. Thus, he says: God is the *meaning* beyond mystery; and God *means* togetherness of all beings in holy otherness.

By this latter statement, Heschel is asserting the doctrine of panentheism—that all is *in* God but God transcends the all. By togetherness of all beings, Heschel is referring to the inclusive nature of God, that God *encompasses* the world, that God is, to use a suggestive metaphor, "the circle moving around humanity."[27] By *holy otherness*, Heschel is stressing the transcendence of God—that God is essentially transcendent and only accidentally immanent. This is the exclusive nature of God. Like Leo Baeck, Heschel uses *polar* concepts or polarities such as togetherness and otherness to express the nature of God. God, for Heschel, is the transcendent unity of these polar concepts.

It is important to note that Heschel does not differentiate the term "God" from the reality God. When he talks about God, he is making statements about the reality of God, even though these statements are admittedly understatements. Therefore, we must still press our question: What is the source of Heschel's certainty?

The third reason that the answer is already known to Heschel is that the Bible, in large measure, is the source of his certainty. Here Heschel's thought takes a turn which is diametrically opposed to existentialism. An existentialist is one who relies on the authority of his own experience. Heschel, in the last analysis, relies not only upon his own experience but primarily on the experience of his forefathers.

The distinctiveness of the Bible, according to Heschel, is that it speaks of God's search for man:

> The Bible speaks not only of man's search for God but of *God's search for man.* . . . This is the mysterious paradox of Biblical faith: *God is pursuing man.* It is as if God were unwilling to be alone, and He had chosen man to serve Him. . . . All of human history as described in the Bible may be summarized in one phrase: *God is in search of man.* Faith in God is a response to God's question. Religion consists of *God's question and man's answer.*[28]

This is the famous Copernican revolution of Heschel—God is not the problem, man is the problem. The Bible is not man's theology but God's anthropology. Man's quest for God is a pale reflection of God's search for man.

This is, to be sure, a prevalent theme, and not only in Biblical literature. The idea of the verse from Job (10:16), "Thou dost hunt me like a lion," is echoed in Francis Thompson's poem "The Hound of Heaven." Judah Halevi also expressed this thought in one of his poems: "And going out to meet Thee, I found Thee coming toward me." But the classical source of this idea is the prophetic consciousness. Whereas the "mystic experience is man's turning to God; the prophetic act is God's turning toward man."[29]

Despite its literary antecedents, the concept of God in search of man is not congenial to the modern mind. Few people today experience the irresistible compulsion of being seized by God, as did the ancient Hebrew prophets. The problem is that most people today do not know how to experience the Divine at all. Finally, therefore, it is the Biblical prophetic experience, appreciated and remembered by the religiously sensitive mind, which is the ultimate source of certainty for Heschel.

Heschel's faith in the prophet's certainty is expressed in this passage:

> Vain would be any attempt to reconstruct the hidden circumstances under which a word of God alarmed a prophet's soul. Who could uncover the divine data or piece together the strange perceptions of a Moses? The prophet did not leave information behind. *All we have is the prophet's certainty,* endless awe and appreciation. All we have is a book, and all we can do is to try to sense the unworded across its words.[30]

To try to reconstruct the past is thus a barren enterprise, according to Heschel. To understand the prophetic experience, we must rather be open to uniqueness, to the unprecedented, the singular, that which only happened at a particular historical time. We must realize that there are certain events which cannot be subsumed under laws.

Perhaps the clearest indication of Heschel's emphasis on the past is the following statement:

> The essence of Jewish religious thinking does not lie in entertaining a concept of God but in the ability to articulate a memory of moments of illumination by His presence. Israel is not a people of definers but a people of witnesses: "Ye are my witnesses" (Isaiah 43:10).[31]

The essence of Judaism, for Heschel, thus lies in the collective memory of the Jewish people.

That Heschel highly prized memory is illustrated by the following incident. The present writer once had occasion to ask Dr. Heschel this question: How can a spirit of religiosity attained during morning services be preserved throughout the mundane occurrences of the day? Heschel answered: "Remember that you prayed."

This incident, I believe, epitomizes the essence of Heschel's philosophy. There are two sections of *Man Is Not Alone* that support this contention. The first is entitled "To Believe Is to Remember."[32] The second is entitled "Faith as Individual Memory."[33]

In the first section, Heschel writes of the collective memory of the Jewish people. He refers to the fact that some prayer books contain, in addition to the thirteen articles of faith of Maimonides, a list of *Zechirot* or remembrances. Remembering these events, such as the Exodus and the Revelation at Sinai, are deemed more important by Heschel than abstract ideas. Jewish faith, Heschel states, "is a recollection of that which happened to Israel in the past."[34]

This does not imply that Judaism is merely a recollection of the past. On what present experiences, then, are we to rely? Heschel's answer provides an interesting analogy: Just as the collective faith of the Jewish people is based on its memory of unique, unrepeatable events, so in our individual lives our faith rests on our memory of those moments when we experienced the Divine. Accordingly, Heschel writes:

> Each of us has at least once in his life experienced the reality of God. . . . The remembrance of that experience and the loyalty to the response of that moment are the forces that sustain our faith. In this sense, *faith is faithfulness,* loyalty to an event, loyalty to our response.[35]

Hence, when Heschel said, "Remember that you prayed," he was expressing an important teaching in his philosophy. In his own words: "The meaning and verification of the ontological presupposition are attained in rare moments of insight."[36]

But what if one has never had such moments of insight? Suppose an individual has never experienced the momentous reality of God? About such an individual or such an attitude Heschel writes: "There can be no honest denial of the existence of God. There can only be faith or the honest confession of inability to believe, or arrogance."[37]

Here the availability of Heschel's philosophy is delimited. It is available only to those who have experienced the reality of God, to those who have had moments of insight. In the same vein, Heschel writes:

> The meaning of revelation is given to those who are mystery-minded, not to those who are literal-minded, and decisive is not the chronological but the theological fact; decisive is that which happened between God and the prophet rather than that which happened between the prophet and the parchment.[38]

Heschel here is arguing against a literal, fundamentalist approach to the Bible. And he is arguing for an acceptance of the theological fact—namely, that God revealed His will to the prophet. To be open to this possibility in the past, one must be open to the mystery in the present. The meaning beyond mystery can be understood only by those who have experienced the mystery.

The Availability of Heschel's Philosophy

Heschel's philosophy, we have seen, is predicated on an experience of the realness of God. One must have experienced the momentous reality of God in order to be open to an understanding of the prophetic experience of Divine concern for man. Heschel's aim has been to awaken and arouse in the reader a memory of the moments of religious insight in his life—those moments when he experienced the religious situation. This is the first step. Granting that the first step has been successfully taken, the second step has been to show that such moments can possess cognitive value, that there is no reason to assume *a priori* that these experiences are subjective. On the contrary, Heschel has tried to show that latent within each of us is an ontological presupposition, an underlying awareness of the *reality* of God's being. We concluded our last section with Heschel's statement that there can be no honest denial of the existence of God. And we noted that this statement raises the question of the availability of Heschel's philosophy to the agnostic or the atheist. Before proceeding further with an explication of Heschel's thought, it is important to pause and reflect on this issue.

It is clear that Heschel maintains that the nonbeliever is simply mistaken. What arguments does he marshal to show that nonbelief and unbelief are mistakes?

In *Man Is Not Alone,* there is a chapter entitled "Doubts."[39] In this chapter, Heschel argues that doubt and denial of the existence of God are not real options.

According to Heschel, doubt or agnosticism—the suspension of belief—is simply not a live option. Heschel says:

> Man cannot afford to be noncommittal about a reality upon which the meaning and manner of his existence depend. He is driven toward some sort of affirmation. In whatever decision he makes, he implicitly accepts either the presence of God or the absurdity of denying it.[40]

This is a familiar argument. It is similar to William James's contention that the exigencies of life create forced options. In matters of belief, one cannot be a fence-sitter. One either affirms or denies the existence of God. Agnosticism is an untenable position.

I have always found this argument unconvincing. Although I do not agree with his position, I do not find anything inconsistent or untenable in the position of the agnostic. It is totally possible for an individual to go through life tenaciously holding to the fact that he does not know the existence of God to be a fact, and further, tenaciously holding to his right not to affirm or deny this belief. There is nothing inconceivable or inconsistent about agnosticism.

Heschel is much stronger in his argument against atheism. He contends:

> The nonsense of denial is too monstrous to be conceivable, since it implies that the universe is all alone except for the company of man, that the mind of man surpasses everything within and beyond the universe.[41]

Furthermore, Heschel argues not only against the position of atheism but also against the credibility and sincerity of the atheist:

> No one can be a witness to the nonexistence of God without laying perjury upon his soul, for those who abscond, those who are always absent when God is present, have only the right to establish their alibi for their not being able to bear witness.[42]

The problem here is not merely an inability to appreciate the problems of the agnostic and the atheist. This has been one of the chief criticisms of Heschel's thought.[43]

A more profound philosophical issue is involved. Heschel's attacks on agnosticism and atheism are worthy of serious consideration only if he supplies us with a coherent and systematic explication of his *conception* of the universe and of God. It is not enough to say that it is inconceivable that the universe is all alone except for the company of man. What does "universe" mean? Does it makes sense to say that "the universe is all alone." Is the universe alone in the sense that a husband is alone after his wife dies? Can man make *any* meaningful statements about the universe, the totality of everything that is? Heschel is right in his assertion that conceptual clarity is not enough. But it is also true that mystery is not enough. The mystery must be "cornered." A feeling for the nonrational must be accompanied by a quest for conceptual clarity. It is because of his lack of conceptual clarity that Heschel's availability to the atheist and the agnostic is doubtful.

Nor does Heschel's thought allow for a healthy skepticism:

> He who seeks God to suit his doubts, to appease his skepticism or to satisfy his curiosity, fails to find the whereabouts of the issue. Search for God begins with the realization that it is man who is the problem; that more than God is a problem to man, man is a problem to Him.[44]

Heschel has no time for doubt, skepticism, or curiosity. But why? Surely doubt, skepticism, and curiosity stimulate further inquiry. But for Heschel there can be no inquiry with respect to God. Man should rather inquire of himself. Man is the problem, not God. More precisely, man is a problem to God.

It is true that man is a problem. It is also true that to the prophetic consciousness man is a problem to God. But it is also a fact that to the modern mind, God is a problem to man.

God is a problem not only because man is arrogant. God is a problem not only because man has become too immersed in mundane affairs. God is a problem also to the intellectual, questing mind seeking an adequate conception of the Divine. To such a mind, Heschel's Copernican revolution simply begs the question. The problem of God is not relieved by a transposition to the problem of man. It is intensified. If man is such a problem, it follows that he needs more than ever to understand the meaning of God.

To Heschel, such a quest is misguided, and for this reason: "However subtle and noble our concepts may be, as soon as they become descriptive, namely, definite, they confine Him and force Him into the triteness of our minds."[45] Mind, the noblest attribute of man, is considered trite by Heschel. Surely man will continue to be a problem as long as he considers his mind to be trite. It is true that our concepts cannot capture the essence of God, but the attempt to frame a concept of God is one of the noblest aspirations of the human mind. And Heschel is a notable example of this aspiration despite his protestations to the contrary.

Why does Heschel demean man's critical capacities? The reason is that his yardstick is the past: "In calling upon the prophets to stand before the bar of our critical judgment, we are like dwarfs undertaking to measure the heights of giants."[46] To be sure, we must examine figures of the past with reverence. We cannot dismiss the past as obsolete. Nor is it fair to apply our perceptions of reality to the judgment of the experiences of Biblical man. The most appropriate attitude is phenomenological—an attempt to understand the life-world of the prophets. And we must conduct such a study with a respect for the integrity of their minds.

But just as we are not giants and they are not dwarfs, we are also not dwarfs and they are not giants. Our critical judgment is our highest faculty. Why should it be demeaned? Why can't a reverential attitude be taken both to our present reality and our past history? They need not be mutually exclusive. This is the fallacy involved in Heschel's treatment of the consciousness of modern man. And it is thereby doubtful that Heschel's philosophy will speak to atheists, agnostics, and skeptics.

However, let us assume that we are speaking about someone with a spark of belief. How will Heschel's philosophy fan that spark into a flame? Having made this person conscious of his ontological presupposition of the reality of God, how does Heschel's thought proceed from this juncture?

The third step is to instill in this person a sense that something is asked of him. More precisely, this is the sense that something is at stake in human existence, that man is the focus of Divine concern, that God requires something of him. In short, the third step in Heschel's procedure is to awaken in contemporary man a sense of the prophetic consciousness.

The essential element in prophetic consciousness is Divine pathos: "The basic feature of pathos and the primary content of the prophet's consciousness is divine attentiveness and concern."[47] It is important to note that pathos is an accidental and not an essential trait of God's being. The prophet refers not to God's being in itself but to God only as related to the people. Only one aspect of God's Being, His directedness to man, is known to man.

Whereas many medieval philosophers denied the passibility of God, that is, God's capacity of feeling, the prophets emphasized that God is intimately affected by the acts of man, that He possesses not merely intelligence and will, but also feeling and pathos. But pathos is not *mere* feeling. Otherwise, God would be a capricious Being.

> The Divine pathos, whether mercy or anger, was never thought
> of as an impulsive act, arising automatically within the divine
> Being as the reaction to man's behavior and as something due
> to peculiarity of temperament or propensity. It is neither ir-
> rational nor irresistible. Pathos results from a decision, from
> an act of will. It comes about in the light of moral judgment
> rather than in the darkness of passion.[48]

Not being a mere feeling essential to God's nature, but a state
conditioned by man's behavior, it is, technically, an accident.
Thus, Heschel attributes feelings to God but not to God's essential being. This attribution of emotion to God is called an-
thropopathy. It is interesting that Heschel, with all his anthro-
popathy, is reluctant to attribute feelings to God's *essential* being.

Nevertheless, Heschel does assert that God suffers.[49] Furthermore, God is in need of man, and man can help God by reducing
human suffering, human anguish, and human misery.[50] Does
this imply that Heschel believed in a finite God? If God is in
need of man, it would seem to follow that God is not omnipotent. Heschel's answer is implied in this statement: "His need is
a self-imposed concern. God is now in need of man, because He
freely made him a partner in His creation."[51] God's need is
self-imposed since it flows from His freedom; it need not imply
any deficiency.

Thus, the third step in Heschel's philosophy is to create an
awareness that God is in need of the person, that what the Jew
does is significant to God and can actually help God.

What ought a Jew to do? This is the fourth step. In contrast
to the leap of faith, Heschel sees Judaism as requiring "a leap
of action."[52]

Mitzvot or commandments are the way God confronts the
Jew in particular moments. By a leap of action, the Jew "is
asked to surpass his needs, to do more than he understands in
order to understand more than he does."[53]

Implicit in Heschel's conception is the idea of man as self-
transcending, reacting to a transcendent God: "Faith is an act
of man who transcending himself responds to Him who transcends the world."[54]

Jewish law is therefore more than a praxis. It is "a source
of deeds."[55] Its main concern is to teach man "how to live with
Him at all times."[56]

If the Jew can accept these four steps, he can move toward

the goal which Heschel envisages. He can strive to become a pious man—to live a life compatible with a sense of the ineffable, "alert to the dignity of every human being."[57] This is the fifth step and goal of Heschel's progression—to sensitize the Jew to religious reality so that he will strive to live a life of piety.

To summarize: Heschel's philosophy is available to those who:

1. Have moments of religious insight in their lives.
2. Consider these experiences as having cognitive import—that is, they accept the reality of God as the premise of their thought and the source of their religious experience.
3. Interpret the reality of God as signifying God's need for their devotion to Him, based on the record of prophetic experiences of the past.
4. Are willing to take "the leap of action," viewing the commandments as the way God confronts them in particular moments.
5. Have as their goal a life of piety, a life "compatible with the sense of the ineffable."

If we are to take Heschel's writings as a coherent philosophy, this philosophy is available to those who are willing to accept these premises.

The other alternative is to take Heschel's writings as a poetic philosophy. This would entail that we do not attempt to view Heschel's thought as an organic whole but rather treat his aphorisms as self-contained units, some of which will be meaningful to us, while others may not be.

According to the first approach, everything Heschel has written is taken as a brick which must fit into the entire edifice.

According to the second approach, Heschel's writings are considered the same way one might listen to mood music. One picks out certain melodies to which one is responsive and adds one's own interpretation to the melody.

So far, we have taken the first approach. Let us try the second approach and then compare it with the first.

Heschel's Philosophy of Human Dignity

The aspect of Heschel's philosophy to which we are most responsive is his theory of man. In the present writer's opinion, his most profound work is his book *Who Is Man?* This book is

Heschel's major statement of human dignity. Its focus is philosophical anthropology: the problem of man.

To begin with, it is important to note that Heschel states unequivocally that human existence is a problem. Thus, he writes that "man is a problem, intrinsically and under all circumstances."[58] Furthermore, he correctly observes that man's consciousness of the problematic character of his existence gives rise to anguish: "To be human is to be a problem, and the problem expresses itself in anguish, in the mental suffering of man."[59] Why is human existence a problem?

A clue to an answer is given by the etymology of the term "existence." The word existence derives from a Latin root meaning "to stand out from" or "to emerge." Human existence, for Heschel, is a problem because man "is not completely a part of his environment."[60] Unlike an animal that lives in harmony with its natural surroundings, man is rarely at home in his environment. Man, in short, is a unique being who constantly transcends his immediate situation in space and time.

This distinctive human mode of self-transcendence is expressed by Heschel in terms of a dialectical conflict between existence and expectation: "The problem of man is occasioned by our coming upon a conflict or contradiction between existence and expectation, between what man is and what is expected of him."[61] The aim of Heschel's theory of man is to resolve this conflict.

Heschel attempts to resolve the conflict between existence and expectation by showing that one cannot talk about human existence without making normative claims. More precisely, we cannot say anything about what man *is* (descriptively) without at the same time making a value judgment of what man *ought to be* (normatively). Thus, Heschel writes: "The task of a philosophy of man cannot be properly defined as a description of human being. . . . We question what we are in the light of an intuitive expectation or a vision of what man ought to be."[62]

For Heschel, there is no existence without essence, no conception of what man is without an implicit vision of what he ought to be. To Heschel, the normative dimension of human being is inescapable. Man has intrinsic value. This belief in the intrinsic value of man is Heschel's philosophy of human dignity.

The term "dignity" derives from the Latin *dignus,* meaning worthy. Hence, the dictionary definition of dignity is "the quality or state of being worthy: intrinsic worth."[63] By intrinsic worth, we mean that value is not only something that a person acquires but is inherent in his very being. Value is inherent in or intrinsic to persons—this is the essence of Heschel's philosophy of man: "The basic dignity of man is not made up of his achievements, virtues, or special talents. It is inherent in his very being."[64]

This philosophy challenges the idols of the marketplace in American life. People in America are generally evaluated in terms of what they own or what they have accomplished. An employer, for example, is primarily interested in value received and not in the intrinsic value of his employee. Rarely is a person asked who he is. The usual question is rather: "What do you do?" And the answer to this question enables the inquirer to determine the niche or slot in society to which this particular man belongs.

But the real tragedy of this state of affairs is more profound. The individual's economic place and role in society often determines his own self-worth. It is extremely difficult for a man whose position is looked down upon by society to esteem himself highly, for our self-image is molded by the opinion of others.

The significance of Heschel's philosophy of human dignity lies in his effort to transcend the utilitarian concepts of everyday life and to offer each individual a sense of his own self-worth. Heschel not only expounded this philosophy in his writings; his quest for human rights in action and in life was an embodiment of the philosophy he taught.

Two Ways of Treating Heschel's Philosophy

The above reflections on human dignity illustrate the second way of treating Heschel's philosophy. His lovely, suggestive aphorisms about man are taken as self-contained units, as stimuli to further thought and deeper reflection on the part of the reader. According to this way of reading Heschel, his words are taken as poetry.

If Heschel's work is taken as an organic totality, however,

such an approach is precluded. According to this, the first approach, one cannot treat Heschel's theory of human dignity in isolation. One basis of human dignity, according to Heschel, lies in his concept of man as a symbol of God. Heschel contends that, in the Bible, nothing in heaven or earth can serve as a symbol of God except man: "And yet there is something in the world that the Bible does regard as a symbol of God. It is not a temple nor a tree, it is not a statue nor a star. The symbol of God is *man, every man.*"[65]

This basis of human dignity, then, lies in the belief that man was created in the image of God. Now the concept of man in the image of God is generally interpreted to refer to man's moral, spiritual, and intellectual capacities—particularly, as Maimonides interpreted, man's reason. How can Heschel's concept of man as a symbol of God be reconciled with his statements about the triteness of the human mind?

A further basis of Heschel's conception of human dignity lies in his belief that God is in need of man. In this view, the dignity of man is purchased at the expense of the dignity of God.

This should suffice to show the problems that result when we take Heschel's philosophy as an organic totality. Yet, most assuredly, this is how he would have wished to be read. Certainly, he was a man who eschewed detachment. He would not have wished for people to read his aphorisms as self-contained units. He would not have expected readers to place in phenomenological brackets the views they cannot accept. Surely, Heschel, as a philosopher, would not have wished that people read his works as poetry.

Hence, the conclusion to be drawn is that the first approach is the only authentic approach. His work must be studied and appraised as an organic totality. This means that it must be evaluated according to our criteria: namely, consistency, empirical reference, and pragmatic value.

Before undertaking this task, however, it is important to discuss his conception of the Jewish people.

Conception of the Jewish People

Heschel's conception of the Jewish people is in consonance with the spiritual thrust and quest for transcendence inherent in his philosophy as a whole.

Normal or natural Jewish existence would be as much of a contradiction for Heschel as a square circle. Thus Heschel writes: "We are the most challenged people under the sun. Our existence is either superfluous or indispensable to the world: it is either tragic or holy to be a Jew."[66]

Like Emil Fackenheim, Heschel states that survival itself is a spiritual act: "Belonging to Israel is itself a spiritual act. It is utterly inconvenient to be a Jew. The very survival of our people is a Kiddush Hashem."[67]

Nevertheless, despite the fact that, after Auschwitz, survival itself is a value, the Jewish people still must pursue essence: "Still we are patient and cherish the will to perpetuate our essence."[68] This essence involves the spiritual order, the kinship with eternity which is the essence of Israel's destiny.

> Judaism is an attempt to prove that in order to be a man, you have to be more than a man, that in order to be a people we have to be more than a people—Israel was made to be a holy people. This is the essence of its dignity and the essence of its merit. Judaism is a link to eternity, kinship with ultimate reality.[69]

The existence of the Jewish people must therefore be coupled with a concern for the self-transcendence of the Jewish people. The Jews must be more than a people. They must constitute a spiritual order. The task of Jewish philosophy, says Heschel, is "to make our thinking compatible with our destiny."[70]

Israel's destiny, according to Heschel, is predicated on its chosenness. God discovered Israel. God chose Israel. It is not the product of evolution. Thus, Heschel writes:

> Israel's experience of God has not evolved from search. Israel was discovered by God. Judaism is *God's quest for man*. . . . We have not chosen God; He has chosen us. There is no concept of a chosen God but there is the idea of a chosen people.[71]

Clearly, according to Heschel, the initiative belongs to God.

Furthermore, "chosenness" conveys the notion that Israel is God's people. No notion of superiority is intended:

> We do not say that we are a superior people. The chosen people means a people approached and chosen by God. The significance of this term is genuine in relation to God rather than in relation to other peoples. It signifies not a quality in-

herent in the people but a relationship between the people and God.[72]

Heschel's aim here is to uphold the spirituality of Israel's chosenness and to rid the notion of any taint of superiority. Thus chosenness is a term of relationship rather than a quality inherent in the people.

Heschel's conception of the Jewish people is thus in consonance with his general approach. The emphasis is on God's quest for man, on a spiritual order, on holy existence, on kinship with eternity. Heschel's emphasis on the spiritual aspect of existence is epitomized in his stress on the spiritual aspects of Jewish existence.

Critique of Heschel

It is out of concern that Heschel's writing be considered as philosophy that we now undertake this critique. Unless his work is examined by objective criteria, it will constantly be regarded as poetry and not philosophy.

First, let us examine Heschel's work from the point of view of inner consistency.

We have noted that Heschel begins by striving to evoke a sense of the religious situation. He then claims that religious experience points to the existence of God as an objective reality and not merely as a subjective idea. Assuming that this feeling is elicited in the reader, Heschel then strives to open the reader to what he considers to be the reality of the Biblical message—namely, God's quest for man. And the appropriate response to God's quest is the "leap of action."

The immediate question that arises is this: Why doesn't Heschel begin with the Biblical message as his starting point? Why does he seek to awaken man's religious sensibilities?

Here it is important to compare Heschel's approach with that of the Protestant theologian Karl Barth. According to Barth, apart from the self-revelation of God, there is no knowledge of God. Barth followed the Calvinistic principle that the finite is not capable of the infinite (*finitum non capax infiniti*) and that there is a qualitative difference between God and man. "The truth concerning God comes to man; it is inaccessible to human reflection in philosophy or to human religious sensibilities."[73]

According to Barth's neo-orthodoxy, theology starts not with man's ascent to God but rather with God's revelation to man, as it is expressed in Holy Scriptures: "Man's knowledge of God must be reversed into God's knowledge of man."[74]

Needless to say, Barth's theology raises difficulties. If the Bible is the only norm, how do we reconcile contradictions within Scripture? Clearly an external rational standard is required.

Now there is a definite similarity between the approaches of Barth and Heschel. Both stress God's revelation to man rather than man's search for God. Nevertheless, there are significant differences. Heschel is not quite as severe as Barth is on philosophy. Philosophers are quoted throughout Heschel's works. Nor would Heschel deny that truth is accessible to human religious sensibilities. On the contrary, Heschel's effort is precisely to awaken these sensibilities to an openness to God's revelation.

However, in the final analysis, Heschel and Barth share the same emphasis: God's quest for man.

The problem is that Heschel is not straightforward in his approach. He constantly shifts his ground. At one point, he will be arguing on the basis of man's latent propensity for religious experience. As we attempt to follow the argument, a Biblical quotation will appear. Then, perhaps, an excerpt from a philosopher will follow. The basic problem in Heschel's writings is the lack of sustained argument.

This leads to various inconsistencies. From his stress on religious experience, one is almost led to draw the premature conclusion that Heschel is an existentialist. But if we read further on, we will note that Heschel regards our generation as dwarfs in comparison with the prophets, who were giants. Such reliance on the past and devaluation of the present are foreign to any existentialist.

Again, a theme stressed throughout Heschel's philosophy is human dignity. How is this emphasis to be reconciled with the "triteness" of our minds in framing concepts of God?

Heschel constantly inveighs against concepts of God, favoring situational rather than conceptual thinking. Yet he is not averse to defining God as *togetherness of all beings in holy otherness*. Is this not a concept?

To be sure, one can find inconsistencies in any and every philosophy. The disturbing feature of Heschel's thought, if taken as a coherent, organic whole, is a studied indifference to inconsistency. On reading Heschel, one gets the impression that inconsistency is not only tolerated but is made a virtue. The feeling is generated that there is a secret behind every paradox, a meaning beyond every mystery. And after a while, we read Heschel for the aesthetic delight in his magnificent use of words. We stop looking for inconsistencies because we have grown accustomed to them.

In terms of empirical reference, Heschel's philosophy will appeal to those who have had religious experiences. It will not speak to the atheist or the agnostic. And it is doubtful that it will speak to those who are seeking an intellectually justifiable faith.

Heschel relies heavily on his conception of revelation as God's quest for man. To many minds, this conception is simply too anthropomorphic to stand the test of rational scrutiny. Moreover, to those seeking a tenable idea of God, Heschel's "Copernican revolution" begs the question. Consider an intellectual person seeking a tenable idea of God, who is told that God is seeking him. Such a person would probably consider the idea of God's quest for man as an arbitrary way of terminating open-minded theological discussion and inquiry.

At this point, the objection may be raised that Heschel's concept of God's quest for man is intuitive and poetic rather than rational and discursive. To be sure, we have pointed out other poetical references to the theme of God's quest for man, such as Francis Thompson's poem "The Hound of Heaven". There are obviously people who are responsive to this kind of poetry. However, it must also be mentioned that there are those who object to this type of poetry also on purely intuitive grounds: that is, they do not find the idea of God's quest for man intuitively compelling, even as a metaphor.

Herein is crystallized the problem of a philosophy of Judaism, such as Heschel's, which relies so heavily on intuition. The problem is that there are those who have had contrasting and contradictory intuitions.

Therefore, it must be concluded that religious experience, taken by itself, does not constitute a sufficient basis for a philosophy of religion. Rather, religious experience must be examined in the light of man's total, synoptic view of reality. Heschel's emphasis on the religious situation must be complemented by conceptual rigorousness and communicable ideas. Religious perception is not enough. It must be united with religious conception.

Heschel does adumbrate various conceptions of the Divine. Most noteworthy is his idea of God as togetherness of all beings in "holy otherness." One wishes that he would have developed more logically this fascinating conception of transcendence within immanence.

With respect to pragmatic value, Heschel's influence is immense. He has provided a depth and scope to contemporary Jewish theology. He has added aesthetic richness and literary grandeur. His writings are studded with insights that make the doctrines of Judaism alive and real.

The pragmatic value of Heschel's thought is that it can make modern man aware of the ultimate questions. The greatest quality of Heschel's work is its depth. It compels the modern Jew to seek greater depth in his interpretation of Judaism. It urges him to see in Judaism a way of thinking, as well as a way of acting.

Heschel's philosophy may not provide the answers to man's ultimate questions. One wonders whether any philosophy could. But if it succeeds in evoking in modern men a sense of the ultimate questions, this itself would warrant an appraisal of its eternal value in the world of Jewish ideas.

"Eternity is another word for unity. In it, past and future are not apart; here is everywhere, and now goes on forever."[75] These words of Heschel distill the essence of his philosophy. It is a philosophy of transcendence which reaches into eternity. It is, to use one of Heschel's own phrases, an echo of eternity.

NOTES

1. "Abraham Joshua Heschel: "Last Words," *Intellectual Digest*, June 1973, p. 77.
2. Abraham J. Heschel, *Between God and Man: An Interpretation of Judaism*, ed. and introd. Fritz Rothschild (New York: Free Press, 1965), p. 7.
3. A. J. H. Heschel, *The Prophets*, 2 vols. (New York: Harper & Row, 1969–71), p. xvi.
4. *Idem.*
5. A. J. Heschel, *God in Search of Man: A Philosophy of Judaism* (New York: Octagon Books, 1972), p. 7.
6. *Ibid.*, p. 3.
7. *Ibid.*, p. 5.

8. A. J. Heschel, *Man Is Not Alone* (New York: Farrar, Straus and Cudahy, Inc., 1951), p. 12.

9. Norman Malcolm and George H. Von Wright, *Ludwig Wittgenstein: A Memoir* (Oxford University Press, 1967), p. 70.

10. *Funk and Wagnalls Standard College Dictionary* (New York, 1968).

11. *Man Is Not Alone*, p. 21.

12. *Ibid.*, p. 20.

13. *Ibid.*, p. 22.

14. *Ibid.*, p. 23.

15. Milton K. Munitz, *The Mystery of Existence*, p. 17.

16. *Between God and Man*, p. 45.

17. *Ibid.*, p. 54.

18. *Ibid.*, p. 49.

19. *Ibid.*, p. 67.

20. See Arthur A. Cohen. *The Natural and the Supernatural Jew* (New York: Pantheon Books, 1962), p. 240.

21. *Man Is Not Alone*, p, 6.

22. *Idem.*

23. *Ibid.*, p. 22.

24. *Ibid.*, p. 67.

25. *Idem.*

26. *Ibid.*, p. 109.

27. *The Prophets*, p. 487.

28. *Between God and Man*, pp. 68–69.

29. *Ibid.*, p. 78.

30. *God in Search of Man*, p. 188 (italics added).

31. *Between God and Man*, p. 70.

32. *Man Is Not Alone*, p. 161.

33. *Ibid.*, p. 164.

34. *Ibid.*, p. 162.

35. *Idem.*

36. *God in Search of Man*, p. 114.

37. *Between God and Man*, p. 66.

38. *God in Search of Man*, pp. 257–258.

39. *Man Is Not Alone*, pp. 81–85.

40. *Ibid.*, pp. 81–82.

41. *Ibid.*, p. 82.

42. *Ibid.*, p. 81.

43. *The Natural and the Supernatural Jew*, p. 252.

44. *Ibid.*, p. 83.

45. *Between God and Man*, p. 78.

46. *God in Search of Man*, p. 222.

47. *The Prophets*, p. 483.

48. *Ibid.*, p. 298.

49. *Between God and Man*, p. 120.

50. "Abraham Joshua Heschel," p. 79.

51. *Between God and Man*, p. 141.

52. *Ibid.*, p. 81.

53. *Idem.*

54. *God in Search of Man*, p. 117.
55. *Between God and Man*, p. 87.
56. *Idem.*
57. *Man Is Not Alone*, p. 286.
58. A. J. Heschel, *Who Is Man?* (1965), p. 3.
59. *Idem.*
60. *Ibid.*, p. 2.
61. *Ibid.*, p. 3.
62. *Ibid.*, p. 5.
63. *Webster's Third New International Dictionary.*
64. Abraham J. Heschel, *The Insecurity of Freedom: Essays on Human Existence* (New York: Farrar, Straus & Giroux, 1966), p. 153.
65. Abraham J. Heschel, *Man's Quest for God: Studies in Prayer and Symbolism* (New York: Scribner, 1954), p. 124.
66. *God in Search of Man*, p. 421.
67. *Ibid.*, p. 424.
68. *Idem.*
69. *Ibid.*, p. 422.
70. *Idem.*
71. *Ibid.*, p. 425.
72. *Ibid.*, pp. 425–426.
73. C. J. Curtis, *Contemporary Protestant Thought* (New York: The Bruce Publishing Co., 1970), p. 99.
74. *Ibid.*, p. 102.
75. *Between God and Man*, p. 102.

9 Mordecai M. Kaplan:
The Natural and the Transnatural

History, it is said, is a pattern of challenge and response. This is especially true of Jewish history. The remarkable capacity of the Jewish people to survive throughout the ages has been due in large measure to their ability to respond creatively to challenges in their environment by reconstructing their inner life to meet these problems.

Of all contemporary Jewish thinkers, Mordecai M. Kaplan has reacted most vigorously and responded most creatively to the unique, unprecedented challenges of the modern age. Kaplan's philosophy of religion has emerged out of a need to grapple with these problems facing the Jewish people. When he arrived in this country at the age of eight, in 1889, the Jewish community was experiencing a process of rapid change. Those who had come from the concentrated Jewish communities of Europe were being exposed to social and intellectual forces that threatened the very survival of Jewish life.[1]

The first of these forces was democracy. Under American democracy, the Jew enjoyed rights by virtue of the fact that he was a human being, endowed by his Creator with the rights to life, liberty, and the pursuit of happiness. In return for these rights, the Jew was expected to participate fully in the political, cultural, and economic life of the nation. Why was this new freedom and equality a challenge to Jewish life?

The source of the challenge resided in the fact that the American Jew faced a different kind of relationship to the larger social entity than his forefathers experienced. Until virtually the middle of the nineteenth century, the European Jews lived without rights.

More precisely, they had privileges, doled out by the sovereign power, whether religious or secular. They suffered frequent expulsions and persecutions—but almost always as a group, as a corporate body. Hence the security or insecurity of the individual Jew was coextensive with the state of the group.

Despite the liabilities of this position, there was, therefore, a positive note. The Jewish people were an identifiable, self-contained unit. The dependence of individual Jews upon the group extended to their very literacy. They went to Jewish schools, learned Jewish subject matter, and practiced their faith together with their fellow Jews. The Jewish community, therefore, had a clear *raison d'être:* it furnished the Jew with his sense of identity.

Under American democracy, however, this sense of identity was weakened. In America, Jews possessed rights not by virtue of their Jewishness but only by virtue of their humanity. Hence the dependence of the individual Jew upon the Jewish group diminished. Assimilation became a major problem. And the most severe symptom of assimilation, intermarriage, has reached epidemic proportions in our time.

The other major factor making for assimilation, in addition to democracy, was naturalism. It is important, at the outset, to define this term since it will be prominent in this chapter. Naturalism is used in a broad sense to connote "all those disciplines which tended to recognize the natural world and the human world as subject to knowable laws, laws built into, as it were, the very character of reality. Naturalism is best understood as the opposite of super-naturalism, the latter based upon the postulate that all existence is governed by the conscious will of a Deity who controls—and hence can direct—the course of natural or human events."[2]

Now the intelligent American Jew experienced a conflict between the supernaturalism of traditional Judaism and the naturalistic framework inherent in modern scientific thinking. As a Jew he was called upon to believe in the supernatural revelation of the will of God and miraculous Divine interventions in the career of His chosen people. Modern scientific thinking challenged this assumption. Furthermore, and more decisive, the individual, through his own experience, often began to doubt these teachings. When he realized that no amount of praying can change the natural course of events by bringing health, prosperity, or safety, he experienced a decisive conflict with the traditional teachings of Judaism. Thinking that Judaism is synonymous with supernaturalism, the modern Jewish intellectual was inclined to jettison "the baby with the bath" and discard Judaism as a live option.

Mordecai Kaplan realized that the combination of democracy and naturalism could lead to a complete dissolution of the Jewish people as a self-perpetuating entity. The only factor operating for Jewish survival, paradoxically, was anti-Semitism. Anti-Semitism forced the Jew to be aware of his existence as a member of a distinct people. It prevented the Jew from enjoying the fulfillment of the democratic promise. Nevertheless, Kaplan recognized that anti-Semitism, being an external force, could not for long maintain the survival of the Jewish group. The natural forces of assimilation, sooner or later, were bound to operate. And this is precisely what is happening in our time with the rise of intermarriage.

Kaplan realized that an internal force was needed to insure Jewish survival—namely, a reinterpretation of Judaism and a new rationale for Jewish survival.

Kaplan's response was to reinterpret Judaism as the evolving religious civilization of the Jewish people. The Copernican revolution in Kaplan's thinking was his thesis that Judaism existed for the Jewish people. Furthermore, Judaism is more than a religion. It consists of the entire civilization of the Jewish people—the Hebrew language, the land of Israel, Jewish culture and the arts, mores, and ethics. Finally, Judaism is an evolving process and is still in the making. Hence it can be renewed and reconstructed.

Kaplan's magnum opus, *Judaism As a Civilization,* promulgating this thesis, was first published in 1934. Its immediate effect was the formation of a small group of Rabbis and laymen who launched the *Reconstructionist* magazine in January 1935. This started the Reconstructionist movement, which is "dedicated to the advancement of Judaism as a religious civilization, to the upbuilding of Eretz Yisrael, and to the furtherance of universal freedom, justice, and peace."

Reconstructionism, in the present writer's opinion, contains an ideology and a theology which can render Judaism meaningful and relevant to the modern intellectual, questioning Jew. Moreover, in the present writer's opinion, Mordecai M. Kaplan is the greatest living Jewish philosopher. Why, then, has the Reconstructionist movement not penetrated to the mind and heart of every intelligent Jew, transforming his outlook and fostering his will to live as a Jew? The reason is that, throughout the years, various misconceptions have arisen about Reconstructionism. If the present writer did not have the good fortune to personally meet Dr. Kaplan and Dr. Ira Eisenstein, he himself would still be misled by these misconceptions.

What are these misconceptions and what was the process of clarification? It is to an explanation of this phenomenon that we now turn.

The Beginning of an Intellectual Adventure

Approximately two weeks before I was to take my oral examination for a Ph.D. in philosophy at Boston University, Mordecai Kaplan came to speak at our synagogue. I was at that time studying the philosophical discipline known as phenomenology, about which I have written in the previous chapter and which was the field of study for my examination. Conversant with the latest trends in philosophy, I had begun to despair of finding an intellectual rapprochement between philosophy and Judaism. I was, at that time, quite excited about phenomenology. Here was a method that enabled one to study, dispassionately and objectively, ideas as experienced by individuals without forming a judgment as to whether these ideas corresponded with objective reality. By "bracketing," or suspending judgment about objective reality, thereby avoiding the interminable dispute between realism and idealism, one could first study experienced reality. Then, after exhausting this study, one could remove the brackets and make a more intellectually honest decision about the nature of objective reality. This field of study has important ramifications for an understanding of the religious consciousness. It enables one to study the religious consciousness of ancient man and the data as experienced.

Important contributions to this field have been made by such thinkers as Mircea Eliade and G. Van Der Leeuw in his *Religion in Essence and Manifestations.* Unfortunately, I had not yet come across any similar intellectual approaches to Judaism.

I did not expect to have any intellectual awakening through Reconstructionism. I was under the spell of various misconceptions.

First and foremost, I had thought that Reconstructionism was purely an ideology with little interest in theology.

Secondly, I thought that the sparse theology that it did possess was inadequate. Countless times I had heard Reconstructionism criticized for the audacity of defining God.

Thirdly, I had been told innumerable times that Reconstructionism was dated. It was valid in the thirties when John Dewey's philosophy was popular but was now out of date.

Despite these misconceptions, I was ready and eager to listen to Dr. Kaplan. After all, I had not yet found a rapprochement between Judaism and philosophy. Perhaps Reconstructionism did have something to offer.

At that time, Dr. Kaplan was 89 years old. The vigor with which he spoke, for a man of his age, was itself a remarkable fact. And, amazingly, he spoke for over an hour.

After he finished his lecture, he invited questions. The first thing that impressed me was the way he answered questions. He had a respect for the person asking the question. And he answered the questions, directly and honestly.

Eventually, I decided to raise a question. "Dr. Kaplan," I asked, "how did you arrive at your definition of God as the power in the universe that makes for salvation?"

He answered: "You realize that we are speaking of the term 'God' and not the reality of God—namely, how man experiences the Divine. Furthermore, the term 'God' means not only the power in the universe that makes for salvation or self-fulfillment but also the *power in ourselves.*"

Immediately, I was gripped. Here was a theologian who had a respect for the integrity of the human mind and who sought the Divine, not only in the cosmos, but in human consciousness. Here was an approach, though different in certain respects from phenomenology, that nevertheless shared its *intellectual modesty.* No claims were made about Divinity in itself—only Divinity as experienced by man.

An intellectual adventure had begun. The more I spoke to Kaplan, the more I realized how unfounded the standard cliches about Reconstructionism were. Reconstructionism was a theology as well as an ideology.

Furthermore, it contained a significant theology, perhaps the one with the most promise for the contemporary Jew.

Finally, not only was Reconstructionism not dated. It was the most relevant conception of Judaism I had heard advanced.

The more I talked to Kaplan, the more I realized how false was the charge that his philosophy was simply a combination of John Dewey and Judaism.

The intellectual influences in Kaplan's thought were manifold: Ahad Ha-am, Emile Durkheim, Kant, Bergson, Matthew Arnold, William James, and Graham Wallas.

And his knowledge of Judaism matched his secular knowledge. I learned that the changes introduced by Reconstructionism were not haphazard but based on a dynamic interpretation of Judaism.

I asked Kaplan about his views on *Halacha.* He replied: "The really important concept is *Takanna,* not *Halacha.* Look up both concepts in the *Jewish Encyclopedia* and see which one receives more treatment." I found a few short paragraphs on *Halacha* in contrast to numerous pages on *Takanna.*

Here was an insight into Kaplan's philosophy of Judaism. *Takanna,* referring to enactments to meet changing conditions, becomes more important than the stable concept of *Halacha.* Yet the continuity of Judaism is maintained by Reconstructionism through its concept of *sancta*—the persons, places, events, and writings through which the Jewish people commemorates those values which make up the sum total of its conception of salvation.

I realized that Reconstructionism contains a total, encompassing, dynamic, and pulsating philosophy of Judaism. I had experienced an orientation to a new approach to Jewish life.

The first thing I wanted to learn about was how Kaplan "evolved" his philosophy of Judaism. It is to this task that we now turn: the evolution of Kaplan's thought.

The Evolution of Kaplan's Thought

The present writer once had occasion to note that Kaplan's views had changed on a certain subject. I asked him, "Doesn't what you are saying now contradict the views you heretofore held on this subject?" "Of course," he replied, "I evolve too." The singular virtue of Mordecai Kaplan is that he is always thinking, always evolving. Here is the story of the evolution of his thought.

It would be an oversimplification to say that Kaplan's thought is merely the sum total of the intellectual influences he received. Kaplan's mind is original, dynamic, and organic. By "organic," a term that is prominent in Kaplan's philosophy, we mean that the development of his thought is more than the sum of its parts. It is the *Gestalt,* the unique pattern of interweaving ideas and interpreting them as instruments for action that is the distinguishing feature of Kaplan's mind.

Finally, then, the intellectual edifice he constructed is the product of his own thinking. Those figures who influenced his thought are more properly regarded as stimuli to the awakening of the latent features in his own total orientation to life.

The cast of Kaplan's mind is scientific. Its method is one of inquiry. It is a process of establishing and verifying hypotheses. And its essence is intellectual honesty.

Kaplan learned intellectual honesty at an early age. Reared in a traditional home, he was nevertheless encouraged to ask "good questions" by his father, Rabbi Israel Kaplan. Thus the pattern of intellectual quest and honesty, united with a love and respect for Jewish tradition and observance, was established in Kaplan's life.

A frequent visitor at the Kaplan home was Arnold Ehrlich, the brilliant Bible critic. Ehrlich's naturalistic interpretation of the Bible, combined with his appreciation of its literary character as an expression of the spiritual genius of Israel, prefigured Kaplan's later openness to Matthew Arnold's theory of the Bible as literature.

In his college years, Kaplan learned how to apply scientific method to social realities. At Columbia University, he studied with Nicholas Murray Butler and was introduced to the disciplines of anthropology and sociology. These studies undermined the conception of religion as supernatural intervention and prepared the way for evaluating religion as a normal and indispensable expression of human nature.[3]

The theories of the French sociologist Emile Durkheim had a lasting effect on Kaplan's thought. In his classic work *The Elementary Forms of the Religious Life,* Durkheim emphasized the social function of religion—namely, the role of religion as an instrument of social cohesion and a unifying bond of the collective consciousness.

To Durkheim, society was a reality *sui generis* which has a distinct existence and nature peculiar to it. Durkheim's social realism made an indelible imprint on Kaplan's mind. It was Durkheim's concept of collective representations that was the intellectual basis of Kaplan's emphasis on the collective consciousness and collective conscience of the Jewish people. And through his study of the sociology of Durkheim and others, Kaplan realized that sociological conditions must be shared by all who hope to share the religious experience. As Kaplan himself expressed it, "To have religion in common, people must have other things in common besides religion."[4]

During his college years, Kaplan pursued, at the Jewish Theological Seminary, studies of Biblical exegesis, Talmud, and Jewish history. Here his growing scientific awareness came into conflict with his traditional beliefs. He experienced the pangs of inner conflict and gnawing doubt. The more he studied Scripture scientifically, the more his belief in the Mosaic authorship of the Torah and historicity of the miracles was undermined. Despite these doubts, after graduating from the Seminary and after a year of postgraduate studies, both Jewish and general, Kaplan accepted a call to an Orthodox pulpit.

How was it possible for Kaplan to accept such a pulpit in that turbulent state of mind? He explains that two factors contributed to his ability to accept the situation.[5] The first was his conformity to Jewish ritual, to which he adhered despite his intellectual doubts. And the second was the abundance of Jewish preaching and teaching material available which did not necessitate involvement in theological problems.

Kaplan, however, was too honest to repress his doubts and

to continue in this situation for long. Most revealing is the following retrospective comment:

> It is true that none of my congregants ever asked me point blank whether or not I believed in the dogma of *Torah min ha-shamayim* (Divine revelation—literally, "Torah from heaven"). But I could not help feeling that they expected me to believe in it. . . . That gave rise in me to a growing sense of sailing under false colors, and to a restless urge to find a way out of the ministry.[6]

A lesser man might have drifted and continued to sail under these false colors.

On the other hand, an honest person, but one with less feeling for the Jewish people, might have abandoned Jewish life entirely. This course seemed irresponsible to Kaplan:

> To abandon my calling and to turn to some other in which I could escape the need of grappling with the problems of Jewish survival I felt would be to act irresponsibly and, therefore, unethically.[7]

Here we find the very *raison d'être* of Kaplan's being: his commitment to Jewish survival. Fortunately, he was soon invited to head the newly proposed teachers' training department of the Jewish Theological Seminary. It is to the lasting credit of the Jewish Theological Seminary that it created the conditions for Kaplan's theories to be expounded, even though his views differed from those of his colleagues. At the Seminary, Kaplan was able to inspire his students with the unique method he developed of grappling with the problem of Jewish survival.

This method was pragmatism. Pragmatism is generally misunderstood and oversimplified. It is usually equated with the simple-minded doctrine that something is true if it works. Actually pragmatism involves a more subtle concept. The originator of pragmatism as a philosophical method was C. S Peirce. In an essay entitled "How to Make Our Ideas Clear," Peirce stated that the essence of the pragmatic method is that the meaning of a concept can best be understood by its effects on life.

William James made pragmatism into a school of philosophy. James characterized the essence of pragmatism as follows:

> Pragmatism asks its usual question—"Grant an idea or belief to be true," it says, "what concrete differences will its being true

make in any one's actual life?" . . . The truth of an idea is not a stagnant property inherent in it. Truth *happens* to an idea. It *becomes* true, is *made* true by events. Its verity *is* in fact an event, a process, the process made of its verifying itself, its verification.[8]

According to James's doctrine, truth could have meaning only in relation to total experience. This further implied that any appeal to a truth which lies beyond possible experience is meaningless. This pragmatic conception of truth is of immense importance in Kaplan's philosophy, for Kaplan eschews any appeal to supernatural and ineffable truth.

But Kaplan found James's version of pragmatism lacking because it did not sufficiently stress the social character of truth and the role of social conditioning in religious experience.

The emphasis on the reality of social forces which Kaplan found wanting in James, he discovered in the thought of John Dewey. The major pragmatic principle which Kaplan derived from Dewey was that all human experience must be understood in the light of its context. Dewey's conception of religion was elaborated in *A Common Faith*—namely, the identification of the Divine with those forces in nature and society that generate and support ideals. This idea was to play a major role in Kaplan's thought. Moreover, Kaplan derived from his study of Dewey the method of functionalism—the idea that to understand something entails knowing what it does and how it functions. And most important, Dewey's conception of thought as a reconstruction of reality, advanced in his *Reconstruction in Philosophy*, gave impetus to the ideology which Kaplan was to promulgate. Ideas are instruments for changing reality—this was the teaching of John Dewey.

Kaplan found pragmatism to be that method most in consonance with Judaism's universe of discourse. Kaplan writes that he arrived at a clearer understanding of

> Judaism's universe of discourse, at what I soon recognized to be pragmatism, the philosophical method which insists upon rendering thought . . . relevant to man's needs. Any idea, to have meaning, must be seen in a context of natural conditions and human relations.[9]

Pragmatism or functionalism is thus the philosophical method Kaplan adopted in his quest for truth and understanding.

One reason that Kaplan found pragmatism so satisfying as a method was its appeal to experience. It was this emphasis on experience which also attracted Kaplan to the thought of Matthew Arnold. In his *Literature and Dogma,* Arnold maintained that the Bible ought to be read as a record of the most articulate striving of man to achieve his salvation or self-fulfillment through righteousness. Kaplan was most impressed with Arnold's conception of God as "a Power that makes for righteousness—not ourselves." Here was a conception of God rooted in experience. As Kaplan explains this idea, "Man needs the assurance, which only faith in God as the Power that makes for righteousness can give him, that his virtuous strivings are not in vain."[10]

Thus the first stirrings of Kaplan's conception of God as the Power that makes for salvation are found in his response to the writings of Matthew Arnold.

The most important Jewish influence on Kaplan was the thought of Ahad Ha-am. Kaplan gleaned from Ahad Ha-am's spiritual Zionism the concept of the centrality of the Jewish people. Kaplan explains the significant impact of Ahad Ha-am's writings upon him:

> That impact effected in me nothing less than a Copernican revolution. I discovered that throughout Judaism's universe of discourse, the people of Israel was the central reality, and that the meaning of God and of Torah can be properly understood only in relation to that central reality. The main concern of Judaism was the Jewish people, its origin, its vicissitudes, its sins and repentance, and the laws it had to conform to in order to achieve its destiny.[11]

Reading Ahad Ha-am thus led Kaplan to the discovery that the constant factor abiding throughout the changes in Jewish history was the Jewish people. Furthermore, Kaplan found inspiration in Ahad Ha-am's conception of cultural Zionism, whereby the state of Israel was envisioned as the hub, the spiritual center of Jewry.

To summarize: The intellectual currents in the evolution of Kaplan's thought became crystallized in a total orientation to Judaism. Basic to this orientation were the following elements:

1. The pragmatic method.
2. The centrality of the Jewish people.
3. The need for a reconstruction of the Jewish religion and a reinterpretation of the idea of God.

These ideas converged in Kaplan's monumental conception of Judaism as a civilization. It is to an explanation of this conception that we now turn.

Judaism as a Civilization

In order to understand any phenomenon, one must apply categories that are applicable to the phenomenon as a totality. Kaplan's major critical contention, in *Judaism as a Civilization*, was that the "categories under which it has been customary to subsume Judaism have been inadequate."[12] These categories, Kaplan maintained, are inadequate because they do not do justice to Judaism as a totality. Each version of Judaism, by emphasizing only a part of the total fabric, offers only a limited understanding of Judaism.

Thus, Reform takes into account the fact that Judaism has evolved and must continue to do so. Reform also contributed the emphasis on ethical monotheism. But Reform, in its original version, detached religion from the organic culture of the people that gave rise to it. Accordingly, Kaplan criticizes Reform on these grounds:

> By the same token that Reformism has etherealized Israel, the nation, into Israel, the religious community, it has sublimated Torah, the all embracing system of concrete guidance, into Torah, the vague abstraction known as moral law.[13]

It is a tribute to Kaplan's influence on the contemporary Jewish scene that later Reform attempted to alleviate these deficiencies by more stress on peoplehood and *sancta*.

Neo-Orthodoxy has the virtue of advocating adherence to a maximalist program of Judaism—i.e., Judaism as a way of life permeating every aspect of Jewish existence. The deficiency of the Neo-Orthodox version lies in its failure to evolve Maintaining a belief in supernatural revelation, they envisage Judaism as a static phenomenon. This fails to do justice to Judaism as an organic, evolving phenomenon and also fails to reckon with the naturalistic temper of our times.

Conservative Judaism grew out of the concept of positive historical Judaism advanced by Zecharias Frankel in the nineteenth century. This concept correctly emphasized the scientific study of the Jewish past as an evolving historical phenomenon. But Frankel failed to draw out its necessary implications:

> The concept of a positive historical Judaism which he suggested might have furnished the much needed guidance in formulating the process of Jewish adjustment, had he met the following two conditions: First, had he been clear as to the kind of principle that is needed; and second, had he pursued the adopted principle to its logical conclusion. . . . The way to arrive at the kind of principle which Frankel was groping after is to view Judaism as a totality, and to avoid the mistakes of identifying it merely with some particular phase of its functioning.[14]

This means, for Kaplan, that Jewish life must be considered "as a distinct societal entity"[15] and that its chief preoccupation cease to be religion. Accordingly, Kaplan wrote this statement, which has had far-reaching implications for American Jewish life: *"Paradoxical as it may sound, the spiritual regeneration of the Jewish people demands that religion cease to be its sole preoccupation."*[16] Kaplan was not merely an academician. His practical idea of a congregation as a Jewish center—not merely a place of worship but one where leisure activities of all kinds were to be conducted—spelled out this social conception of Judaism in concrete terms.

What was needed, therefore, was a conception of Judaism which did justice to its totality. Kaplan supplied this need by his conception of Judaism as a civilization. What precisely does Kaplan mean by a civilization? For him a civilization is:

> the life-style of an organic society like a nation or a self-conscious people that is self-perpetuating and self-governing by means of a spiritual heritage which is transmitted from generation to generation and which responds to changing conditions and ever-increasing needs of human existence.[17]

Three important elements thus constitute a civilization. First, it is organic:

> A civilization is not a deliberate creation. It is as spontaneous a growth as any living organism. Once it exists it can be guided and directed, but its existence must be determined by the imperative of a national tradition and the will to live as a nation.[18]

Thus, a civilization is a living, pulsating, dynamic, natural phenomenon. This is what is meant by organic.

Second, a civilization is self-perpetuating by means of transmission of a social heritage. This transmission takes place "by the method of suggestion, initiation, and education of the young."[19] The term "social heritage" is an important one in Kaplan's thought. Kaplan learned the significance of this concept from Graham Wallas, who wrote a book entitled *Our Social Heritage*. As applied to Judaism, a social heritage, writes Kaplan, is "the sum of characteristic usages, ideas, standards and codes by which the Jewish people is differentiated and individualized in character from the other peoples."[20]

Third, a civilization is responsive to changing conditions and to human needs. Herein, Reconstructionism differs from Orthodox Judaism. Being responsive to changing conditions, Reconstructionism accepts the theory that genuine innovation is legitimate.

There is no doubt that the term civilization explains the phenomenon of Judaism far more scientifically than other concepts, precisely because it provides a synoptic and totalized conceptual framework. The question that now arises is that of the function of the Jewish religion. Judaism, Kaplan says, is "the evolving religious civilization of the Jewish people." Considering Judaism as a social phenomenon, we ask: what social function does religion play? Furthermore, given the evolving character of Judaism, what constitutes identity in change, and what is the source of continuity in Judaism's religious evolution? To answer these questions we now turn to Kaplan's concept of religion.

Conception of Religion

Religion, for Kaplan, cannot be isolated from its cultural matrix. It is, rather, an organic element in a civilization. Religion is "the central phenomenon, the controlling force, the organizing power, the vertex around which all other elements of a culture revolve."[21] Accordingly, religion does not originate as an answer to ultimate, metaphysical questions. Rather, religion is a civilization's way of attempting to achieve salvation or self-fulfillment.

Salvation has been variously conceived during the various stages of Jewish history. In Biblical times, salvation was conceived as deliverance from this-worldly evils such as defeat in war or persecution at the hands of enemies. In Rabbinic times, salvation was conceived of as bliss in the hereafter. In our time, salvation is conceived of as self-realization.[22]

It is Kaplan's contention that the concept of salvation or self-fulfillment is meaningless apart from the individual's social group. Unlike existential philosophy, which conceives of the salvation of the individual in opposition to and in defiance of the group, Kaplan maintains that group life is precisely the factor which relieves the individual's sense of loneliness and alienation:

> Religion creates a sense of belonging and fellowship among the members of a community. It helps the individual achieve self-fulfillment and happiness through the fostering of his potentialities and opportunities. . . . That kind of belonging redeems us from the devastating sense of alienation. Religion helps the human being overcome the fear of being alone, which, according to Aristotle, only a superhuman or a subhuman being can endure.[23]

How does religion create this sense of belonging? It accomplishes this end by fortifying the collective consciousness of the group:

> In ancient civilizations the collective consciousness was hypostasized or deified in a totem, fetish, or potentate. Each religion would elevate its heroes, historic events and places, holy texts and myths into *sancta* which enhanced the organic group spirit.[24]

In this passage, the influence of Durkheim's conception of religion is manifested.

Following Durkheim, Kaplan interprets religion as a way of fortifying the collective consciousness of a group by means of collective representations. These collective representations are embodied in *sancta,* which are the persons, places, events, and writings which any culture creates out of its experience, and through which it celebrates or commemorates those values which make up the sum total of its conception of salvation. In Judaism, the Torah, the land of Israel, and Moses are examples of *sancta. Sancta* not only enhance the organic group spirit but also provide the element of identity or continuity in change in the evolution of a civilization:

> The sense of unity and even of like-mindedness is not contingent upon the sameness of interpretation, but upon the sameness of the constellation of realities interpreted. The latter sameness is far more unifying than agreement in abstract generalizations. If Jews will thrill to the *sancta,* or constellation of historical realities which figure in their tradition, and maintain those

realities as centers of ethical and spiritual reference, no matter
how far apart they are in their views about life—they will be
sufficiently united to function in their collective capacity as an
instrument of salvation to the individual Jew.[25]

Religion, through its *sancta,* thus fortifies the collective consciousness and also provides the element of continuity or
sameness that persists in the flux of evolution.

Accordingly, religion enables the individual to achieve self-
fulfillment by fostering his sense of belonging to an organic
group. But this is only the first step. Secondly, the function of
religion is to enhance the individual's morale. How does religion function in this capacity?

Human nature is a constellation of needs. When man's
physical needs are satisfied, other needs seek fulfillment. These
other needs are psychosocial and spiritual in character.

The sense of belonging helps to satisfy man's psychosocial
needs. But man also has spiritual needs. He needs to feel that
the universe in which he lives is hospitable to human values.
He needs to feel that life is worthwhile. And he needs to maintain his faith in life and in the inherent justice of the world
despite continued disappointment and disillusionment. In
order to fulfill these spiritual needs, man needs to conceive
of the universe as so constituted that it enables man to achieve
salvation. Here we arive at the most important and most controversial element in Kaplan's theory of religion—his concept
of belief in God.

It is, first of all, important to differentiate between the belief
in God and conceptions of God. Belief in God is not arrived
at rationally or philosophically. Philosophical or intellectual
conceptions of God are relatively late stages in the development
of religion. But this does not mean that belief in God is anti-
rational or irrational. It is rather nonrational. It issues not from
logic but from life—namely, from man's will to live:

> Both the will to live and the belief in God are phases of one
> vital process. The belief in God is not logically inferred from
> the will to live. It is the psychic manifestation of the will to
> live. We may state, therefore, that belief in God is the belief
> in the existence of a Power conducive to salvation which is the
> fulfillment of human destiny. We must remember, however,
> that the grounds for that belief are not derived from speculative
> reason, but directly from man's actual strivings for maximum life

or salvation. The inference from the striving for happiness or salvation to the existence of God is not a logical, but a soterical inference (Gr. *soterios*—saving). The biological will to live implies the existence of conditions that are propitious to life. The will to live abundantly, and to achieve one's human destiny, likewise implies the existence of conditions that favor abundant life, or salvation. . . . Religion is thus man's conscious quest for salvation or the achievement of his human destiny.[26]

This passage calls for a careful interpretation. There is no contemporary Jewish thinker more misunderstood than Kaplan. Many of these misunderstandings are based upon Kaplan's idea of belief in God as the power that makes for salvation. And these misconceptions could be obviated by a careful reading of the above passage. What are these misconceptions?

First, there is the misconception that Kaplan has a naively optimistic attitude toward reality. Thus one author reproaches Kaplan on the grounds that most lives are unfulfilled.[27] This critic fails to reckon with the fact that salvation, for Kaplan, is not an automatic process. Thus, the important term in the above passage is *conditions*—that is, there are conditions that are congenial to self-fulfillment in the cosmos. This is illustrated by Kaplan's belief that there is enough in the world for man's needs but not enough for man's greed. By *conditions,* then, Kaplan refers to those factors that the human species must take into consideration in order to insure its survival. In terms of the individual, this means that if a person cultivates *wisdom* or a mature sense of values and holds to these values (such as courage, responsibility, honesty) tenaciously, he will find a sense of personal fulfillment in life. Kaplan does *not* mean that all the individual's ambitions and goals will be fulfilled. He would doubtless reply to the above-mentioned criticism by saying that most lives are unfulfilled because most people pursue the wrong goals—namely, success instead of fulfillment, power instead of creativity, self-aggrandizement instead of cooperation. To believe in God, therefore, means to cherish the right ideals, such as justice, honesty, and compassion, to live by these ideals no matter what discouragement we face, and to believe that these ideals will ultimately be vindicated.

Another frequent criticism is that Kaplan simply identifies the Divine with the good. This is inexact. Here an understanding of predicate theology is important: Kaplan is not merely asserting that the Divine is good, but rather that the good is Divine, or, to put it differently, not that reality is good but that goodness is real. This means that goodness is intrinsic to the character of the universe. By means of predicate theology, Kaplan avoids the hopeless problems of theodicy and gives cosmic impetus to man's striving for the fulfillment of his ideals. The problem of evil is thereby converted from a barren metaphysical issue to a practical problem—namely, how can we eradicate or conquer particular evils. And in fighting against evil, man realizes the Divine. I shall have more to say about Kaplan's theology and the problem of evil later on in this chapter.

The most serious criticism, however, is the following:

> The Reconstructionist method of drawing conclusions from the higher aspirations of man to the structure of universal reality is tantamount to fashioning the cosmos in the image of human aspirations and values. . . . Outside human consciousness and strivings we find only facts and not values.[28]

This criticism takes us to the heart of the issue—namely, shall we conceive of the cosmos as blind, indifferent, and meaningless? Or shall we consider the cosmos as the source of value?

The very term "cosmos" means order. Kaplan's argument is that just as there are conditions in the cosmos propitious to life, so too are there conditions propitious to life abundant or salvation. Kaplan is not projecting human values into the cosmos. Rather, the cosmos, as an ordered, organic totality, integrated by cosmic laws, is a source of value-potentialities. To assert, as Kaplan's critic does, that outside of human consciousness there are only facts and not values is to do the very thing he attributes to Kaplan, namely, to deify man.

The essence of Kaplan's position is that values are just as real as facts:

> Values, though invisible and intangible, are as real as visible facts or realities. As psychic and social facts or realities, values are far more potent as fact makers or factors, in the sense of producing results. The God-concept, properly understood as a factor in ordering the life of men and nations, is the most potent and creative factor in human existence.[29]

The distinction between fact and factor is a significant one. A fact is an object of *reason;* factors are realized through wisdom, which Kaplan now sees as the essence of religion. Wisdom, or a sense of values, deals with factors. A value is defined by Kaplan as "whatever satisfies a human need."[30] He goes on to say that values are fact makers—that is, they produce results.

To claim that values have no roots in the cosmos is to make nonsense of the very real interaction between man and the world. If there were no factors or value-potentialities in the cosmos which man realizes in his response, there would be no cosmos but only chaos. It is a necessary condition of the meaning of the very term "cosmos" that values are not created *ex nihilo* by man but are integral to man's interaction with the universe in which he lives.

To summarize: Kaplan defines religion as man's conscious quest for salvation or the fulfillment of his human destiny. This quest is based on the human will to live abundantly. Kaplan argues that this quest implies that there exist *conditions* that are propitious for human salvation or self-fulfillment. There are those who argue that these conditions are not inherent in the cosmos. I have attempted to show that it is more logical to assume that these conditions or value-potentialities exist in reality. To deny value to extrahuman reality is to deny God.

It is singularly peculiar that Kaplan's critics are not atheists but supernaturalists. They fail to see that to attribute values only to human consciousness leads to the very deification of man they wrongly assign to Kaplan. It further indicates the trouble with supernaturalist God concepts: they are remote from human experience. Kaplan's fundamental aim is to relate the God-idea to human experience. Thus, he writes: "The nearer we get to knowing the actual conditions essential to genuine salvation, the truer is bound to be our conception of God."[31]

Accordingly, before discussing Kaplan's conception of God, it is important to explicate the conditions he deems essential for collective Jewish self-fulfillment or salvation.

Zionism and the Reconstitution of the Jewish People

Kaplan places the center of gravity in Jewish peoplehood. It was Ahad Ha-am, Kaplan states, who impressed him with the concept of the spiritual reality of the Jewish people.

The spiritual reality of the people is inextricably interwoven with the land of Israel. Kaplan defines a people as "a chain of generations united by a common history and culture the origin of which can be traced to life in a particular land."[32] In order for this people to function to its fullest capacity in the present, Israel ought to be the spiritual center of world Jewry, radiating guidance and inspiration to the Jewish communities of the Diaspora. This is Ahad Ha-am's doctrine of spiritual Zionism.

But Kaplan sees in Ahad Ha-am's concept of cultural or spiritual Zionism an even more profound teaching. Accordingly, Kaplan writes that Ahad Ha-am

> saw more clearly than any of his predecessors that, under the conditions of modern life, which are so radically different from those that preceded the Emancipation and the Enlightenment, the Jewish people would have to undergo nothing less than a complete metamorphosis in order to become a creative force in human life.[33]

This metamorphosis, Kaplan argues, can only be accomplished by calling together the Jews of the world, through their representatives, to adopt a formal covenant reconstituting the Jews as a people. Underlying this proposal is Kaplan's concept of the transnatural Jewish community, through the expansion of the Zionist ideal into a "Greater Zionism." The purpose of the "Greater Zionism" is "to reinstate the spiritual unity of the Jewish people through the reclamation of *Eretz Yisrael* as the homeland of its tradition, culture, and religion."[34]

What does Kaplan mean by spiritual unity and how is it to be constituted?

By spiritual unity, Kaplan means organic unity. Organic unity refers to that process whereby totalities act upon each of their parts and the parts upon the totalities. But not all the parts of an organism are equally vital to its life:

> Thus, in the human organism, many organs can be dispensed with, as is evident from the number of operations involving their excision, but one cannot take out a human heart and expect the body to go on living. The same is true of social organisms.[35]

How does this theory apply to Israel and its relation to the Diaspora?

The medieval poet Judah Halevi wrote these words: "Israel among the nations is like the heart among the organs of the body." Kaplan draws out the implications of this analogy:

> Israel is today the focal center of all that is vital in Judaism.

It is the heart from which currents of that vitality can be cir-
culated through all the Jewries of the Diaspora, provided that
arteries of communications are kept open, so that the vital
blood stream of a living and creative Jewish culture can circulate
freely throughout the entire body of world Jewry.[36]

To Kaplan, this free circulation can come about only through
a reconstitution of the Jewish people. Zionist leadership, he
maintains, should call a "Jewish World Conference to recon-
stitute the Jewish people."[37]

The purpose of this reconstitution is to give *de jure* status
to the Jewish people. Furthermore, this reconstitution should
mark the renewal of the covenant originally entered into on
Mount Sinai under the leadership of Moses. However, this
new covenant would be quite different from the Sinaitic
Covenant.

The Sinaitic Covenant constituted the Jewish people as a
nomocracy—that is, a community subscribing to the same law
code. Such uniformity in the modern post-emancipation age is
no longer possible or feasible. Hence, Kaplan argues that the
type of community which Jews must henceforth constitute will
have to be of a new and different nature, both structurally and
ideologically:

Structurally, it would resemble a wheel with hub and spokes.
The hub would be the Jewish community in Israel, to be known
as Zion, while the Jewish communities in the Diaspora would
constitute the spokes.[38] The rim would consist of the provisions
of the constitution. Among these provisions would be the
following:

1. It should define the relation of the Jewish people to existing
   political bodies, and refute the charge of dual allegiance
   proferred against Jews being outside the State of Israel.
2. It should point the way to Judaism as an evolving religious
   civilization, which is compatible with unity in diversity and
   with continuity in change.
3. It should call upon the State of Israel to guarantee for all
   its citizens freedom of worship as well as freedom of expression in cultural and socioeconomic spheres.
4. It should affirm that the State of Israel is the creation of
   the Jewish people for the express purpose of establishing
   a Jewish community to be known as Zion, which is to function as the spiritual catalyst for Jewish life everywhere.

5. It should call for the structuring of Jewish populations in
the Diaspora on lines of organic community in which every
Jew is registered and in which all activities, institutions, and
organizations are coordinated.[39]

It is obvious that Provision 3 is a necessary condition for
Provision 4.

Before Israel can become a spiritual catalyst, the control of
its religious life must be wrested from the hands of the in-
transigent Orthodox Rabbinic leadership. It is a major tragedy
of Jewish life that these Orthodox leaders do not share Kaplan's
liberalism and concern for the totality of Jewish peoplehood
and civilization.

Until such time as the power realities of the Orthodox control
of religious life are changed, Kaplan's program will remain an
idealistic vision. But it is an idealistic vision that reckons best
with the reality of the collective needs of the Jewish people.

In the meantime, what can the American Jew do to foster
Jewish unity? This involves Kaplan's concept of organic community, mentioned in Provision 5. We turn now to an examination
of this concept.

The Concept of Organic Community

Kaplan defines an organic community as *"one which is held
together by a sense of mutual responsibility on the part of all
who belong to it."*[40] In pre-emancipation times, Jews lived in
organic communities because this was expected of them by non-
Jewish governments. In contrast, the fate of American Jewry,
according to Kaplan, depends upon its ability to maintain its
organic unity *voluntarily*.

To achieve this type of community, the synagogue will have
to undergo a radical transformation. First, it will have to sur-
render part of its sovereignty to the community. Second,
Rabbis will be in the service of the community in the same
way as educators who head the bureaus of Jewish education
or directors of community centers.[41]

The function of each organic community will be fourfold.[42]
First, it must reinstate the ancient Jewish attitude toward the
study of Torah. Second, it ought to promulgate highly ethical
standards on the part of its adherents. Third, it should seek to
provide for the health, well-being, employment, and social wel-
fare of its members by cooperating with local government

agencies. Fourth, it must enlist the talents of those who are able to enhance the ideological and cultural expression of Jewish life.

The advantages of such an arrangement are manifold. It would lessen the competitive nature of Jewish life today and foster cooperation. The jockeying for power of the various organizations on the Jewish scene would give way to a working together in unity and harmony. It would decrease the unfortunate power of the affluent over American Jewish life. Creative affiliation with the community would be placed within the reach of every Jew, whatever his economic status. It would enable the American Rabbi to exercise his creative leadership in a more fulfilling manner. And it would enable the Jew who is interested in Jewish culture and survival but apathetic toward religion to participate more fully in Jewish life.

With the present crisis of the synagogue and the quest for different forms of Jewish identification such as *Havurot,* the conception of the organic community is especially relevant to American Jewry's needs. To be sure, the American Rabbi would have to become more sympathetic to the needs of the secularist Jew. But a dialogue between them would be advantageous to both. This would truly foster a spirit of fellowship on the American Jewish scene.

Living in Two Civilizations

The idea of organic community is only one of Kaplan's major theoretical contributions to American Jewish life. Equally important is his concept of living in two civilizations.

Many American Jews experience a conflict of loyalties. "How can I be both an American and a Jew?" is the typical query. Kaplan supplies a mode of adjustment, a *modus vivendi,* for such a Jew by showing that no such choice is required. Whereas in the past Jews had to choose between being Jews and being citizens of the lands in which they lived, today one can be an American and a Jew at the same time. This implies that one can live in two civilizations, sharing the religion and culture of both.

This implies that Kaplan regards American democracy as a religion. Kaplan maintains that American democracy must be regarded as a religion to combat the claims of totalitarian philosophies. And he shows how American democracy, in fact, functions as a religion.

The values of American democracy are the sacredness of the human soul, its dignity, and the belief that all men are endowed by their Creator with inalienable rights such as life, liberty, and the pursuit of happiness. Furthermore, American democracy, as religion, has *sancta* such as the American flag and the Fourth of July. Finally, to show how this religion of American democracy could be translated into forms of liturgy, Kaplan published *The Faith of America,* containing services for the major American holidays of the year.

Kaplan's conception of living in two civilizations enables the American Jew to live without conflict. And his idea of the religion of democracy could alleviate many of the troublesome questions concerning the teaching of religion in the public schools.

The Concept of Jewish Vocation

It can be seen that Kaplan's program for the American Jew aims to bring about a creative and harmonious adjustment of the Jew to American life. Also central to this aim is Kaplan's replacement of the "chosen people" concept with the idea of vocation.

No amount of reinterpretation of the "chosen people" concept (such as the choosing people rather than the chosen people) can remove the odium of comparison and the implied invidious distinction between one people and another. For example, the most frequent apologetic device for the "chosen people" is the emphasis on "noblesse oblige"—that it carries with it a sense of consecration and responsibility. True as this is, it cannot camouflage the other implications of the "chosen people" idea, such as the invidiousness of the distinction between Israel and the nations. When Israel is compared with light and the nations of the world with darkness, as in the *Havdalah* and *Alenu* prayers, there can be no question that this is a plain assumption of superiority. Accordingly, Kaplan states:

> The assumption by an individual or group that it is the chosen and indispensable vehicle of God's grace to others is arrogance, no matter how euphemistically one phrases the claim to being chosen.[43]

Twist and turn the doctrine as we may, it cannot be divested of the latent assumption of superiority.

A strategic question arises at this point: Don't Jews need the idea of the "chosen people" to compensate for the feeling of inferiority resulting from the Christian belief that they are the true Israel and that the Jews are hence rejected? Kaplan's answer to this question is significant:

> For Jews to accept belief in the chosenness of the Jewish people as an alternative to belief in God's rejection of the Jewish people would be to substitute one error for another, one illusion for another. It is dangerous to avoid the pain of disillusionment by hugging an illusion: we can find true salvation only by the acceptance of reality.[44]

Two wrongs do not make a right. The authentic self-fulfillment of a person or a people can come about only by the acceptance of reality. It is precisely the inability of so many Jews to accept reality that accounts, in part, for their failure to reckon seriously with the thought of Modecai Kaplan.

The alternative that Kaplan suggests for the anachronistic "chosen people" concept is the idea of vocation. Kaplan argues that rejection of chosenness does not mean that Jews need to reject the inspiration of faith in a high destiny for the Jewish people. This faith in the lofty destiny of the Jewish people—a faith that would inspire Jews to make the most beneficent use of their capacities—can be adequately expressed by the concept of vocation. Kaplan defines vocation as "the dedication of a people to the task of giving to the world those universal values which its experiences have revealed to it."[45] The significant feature of this concept is that the holiness of the Jewish people does not exclude the holiness of other peoples:

> Consecration of the Jewish people to its vocation makes it a holy people, but nothing in such a vocation implies that other peoples cannot become just as holy, if they, too, dedicate themselves to serving God by embodying in human life the universal values that their historic experiences have revealed to them.[46]

It is important to note precisely how this concept of "vocation" differs from the Reformist notion of "mission." Kaplan defines the Reformist notion as the affirmation that

> God chose to disperse the Jews among the nations in order that they might fulfill the divine mission of teaching mankind the fatherhood of God and the brotherhood of man. The early

Reformers made of this mission the sole justification of Jewish existence.[47]

According to this notion, what the Jew contributes to humanity is the sole justification for his existence.

At this juncture, it is important to note that Kaplan, in some of his writings, emphasizes that Jewish existence needs no justification, whereas in other passages he argues that Jewish existence requires an "essence," or meaning. In the following passage, both views are expressed:

> Religiously regarded, the will to live of any human individual or group is a manifestation of the divine. That divinity comes to the fore whenever men or societies try to make the most beneficent use of their capacities and opportunities. When people live in that spirit they feel they have a mission in life.[48]

Thus, Kaplan disagrees with the Reformist notion of mission in that he regards the Jewish will to live *abundantly,* making the best use of their capacities, as an end in itself. By being *authentic,* or true to themselves, the Jews gain a sense of vocation. It is not contingent on service to humanity. Moreover, it is significant that Kaplan writes also of the Jewish will to live *well,* making the best use of their capacities. Kaplan is not *only* interested in Jewish survival, as many of his critics have contended.

Furthermore, in this same passage, Kaplan goes on to say that "essence," or meaning, strengthens Jewish existence: "The desire to live as a Jew is strengthened in us, when we are aware of some objective that makes Jewish life worthwhile."[49] Accordingly, it would be correct to say that existence and essence are complementary concepts in Kaplan's thought: Jewish existence is fostered by a sense of meaning, purpose, or "essence." Thus, Kaplan has written: "In terms of contemporary philosophy, Judaism as an evolving religious civilization is *existentially* Jewish peoplehood, *essentially* Jewish religion, and *functionally* the Jewish way of life."[50] Existence, essence, and function are therefore inextricably interwoven in Kaplan's conception of Judaism.

This means that "the average intellectual Jew"[51] has to be assured, first, that the Jewish people is on its way to being constituted (existence) ; second, that the Jewish idea of God is evolving with the progress of the human mind (essence) ; and finally, that the Jewish way of life is capable of giving primacy to those values that are essential to human survival and progress.

This is the full meaning of Jewish vocation. It signifies the "calling" that Jews must make the most and the best out of their existence. Most noteworthy, it neither makes nor implies any invidious distinctions about the religion of other peoples.

Before grappling with the fundamental question of essence —Kaplan's idea of God—it is necessary to comment briefly about his conception of the Jewish way of life, embodied in Jewish law and ritual.

Jewish Law and Ritual

To be sure, the Jewish way of life, for Kaplan, is principally Torah, or study. In his most recent book, Kaplan calls for "more study, less praying."[52] This implies that the synagogue ought to be transformed into a *Bet Ha-midrash,* or house of study, and that the major concentration ought to be on fostering in the adult Jewish population a passionate desire to transmit the Jewish heritage to their children. Unfortunately, the level of Jewish literacy in the adult Jewish community is so low and the desire to learn so minimal that Kaplan's important suggestion has fallen on deaf ears.

The average Jew, unfortunately, is not an intellectual. His conception of Judaism is one of a set of rituals or observances. Judaism, to him, means such observances as *kashrut* and *Shabbat.* Hence, the only way of reaching the average Jew is to give meaning to these concepts.

The first concept that must be updated is the concept of Jewish law. Kaplan has great respect for Jewish law. The fact is, however, that with the breakdown of the authority of the community on the individual Jew in the post-emancipation period, the traditional concept of Jewish law is no longer tenable.

Hence, the modern Jew must recognize that the authoritarianism of the past has no place in today's society. As Kaplan states, most vividly, the past should have a vote, not a veto. This democratic concept of law implies that the "constitution" must be amended. Accordingly, Kaplan contends, as we have mentioned, that *Takkana,* or legislative enactment, is a more important concept today than *Halacha,* or law. The problem is, however, that neither Orthodoxy nor some elements in Conservatism would agree with Kaplan's thesis that the Torah, as the constitution of the Jewish people, can be amended.

Moreover, Kaplan argues that a distinction must be made between ritual practice and law. In the past, ritual acts such as Sabbath observance were in the same category as social legislation, such as the issuing of a divorce. This situation is no longer tenable. Ritual acts can no longer be subsumed under law. They have to be regarded in an entirely different manner. Rituals should serve as symbols of basic Jewish values. For example, Sabbath observance can serve as a symbol of creativity; Passover observance can be viewed as a symbol of freedom. The criteria for observance should involve the question as to whether the value which a given ritual symbolizes is still held sacred by Jews. Furthermore, with new values constantly emerging, new rituals should be created to symbolize them. Creativity in ritual is imperative for modern Jewish survival.

It is the area of teaching the values symbolized by particular rituals that is the most promising avenue of adult Jewish education. Since the rituals are what most Jews associate with Judaism, such education could enable the Jew to move beyond the superstitious and theurgic conception of ritual he presently entertains to a healthier, more rational, and more fulfilling conception of Judaism.

In this manner, modern Rabbis and educators might eventually awaken the American Jew from his lethargy and move him to rethink the most fundamental concept of religion— the idea of God.

Kaplan's Theology

The most crucial aspect of Kaplan's thought is his idea of God. Despite the fact that he emphasizes Jewish peoplehood, it must be pointed out that the most novel and most controversial area of his thought is his theology. In this respect, Kaplan can be compared with Spinoza. Like Spinoza, he has been considered by reactionaries as a heretic, as testified to by the public burning of the Reconstructionist Prayer Book in New York in 1945. It has been observed that Kaplan's "opponents and adherents alike correctly assessed the new prayer book as a revolution in theology."[53] Also, like Spinoza, it can be said that Kaplan is a God-intoxicated philosopher who is constantly revising and rethinking his concepts of God.

In the light of these observations, it is paradoxical in the extreme to view Kaplan as primarily a sociologist or anthropologist. First and foremost, let it be said that Kaplan is a philosopher, a soteriologist, and a theologian. And he has instituted nothing less than a revolution in theology. What is the nature of this revolution?[54]

Throughout his career, Kaplan has endeavored to formulate a conception of God in harmony with the modern universe of discourse. His effort is noteworthy for its attempt to disengage the God-idea from supernatural elements, to steer away from the personification of Deity as a magnified human being. Even more significant is his attempt to avoid hypostatizing God, or conceiving of God as an entity.

To achieve this end, Kaplan advocates that we substitute the notion of process for the notion of entity. Kaplan's theology is, therefore, more than a rejection of supernaturalism; it constitutes an attempt to reorient our habitual ways of thinking about God. This is the revolutionary aspect of Kaplan's theology.

Before explicating Kaplan's idea of God, it is important to refute some of the standard criticisms voiced against it. These criticisms are misleading and prejudice our understanding of the idea. It has been asserted, for example, that Kaplan's conception of God is merely an adjunct of Jewish peoplehood, that for Kaplan, God becomes whatever the Jewish people take Him to be. This criticism is baseless. Kaplan is arguing against what he considers to be traditional Jewish conceptions and is striving to formulate a God-idea compatible with modern modes of thought. To be sure, Kaplan's God-idea is organically related to Jewish peoplehood. But an organic relation between Deity and peoplehood is not a reduction of one to the other. This confusion of relation and reduction may be referred to as the *reductionist fallacy* in evaluating Kaplan's theology.

Another criticism is the following: Kaplan's approach has been labelled non-Jewish on the grounds that he defines God. This objection betrays a lack of acquaintance with contemporary analytic or linguistic philosophy which distinguishes between God and what the term "God" means and how it functions in human discourse. Kaplan, unlike some other Jewish theologians, does not claim to know what God is. Rather, he is striving to determine the meaning of the term "God" and how it operates in human discourse. This approach is a far more intellectually modest one than most other theologies of our time.

What, then, is the meaning of the term "God?" Kaplan proposes three ways of understanding its meaning—as a functional word, as a value term, and as a predicate.

First, Kaplan suggests a functional approach to the God-idea. Accordingly, his conception of knowledge is pragmatic: When we seek to know something, we are inquiring about its effects, its consequences, its operations, its functions. As an example, he cites the scientific concept of energy and asks: "What do we really know about energy except the way it functions?"[55]

Let us examine the application of this approach to the God-idea. Kaplan recommends that the term "God" be considered a functional noun:

> The term "God" belongs to the category of functional nouns. Gold, silver, wood are substantive nouns, but teacher, shepherd, king, are functional nouns. A functional noun is necessarily correlative: one is a teacher of a pupil, a shepherd of a herd, king or God of a people.[56]

The experience of God is thus identified with the way God functions in human life. God and man, or God and people, are correlative concepts: One cannot be understood apart from the other.

In examining how the term "God" functions in human life, Kaplan arrives at a second element involved in the God-idea. He maintains that God is a value term, denoting "a relationship of supreme importance to a people or to mankind."[57] This is analogous to Paul Tillich's conception of ultimate concern —that the term "God" denotes that which is of ultimate value for man. Kaplan, however, goes beyond Tillich in spelling out what this means in terms of human action—namely, individual and collective responsibility.

Does this mean that for Kaplan the term "God" denotes a purely subjective human experience? Kaplan emphatically insists that he does not wish to imply "that God, Divinity is merely an idea. Divinity is the creative, coordinating, integrative process of the universe, insofar as it makes for the salvation of man, both individual and social."[58]

To clarify: Kaplan means that values such as creativity and responsibility are not created *ex nihilo* by man but are rooted in the cosmic process of interdependence. Man's quest for self-integration is rooted in the cosmic drive toward unity, exemplified by the unifying tendency of electrons to combine into atoms.

Kaplan's point, then, is not that human values such as responsibility or creativity exhaust the meaning of the term "God." Rather, he argues that Godhood, or Divinity, as the cosmic process of interdependence and creativity, can be identified in human experience through the ethical values that are its manifestations. For this reason, Kaplan believes that it is instructive to explain the idea of Divinity in terms of predicates or adjectives:

> We therefore learn more about what God or Godhood should mean to us when we use those terms as predicates of sentences than when we use them as subjects. We learn more about God when we say love is divine than when we say God is love.[59]

Kaplan's preference in this passage to explain Godhood as that adjectival property or set of properties in the universe that make for human self-fulfillment points to the central problem in his theology. Previously Kaplan had stated that the term "God" is a functional *noun*. Here he prefers to translate the term "God" into *predicates* or *adjectives*. It is Kaplan's alternation between these two ways of analyzing the God-idea that reveals a fundamental ambiguity in his theology.

This ambiguity is present throughout his theological writing. On the one hand, he repeatedly refers to God as "the Power that makes for salvation." This phrase seems to imply a conception of God as a uniting force that is the source of human fulfillment. But in other passages, such as the following, the term "God" seems to mean a plurality of qualities or forces in the universe: "It is sufficient that God should mean to us the sum of the animating, organizing forces and relationships which are forever making a cosmos out of chaos."[60]

To clarify the problem: Does Kaplan mean by the term "God" those properties or aspects of the universe which foster human creativity and are expressed in human discourse as *predicates?* Or does Kaplan mean to identify the term "God" with *one* central creative process in the universe and in man that impels human beings toward self-fulfillment, expressed in human discourse as a *noun?*

This problem is further manifested in Kaplan's alternation between process and power in referring to Divinity. These two terms, which he often uses interchangeably, are *not* synonymous. The term "process" connotes temporal passage, becoming, growth and change, and would seem to imply the notion of development and dynamic movement in Divinity—a God "in the making." The term "power," on the other hand, would seem to denote the source or energizing ground of this movement. The question thus arises: Are the power and the process two aspects of one Divine reality, or two distinct phases of nature in its positive and creative aspects?

We are now in a position to summarize the questions arising from the central ambiguity in Kaplan's conception of God:

1. What gives the Divine process or set of processes its unity?
2. What is the relationship between power and process?
3. What is the relationship between Divinity and nature?

A clue to an answer to these pressing questions is provided by the following statement of Kaplan: "Nature is infinite chaos, with all its evils forever being vanquished by creativity which is God as infinite goodness. . . . The power of God is inexhaustible but not infinite."[61]

Kaplan here is identifying the meaning of the term "God" with the process of creativity conquering chaos, with the eternal and ongoing active tendency in the universe to bring order out of chaos. This process is unfulfilled without man. The role of man in the universe is to transform the potentiality of the creative process in the universe into actuality in his life, through such values as honesty and responsibility. God, as the power that makes for salvation or self-fulfillment, is the inexhaustible ground or potentiality that generates the process. The process is the ongoing activity of the Divine in the universe, which is actualized when man acts according to justice and law. Kaplan here has cogently translated the Rabbinic concept of the partnership of man and God into the modern universe of discourse.

Nevertheless, the problem is still not resolved. Kaplan views the term "God" as a generic term and not as a proper noun. As a generic term, it denotes the eternal creative power or potentiality, generating the eternal creative process within the universe that is fulfilled in man, if properly used by him. Does this conception provide the unity which the philosophical mind craves?

It is to be noted at this point that this question is not only of philosophical interest. The basic theological principle of Judaism is the unity of God. If Kaplan's theology is to be continuous with Judaism, the unity of God must be preserved, albeit reinterpreted.

Kaplan's critics have seized on this point, seeing here a vulnerable position. Thus, one critic has argued:

> The logic of the Reconstructionist position, however, leads to a modern polytheism. "Process of godhood" and "divine aspect of reality," in the singular, have no logical justification in the Reconstructionist context.[62]

Paradoxically, this same critic who sees in Reconstructionist theology a modern polytheism contradicts himself in the very same essay when he writes:

> It should be noted that in Reconstructionism we are confronted with a form of pantheism. By identifying certain processes in man and the world as divine, we identify the divinity with the world and, indeed, with man.[63]

Now if Reconstructionist theology is pantheistic, the logic of Reconstructionism cannot lead to polytheism. Spinoza's pantheism, according to which God is identified with nature (Deus sive Natura), is the supreme philosophical conception of Divine unity. This critic, however, will not accept Spinoza's conception of Divine unity because of prior religious conviction. He maintains that only the supernaturalist conception of the One God "constitutes the world as a unity, a universe."[64] His argument is that we do not experience unity. The idea of the cosmos is "a metaphysical concept."[65] The very concept of a cosmos implies either a "monistic and deterministic pantheism or a supernatural ethical monotheism."[66] Because of his prior religious belief in supernaturalism, he cannot opt for pantheism. Having rejected supernaturalism, Kaplan, in the eyes of this critic, has rejected monotheism. "Having rejected Jewish monotheism, Reconstructionism has not provided a convincing foundation for Jewish universalism."[67] Despite the fact that this criticism is a tissue of confusion, accusing Kaplan of being both a pantheist and a polytheist, which are incompatible, Reconstructionist theology must nevertheless wrestle with this problem: In what sense is God one? *The metaphysical issue cannot be avoided.*

At the outset, it must be noted that Kaplan is not a pantheist.

He does not equate God with nature. How, then, can the Divine unity be maintained without recourse to supernaturalism?

Kaplan's answer to this question shows him to be a metaphysician of the first order, despite even his own demurrals on this score. He propounds a concept of Divine transcendence which preserves the Divine unity without recourse to supernaturalism. This concept is the idea of the transnatural. Transnaturalism, Kaplan has suggested to the present writer, is Reconstructionism's greatest contribution to contemporary Jewish theology. Let us explore this doctrine.

The purpose of transnaturalism is to evolve a conception of Divine transcendence that does not overstep the limits of natural law. For this purpose, Kaplan employs the term "transnatural" rather than supernatural to describe the God-process:

> As cosmic process, God is more than a physical, chemical, biological, psychological or even social process. God includes them all, but what is distinctive about the God-process is that it is superfactual and superexperiential. Were one to add supernatural the whole point would be missed, since the term supernatural implies miracle or suspension of natural law. On the other hand, it would be correct to say that the God-process is *transnatural*.[68]

Kaplan's aim here is to avoid supernaturalism and yet maintain that the God-process transcends or surpasses the human. The problem is to determine the precise meaning of "transnatural." Kaplan decidedly does not mean that God transcends nature as a distinct entity. This is precisely the view he is striving to avoid. What, then, does the prefix "trans" mean in this instance?

Among the definitions given of "trans" is the usage: "through and through, so as to change completely."[69] This provides the key to unravel the meaning of transnatural. It is Kaplan's contention that the term "God" denotes that process which interweaves through the elements of the universe, transforming them into new emergent organic wholes.

The distinctive feature of an organism, Kaplan maintains, is its capacity to function as an emergent totality that cannot be completely explained by the working of its parts. Intrinsic to Kaplan's conception of organicity is his belief that the whole adds up to more than the sum of its parts—by virtue of the integration of the parts into a new emergent entity. And God is precisely that process which makes of nature an organic whole. Transnaturalism therefore implies a conception of the God-process which pervades nature and transforms it from chaotic disunity to dynamic equilibrium and reciprocity. Hence, transnaturalism offers a concept of Divine unity which constitutes the cosmos as a unity *without recourse to supernaturalism and all its attendant difficulties.*

Now the Divine unity, for Kaplan, is posited, not experienced. Man, however, can and does experience the drive to unity and self-integration. Self-integration, for Kaplan, is the experience of happiness or whole-souled gratitude wherein inner conflict is resolved. Kaplan sees in this experience the analogue of the Divine unity: "Whole-souled gratitude presupposes that we conceive of God as the apotheosis of the interrelated unity of all reality; for it is only such unity that is compatible with life's worthwhileness."[70] Kaplan is *not* attempting to prove the unity of God on the basis of the interrelated unity of all reality, as his critic contends.[71] Rather, on the basis of man's quest for self-transcendence and self-unification, on the basis of man's soteriological or salvational drive, he is positing or presupposing that man is responding to a transnatural cosmic unity. Clearly, this is an act of faith. But it is a nonrational presupposition required to give life meaning and not an irrational leap.

It is clear, therefore, that Kaplan can be accused neither of pantheism nor polytheism. He is not a pantheist because he does not equate God with nature. Rather he conceives of God as the creative process that makes of nature an organic whole. Thus, God transcends nature not as an entity but as process. This concept of transcendence can be illustrated by analogy to the human personality. Kaplan writes:

> *Living beings add up to more than the sum of their parts. . . .* The soul is the creative plus in human nature, as God is the creative plus of nature as a whole. God represents the inexhaustible fund of creative potentiality in nature by virtue of which it transcends the mechanical.[72]

Kaplan's concept of Divine transcendence, then, refers to that creative aspect of nature whereby it transcends the mechanical. Nature conceived of as a machine is a whole whose single function is served automatically by its parts. In contrast, nature conceived of as organism is a whole with parts so integrated that their relation to one another is governed by their relation to the whole.

The question now arises: How is prayer conceived of according to this view? It has become commonplace, in this connection, to raise the question: How can one pray to a process? This formulation of the question prejudices the issue, for it unduly restricts the meaning of prayer as praying *to* Someone. It would be more in the spirit of Kaplan's approach to speak of praying *with;* that is, the function of prayer would be to open ourselves to the creative process as it functions in nature and in us.

In this view, prayer can be viewed as an expression of man's quest for self-transcendence. The process of self-transcendence is the individual's drive to totality or self-integration within the universe.

The ultimate object of transcendence, or of Divine transcendence, is God as the cosmic process which makes of nature an integral whole. The relation between the transnatural or the transcendent God-process and man is that Divinity functions in man "as a compelling drive toward self-integration or individuation in a sense of identity or at-homeness in the world."[73] The purpose of prayer is precisely to open ourselves to this functioning of Divinity in us.

Prayer, in this view, also has the purpose of uplifting man. It is interesting that Kaplan quotes approvingly the conception of the philosopher Samuel Alexander that the mind of man is the prelude to Godhood. According to this conception, Deity is

the next higher empirical quality for any level of existence. . . . There is nothing in mind which requires us to stop and say this is the highest empirical quality which time can produce from now throughout the infinite time to come. It is only the highest empirical quality which we who have minds happen to know.[74]

The function of prayer, then, could also be considered as man's quest to elevate himself—to open himself to a higher level of reality transcending mind.

These nonanthropomorphic conceptions of prayer may seem strange to those who are habituated to the view of prayer as theurgy. Prayer as theurgy is a function of the emotions. Prayer

as a self-transcending process is a function of the higher, creative, intellectual, and spiritual capacities of man. This does
not negate the idea of a "personal" God. The term personal
here simply has to be redefined as person-related. What could
be more personal than the individual's quest for transcendence?

The final question that must be reckoned with is the problem
of evil. Kaplan here has been accused by his critics of identifying God with the good and ignoring the reality of evil in the
universe. His view, it has been said, leads to a cosmic optimism
which is not true to the facts.

In point of fact, Kaplan's world-view is more properly desig-
nated as meliorism—that is, an effort to improve man's situation
in the world. Thus, his method is "to shift the problem of evil
from the field of thought to the field of action."[75] This means
that instead of bewailing the existence of evil and seeking
metaphysical explanation of its origin, it is more appropriate
for man to ask himself, "What must I do to make the world
better?" This is an authentic response to the problem of evil
because it places the responsibility for overcoming evil squarely
on man's shoulders.

Accordingly, when Kaplan defines the process of Divinity
as creativity conquering chaos, he does not mean that this is
an automatic process. Man must cooperate with this process
in order for it to be actualized. Hence, Kaplan maintains that
the Divine process of creativity operates according to laws and
conditions. The consequent view of moral evil, therefore, is
that it

> lies in self-deification, in the assumption that the salvation of
> the individual can be achieved by self-assertion, without reckon-
> ing with a Power, not ourselves, that lays down the conditions
> of such achievement.[76]

The most significant term in this statement is "conditions."

Kaplan conceives of man's relation to the cosmos as a conditional one. This, incidentally, can be regarded as Kaplan's reinterpretation of the concept of covenant: If man lives in accordance with the conditions of the universe—that is, if he acts
in accordance with the polarity of independence and interdependence that exists in the cosmos, he will survive. But
if man sets himself up as a god, as a law unto himself, as the
sole arbiter of value, evil results. Moral evil is thus a result of

man's failure to reckon with the cosmic sources of value as manifested in the lawful character of the universe.

To illustrate: Just as in the nucleus of an atom the positive and negative charges are maintained in equilibrium, so, too, the moral law consists of a delicate balance between opposites. Analogous to this polarity in the cosmos is the polarity of values held together by law. Independence must be balanced by interdependence. Moral evil is the failure to reckon with this law, this delicate and vital balance.

Although Kaplan's view can account for moral evil, in a collective sense, it cannot explain natural evil. But Kaplan simply admits that he does not know why anything exists, let alone evil. This is an example of intellectual modesty unparalleled in theology! It is certainly more honest than the incessant and interminable efforts to reconcile the omnipotence and goodness of a most perfect Being with the evil in the world.

To sum up: We do not know why, metaphysically, an evil like cancer exists. But we can do our best to conquer it. The contribution of Reconstructionist theology is that it offers man this hope—that when he strives with all his power to conquer evil, there is a transcendent Power at work in the universe to which he is responding and which is responsive to his most noble efforts. By viewing evil as something to be conquered, Kaplan converts a theoretical problem into a practical challenge.

The interesting feature, then, of Kaplan's transnatural conception of God is that it offers a communicable doctrine of transcendence which motivates man to goal-directed activity. The transcendence of God is not beclouded in mystery and mysticism. Nor is it opaque to reason, for it does not entail belief in the suspension of natural law. Rather, it has the virtue of transfiguring the vague and inchoate concept of transcendence into a linguistically meaningful and empirically identifiable term in theological discourse.

Critique of Kaplan

The critics of Kaplan are so manifold and the criticisms so vociferous that I have attempted to ferret out those that are unjustified in the course of this explication. Now we must determine which criticisms still stand.

From the point of view of inner consistency, I have indicated the fundamental ambiguity in Kaplan's theology and demonstrated how it can be resolved. The major problem, we have seen, is how the unity of God can be maintained in the face of Kaplan's repeated assertions that God is the sum total of all the forces in the universe that impel man to self-fulfillment. As has been demonstrated, despite the frequency of such phrases, it is abundantly clear that Kaplan conceives of God as a unitary transcendent process that makes of the universe a *cosmos,* or ordered unity.

It remains to ask why Kaplan repeatedly engages in such locutions as "the sum total of all forces that make for salvation," leaving himself open to critics who seek metaphysical unity. The answer to this question suggests the major problem which Reconstructionist theology must reckon with in the years to come.

The answer lies in Kaplan's overemphasis on pragmatic value. To be sure, a philosophy must be evaluated in terms of its effects, consequences, and functions. But the question of truth—a purely philosophical question—cannot be avoided.

The philosophic mind seeks to know reality for itself and in itself whether or not this reality is conducive or propitious to man's salvation or self-fulfillment.

Kaplan repeatedly emphasizes such locutions as "the sum total of all those forces making for self-fulfillment" in order to more properly induce man to move toward such fulfillment by *identifying* these forces. As a result of this emphasis, Kaplan becomes involved in the ambiguity which I have assiduously attempted to resolve. More stress on inner consistency and less emphasis on pragmatic value would have made such efforts to resolve the ambiguity unnecessary.

The question now arises as to why this attempt to unravel the ambiguity was undertaken. This involves the present writer's belief that the promise of American Jewish theology lies in Reconstructionism. And it also involves a curious irony. This irony is that despite his protests against metaphysics, Kaplan is a great metaphysician. The problem is that he is so imbued with the pragmatic method that he does not carry his meta-physical doctrines to their logical conclusions.

Surely he *is* concerned with truth in and of itself. He is the only living Jewish theologian who is constantly thinking and revising his idea of God. But in the development of these ideas, he does not unravel their complete implications. Accordingly, in terms of inner consistency, I have argued, against Kaplan's critics, that the consistency is there but has to be discovered by exploring the implications of Kaplan's concept.

Empirical reference and pragmatic value are the strengths of Kaplan's conception of Judaism and his theology.

Kaplan always seeks empirical reference. He continually endeavors to find in *human experience* the basis of the conceptions he propounds. His conception of Judaism as an evolving religious civilization is one which *fits the facts* of modern Jewish life. And his conception of transcendence is distinguished by being linguistically meaningful and empirically identifiable.

Pragmatic value, as I have suggested, is the main criterion operative in Kaplan's thought. In all areas of his thought, he seeks those conceptions that best foster human self-fulfillment. And he has done more than any other contemporary thinker to foster and enhance Jewish life in America.

Reconstructionism contains the promise of future Jewish thought. To fulfill this promise, a concentrated effort on theological reconstruction is required. Reconstructionsm has the germ idea of the kind of theology needed on the American Jewish scene. But it must develop a solid metaphysics to forestall the shallow criticisms of its opponents. This means that metaphysical issues must be faced and that truth value must be held to be as important as pragmatic value.

In the following chapter, I shall discuss two of the newer Jewish thinkers. One of these thinkers, Jacob Agus, during the course of his development was sympathetic with Reconstructionism but eventually took issue with the metaphysical incompleteness of its theology.

It should be abundantly clear, however, that more than any other person on the American Jewish scene, Mordecai M. Kaplan has stimulated creative thought. He is surely the seminal figure in contemporary Jewish thought.

NOTES

1. For a helpful explanation of these forces as they impinged upon Kaplan, I am indebted to Ira Eisenstein, "The Naturalistic Religious Philosophy of Mordecai M. Kaplan," unpublished paper.
2. *Idem.*

3. See Ira Eisenstein and Eugene Kohn, *Mordecai M. Kaplan: An Evaluation,* p. 18.
4. *Idem.*
5. *Ibid.,* p. 290.
6. *Ibid.,* p. 295.
7. *Idem.*
8. John J. McDermott, ed., *The Writings of William James* (New York: The Modern Library, 1968), pp. 311–312.
9. *Mordecai M. Kaplan,* p. 299.
10. *Ibid.,* p. 297.
11. *Ibid.,* p. 298.
12. Mordecai M. Kaplan, *Judaism as a Civilization* (New York: Reconstructionist Press, 1957), p. 179.
13. *Ibid.,* pp. 121–122.
14. *Ibid.,* pp. 176–177.
15. *Ibid.,* p. 177.
16. *Ibid.,* p. 345.
17. Mordecai M. Kaplan, *The Religion of Ethical Nationhood* (New York: The Macmillan Co., 1970), p. 16.
18. *Judaism as a Civilization,* pp. 180–181.
19. *Ibid.,* p. 181.
20. *Ibid.,* p. 179.
21. Eisenstein, *op. cit.*
22. *The Religion of Ethical Nationhood,* p. 18.
23. *Ibid.,* pp. 71–72.
24. *Idem.*
25. *Judaism as a Civilization,* pp. 519–520.
26. Mordecai M. Kaplan, *The Future of the American Jew* (New York: Reconstructionist Press, 1957), p. 172.
27. See Eugene Borowitz, *A New Jewish Theology in the Making,* p. 119.
28. Eliezer Berkovits, "Reconstructionist Theology: A Critical Evaluation" in *A Treasury of Tradition,* eds. Norman Lamm and Walter S. Wurzburger (New York: Hebrew Publishing Co., 1968), p. 413.
29. *The Religion of Ethical Nationhood,* p. 23.
30. *Idem.*
31. *The Future of the American Jew,* p. 175.
32. Mordecai M. Kaplan, *Questions Jews Ask* (New York: Reconstructionist Press, 1966), p. 43.
33. *Ibid.,* p. 222.
34. Ira Eisenstein, "Mordecai M. Kaplan" in *Great Jewish Thinkers of the Twentieth Century,* ed. Simon Noveck (B'nai B'rith Great Book Series), p. 275.
35. *Questions Jews Ask,* p. 409.
36. *Ibid.,* p. 410.
37. *The Religion of Ethical Nationhood,* p. 123.
38. *Ibid.,* p. 123.
39. *Ibid.,* pp. 132–133.
40. *Questions Jews Ask,* p. 288.
41. *Ibid.,* p. 289.

42. *The Religion of Ethical Nationhood*, p. 133.

43. *The Future of the American Jew*, p. 219.

44. *Questions Jews Ask*, p. 211.

45. *Ibid.*, p. 211.

46. *Idem.*

47. *Ibid.*, p. 208.

48. *Idem.*

49. *Idem.*

50. Mordecai M. Kaplan, *The Purpose and Meaning of Jewish Existence*, p. 300.

51. *Idem.*

52. *The Religion of Ethical Nationhood*, p. 175.

53. *Mordecai M. Kaplan*, p. 211.

54. During the course of this exposition of Kaplan's theology, I shall be quoting at length from my articles "Mordecai M. Kaplan's Theology: A Re-evaluation," *Conservative Judaism*, Summer 1971, and "The Concept of Transcendence in Reconstructionism," *Reconstructionist*, June 30, 1972. I am indebted to both periodicals for permission to quote from these essays.

55. "The Meaning of God for the Contemporary Jew," in *Essays on Jewish Thought and Life*, ed. Alfred Jospe, p. 71.

56. *The Religion of Ethical Nationhood*, p. 4.

57. *Idem.*

58. "The Meaning of God for the Contemporary Jew," p. 71.

59. *Ibid.*, p. 73.

60. Mordecai M. Kaplan, *The Meaning of God in Modern Jewish Religion* (New York: Reconstructionist Press, 1962), p. 76.

61. *The Religion of Ethical Nationhood*, p. 51.

62. Eliezer Berkovits, *op. cit.*, p. 406.

63. *Ibid.*, p. 388.

64. *Ibid.*, p. 407.

65. *Ibid.*, p. 406.

66. *Idem.*

67. *Ibid.*, p. 408.

68. *The Future of the American Jew*, p. 183.

69. *Webster's New Collegiate Dictionary*, p. 902.

70. *The Meaning of God in Modern Jewish Religion*, p. 226.

71. Berkovits, *op. cit.*, p. 405.

72. *The Religion of Ethical Nationhood*, pp. 89, 91.

73. *Ibid.*, p. 79.

74. *Ibid.*, p. 111.

75. *The Future of the American Jew*, p. 236.

76. *Ibid.*, p. 278.

10 Arthur A. Cohen and Jacob B. Agus:
The Supernatural and the Absolute Self

Self-transcendence is an important aspect of human experience. A man dissatisfied with the present needs to transcend his life situation by looking to a better future. A person who finds the mundane world insufficient to fulfill his higher yearnings may seek to find fulfillment through relationship to a supernatural Being or an Absolute Self. The situation of the Jew throughout history has been a prime example of this kind of self-transcendence. Fettered by adverse historical circumstances, the Jew has perennially strived to transcend his unpleasant situation through relationship to a supernatural Being or Absolute Self.

The drive to self-transcendence is thus a dimension of human life and especially of Jewish life. Man needs to rise above his present situation. But the major questions are: To what end shall he direct this urge? What is the legitimate object of human self-transcendence? The two thinkers whose theology we shall examine in this chapter argue that the necessary object of human self-transcendence is a transcendent Being. Our purpose will be to inquire into the grounds of this alleged necessity— namely, must transcendence be conceived of as a Being? Does continuity with the Judaism of the past require that transcendence be conceived of in this manner? What consequences, if any, follow either from an acceptance or rejection of this notion?

The two thinkers we shall examine constitute an interesting contrast. The first thinker, Arthur Cohen, is a professional writer. His mode of self-transcendence is the imagination. But, paradoxically, he does not conceive of the transcendent object of his thought to be imaginary. Rather, his chief concern is to establish that Divine transcendence, conceived of as a supernatural Being, is a real and not a fictive entity.

The second thinker we shall examine is Rabbi Jacob Agus, a philosopher. His mode of self-transcendence is reason. His chief concern is to establish that Divine transcendence, conceived of as Absolute Self or Personality, is the outcome not only of faith but of rationality.

We turn first to the theology of Arthur Cohen. Arthur A. Cohen was born in 1928 and received his education at the University of Chicago. He was a Fellow in Medieval Jewish Philosophy at the Jewish Theological Seminary from 1951 to 1953, and has done additional study at the New School for Social Research, Columbia University, and Union Theological Seminary.

Cohen is a cofounder of the Noonday Press, founder of Meridian Books, and was Director of the Religious Department at Holt, Rinehart and Winston from 1961 to 1964. He is a member of the Advisory Council of the Institute for Advanced Judaic Studies, Brandeis University, and of the Editorial Board of *Judaism.*

Among his books are *Martin Buber, The Natural and the Supernatural Jew, The Myth of the Judeo-Christian Tradition, The Carpenter Years,* and *In the Days of Simon Stern.* He has edited *The Anatomy of Faith* and has contributed to *Religion and the Free Society.*

Cohen's Orientation to Judaism

The key to Cohen's theology is found in the following statement:

> I am afraid less of abnormalizing the Jew than of normalizing him. This is so because my concern is less with Jewish history as such, with the works of the Jewish mind, with the identification of its peculiar cast and accent, its spirit and force, than with a specific phenomenon: the Jewish mind as it has thought and continues to think about its supernatural vocation.[1]

Cohen, thus, undoubtedly contends that natural or normal categories fail to do full justice to the phenomenon of the Jew. To be sure, he does not deny these categories. He says that the "natural Jew is a creature situated in nature and activated by history."[2] But it is his belief that the idea of the "natural" Jew is only a half-truth. The full and complete truth is this:

> Without the command to sustain one's supernatural vocation (that is, the belief that God has called the Jew to Himself) to call oneself a Jew is but a half-truth—a mere designation without ultimate meaning.[3]

Before expounding the meaning of Cohen's doctrine, it is important first to seek its roots and to understand why he is not content with normalizing the Jew. Why is Cohen *less* afraid of abnormalizing the Jew?

The poet has told us that the child is father of the man. The following biographical incident, related by Cohen himself, in a published dialogue with Mordecai Kaplan will help us to understand why he sees Jewish existence as essentially abnormal:

> . . . it is my recollection that in the early forties a rally was held at Madison Square Garden to which Chaim Weizmann spoke (but for all I remember it might well have been Rabbi Stephen Wise). My memory tells me that it was Chaim Weizmann, and I was a boy of fifteen, holding the hand of my father and hearing Weizmann announce that word had just been received that two million Jews were dead. Sobs broke out about me and my father began to cry, and all that I can remember was that I burst into tears, not knowing what it meant for two million people to die, but knowing that that man next to me was my father and indeed he might have died and indeed I

might have died and indeed the twenty thousand Jews who crowded Madison Square Garden all might have been dead. It came to me at that moment and has stayed with me all my life, that the commitment to values that define any civilization makes us liable to the distaste and loathing of the world, that the holding of any truth makes oneself vulnerable, whether it is an individual truth or the posture of a nation, whether it is the values of civilization or whether it is the belief in God. Ultimate truth carries with it ultimate vulnerability.[4]

We see in things what we are conditioned to see. And the earlier the age, the more we are conditioned. According to his own testimony, the above-related experience of the fifteen-year-old boy in Madison Square Garden formed an indelible imprint on the mind of Arthur Cohen. He was seized with a feeling of the insecurity of Jewish existence. Accordingly, his interlocutor in this dialogue, Mordecai Kaplan, responded to him in this vein:

You came to Jewish life at a most tragic point of its existence. You did not have the opportunity as a child to share the full and normal life-style of the Jewish people. Therefore when the awareness of your Jewish identity came to you the way it did, it inevitably led to the conclusion that the fact of your Jewish identity, no matter how true it might sound, was vulnerable.[5]

The impact of this experience and its effect on Cohen's thinking is, of course, a matter of psychological speculation. The point is, however, that an artist is never content with mere experiences. The feeling of Jewish insecurity could not remain with Arthur Cohen simply as a datum. Cohen the artist transmuted this feeling, through the imagination, into a sense of Jewish supernaturalist vocation. True, the Jews are politically insecure. But they are insecure because they are bearers of a supernatural truth. Thus, like the medieval Jewish philosopher and poet Judah Halevi, Cohen transforms a deficiency into a positive characteristic. Judah Halevi's *Cuzari*, we recall, was based on the paradox that the most politically despised people was the bearer of the highest religious truth. Similarly, the reality of Jewish insecurity or vulnerability finds its rationale, for Cohen, in the belief that the supernatural Jew represents the ultimate truth.

Given Cohen's orientation to Judaism, we now ask: What does he mean by the supernatural Jew? What does he mean by ultimate truth, and how does he propose to know it? It is to these questions that we now turn.

The Supernatural Jew

Fortunately, Cohen provides us with a statement of his personal beliefs. He refers to these beliefs as existential dogmas. By the phrase "existential dogmas,'" he means the faith that *he* must believe, because, as he puts it, "without it there is nothing I consider ultimately relevant or meaningful to believe."[6]

Cohen considers these dogmas to be empirical: "My dogmas are conclusions drawn from my understanding of the actual situation of the Jew—in this sense they are *empirical*."[7]

He avers that they are also historical: "They are also judgments upon the events of Jewish history which transmit meaning and instruction regarding the predicament of the Jew amid the nations—in this sense they are historical."[8]

And he asserts that they are also transhistorical: "They define a view of the Jew's involvement with ultimate reality, his connection with a destiny which commands him, with that which makes him, in fact, Jewish—in this sense they are transhistorical, possibly metaphysical, and certainly theological."[9]

Cohen's first dogma is his belief in the supernatural Jew. The Jewish community, Cohen holds, not only believes that it is open before God. More than this, the Jewish community is *supernatural,* being "the one to whom God has opened Himself."[10] How has God opened Himself? Cohen answers:

> God has covenanted with the Jewish people that it shall transcend nature and history to him alone. He has confirmed in the Jewish people the possibility (which all men possess) of intending its transcendence. Moreover, God has converted the fatality of nature and history into the destiny of the Jew, that he transcend his natural situation to Him. Without the command to sustain one's supernatural vocation (that is, the belief that God has called the Jew to Himself) to call oneself a Jew is but a half-truth—a mere designation without ultimate meaning.[11]

We begin to see already that Cohen offers a doctrine of radical transcendence. The supernatural Jew transcends *both* nature and history. It is important to note that, for Cohen, the natural dimension is not negated but transcended by destiny.

And by destiny he means that the Jew "has a beginning which

originates outside of time and an end which will transcend it.
Time, we believe, is but an epoch in eternity."[12] Cohen is
thus a thinker of theological audacity. But his theology is not
supported by epistemological considerations. Rather, epistemology, or theory of knowledge and belief, is unnecessary for
Cohen. He is a theologian and not a philosopher. And as a
theologian, the criterion he seems to be using is whether a given
doctrine possesses *ultimate* meaning.

Ultimate meaning, for Cohen is *Heilsgeschichte*—sacred history. Jewish theology is understood by him to mean "the knowledge of sacred history."[13] Applied to Jewish history, the result
is that

> the historian of Judaism cannot interpret many of the most
> shocking and scandalous assumptions of the Jewish religious
> mind unless he acknowledges that the Jew considered his own
> history to be the central event of a divine drama—a drama of
> covenant, sin, and purgation; a drama of divine dispersion and
> promised ingathering; a drama in which natural history was
> raised up to God and relocated within the order of providential
> causation.[14]

Instead of regarding the ancient Jewish collective consciousness
as mythological, Cohen sees it as normative. His purpose is not
to reinterpret these shocking and scandalous assumptions but
to provide a theological framework for them.

Thus, Cohen's second existential dogma is that the exile is
not merely an accident of history. It is rather "the historical
coefficient of being unredeemed."[15] This means that the exile
shows that the Jew is still unredeemed and *therefore* all history
is still unredeemed.

The third existential dogma follows readily: the Jew is a
messianic being. Cohen contends that "the purpose of the
supernatural vocation of the Jew is to make all history alive
to its incompleteness."[16] There is no redemption for the Jew
unless all history is redeemed.

Fourth, the Jewish people has been elected by God precisely
to redeem the world: "God elects, not the single Jew, but the
Jewish people. . . . The Jewish people has not itself alone to
redeem."[17]

Fifth, there is a dialectical relationship between the natural
and supernatural dimensions of Jewish existence. Thus, the

situation of the Jewish people at any given moment "is fashioned not only by God but by the events of time and history."[18] Take, for example, the exile of the Jews in the year 70 C.E. To Cohen, the exile is not only a historical, natural event caused by man but a cosmic, supernatural happening ordained by God::

> The Exile is a cosmic, not an historical, event in Jewish tradition. The Jew goes forth among the nations. This is God's action. The nation receives the Jew, grants him asylum, establishes his station, defines his limitations, and fences his universe. This is the action of secular history.[19]

Thus does Cohen delimit and demarcate the spheres of God's action and man's action, the supernatural and the natural.

An obvious question arises: Has not Zionism and the return of the Jewish people marked the end of exile? Here Cohen distinguishes between dispersion, a natural-historical category, and exile, a theological category:

> The Dispersion ends when the people are restored. The Zionist movement and the triumph of Zionism in the founding of the State of Israel consummate the natural return of the people to its home.[20]

In contrast, however, the exile is not over. The exile is not over, Cohen holds, because "the Exile of the Jew is the symbol of the 'sin' of the world."[21] As long as the essential character of man and history is not altered, the exile is not over. As long as there is human corruption, the exile is not over. For Cohen, then, exile is a theological concept. In fact, it is his belief that

> the concept of Exile is the Jewish doctrine of the Original Sin, an animadversion upon the corruptibility of all history, the violence of all events, and the defection of all nations. What Original Sin imputes to the individual sinner, the Exile imputes to the collectivity of all nations.[22]

Exile, for Cohen, signifies a state of being cut off from God. The destiny of the Jew is to make the nations of the world aware that they are cut off from God: "The special destiny of the Jew is to witness to the evil which man does, not alone to the individual, but to Providence."[23]

Cohen's concept of the exile is admittedly Christian. But its Christian overtones belie its polemical thrust—namely, to assert the superiority of Jewish to Christian messianism:

The Exile of Israel is, in the order of spiritual history, the first moment and the advent of the true Messiah the last. God creates, man falls; God elects, the community sins; God disperses, the nations ravish. There is no center to history, no midpoint. There are innumerable centers, partial adumbrations, but the final word is indeed a final word. There can be no penultimate finalities, such as Jesus Christ. Jesus may be Christ to the Greek, but not to the Jew.[24]

Cohen employs Christian theological terminology for purposes of an anti-Christian polemic. The Jew bears the truth because the Jew anticipates the consummation, the final redemption, the *ultimate* and not the penultimate revelation of God beyond history. It is precisely this eschatological trust—the trust that he will be witness to the final truth of God—that enabled the Jew to transcend the assaults of Christendom. This eschatological trust, and its concomitant indifference to the actual course of world history, is the hallmark of Cohen's supernatural Jew.

Of course, by definition, we cannot know the content of this eschatological truth. The revelation of eschatological truth belongs to God alone. Cohen's messianism is decidedly *not* of this world. The Messiah, for Cohen, brings "not only social change."[25] Rather, Cohen's messianism requires "the completion of one order of time and history and the inauguration of another."[26] In short, total redemption, which the Jew represents, does not occur within history but only when temporal history ends and the era of eternity commences.

It can readily be seen, therefore, that Cohen is realistic, if not pessimistic, about *actual* history. He maintains that the only meaning *within* history is the discernment by the historian of pattern and purpose. Cohen, in contrast to secular philosophers of history, espouses the view that history becomes meaningful "only when it is seen to commence and to conclude."[27] And what passes between the beginning and the end is but "the inconclusive struggle of man to overcome the demonic."[28]

How, then, does Cohen conceive of the role of the Jew *before* the incursion of eternity into time? What is the function of the Jew in the here and now, before the final moment has come? The special destiny of the Jew, Cohen contends, is to "witness to the evil which man does, not alone to the individual, but to Providence."[29] The present task of the Jew is thus to bear witness to the evil, the incompleteness, the insufficiency of temporal history. The supernatural Jew, for Arthur Cohen, bears testimony of the *ultimate* meaninglessness of history *as such* and the ultimate meaning of a final consummation, beyond history and in eternity, when the world will finally be redeemed from evil. The supernatural Jew therefore represents, for Arthur Cohen, the possibility of God's last word to man.

Cohen's conception of the supernatural Jew is thus pure and unadulterated theology. Its focus is eternity, not time; the supernatural not the natural; the dialectic of Divine and human destiny, not human destiny alone.

Cohen expresses this very clearly when he writes: "It is foolish to speak of human destiny unless we speak of creation and consummation. This is the religious postulate of any metaphysics of creation."[30] Since human destiny, for Cohen, is meaningless without God, it is important to examine his conception of God—the supernatural.

Cohen's Conception of God

Intrinsic to Arthur Cohen's idea of God is his belief that there is a reality corresponding to his conception. Admittedly, the theologian who attempts to frame an idea of God works as best as he can to formulate his conception in consonance with what he perceives as objective reality. But Arthur Cohen insists, perhaps more than any other contemporary Jewish theologian, that his idea must conform to reality.

The reason, Cohen holds, that his idea *must* conform to reality lies in the existential necessity that his idea be no mere fiction. Cohen realizes that he cannot demonstrate empirically the existence of this reality. But he is not content merely to say that he has a need to believe in God. The term "need" is too soft, too modest. Accordingly, Cohen writes:

> I do experience through the witness of history and the record of previous and immemorial encounters between man and God the fact that there is a reality which I cannot demonstrate in an acceptable empirical manner but which, by *force majeure*, I demand of the universe.[31]

We now see why the term "need" is too soft. Cohen, in effect, is storming the heavens for a response to his "demand." He demands that there be a reality corresponding not only to his cry, but to the cry of all Jews and indeed, of all men throughout the ages. He demands that the religious encounter be truly a transaction with a real supernatural Being.

Cohen prefers the term transaction to the idea of encounter. He states explicitly that he regards the relation between God and history as "transactional."[32] By this term he means to indicate that

> there is a transaction between God and man in the medium of history—that is to say, God has an objective persona, objective to us as well as to Himself, and that only if we can take Him seriously as a God, can we take ourselves seriously as men.[33]

Clearly, then, Cohen conceives of God as a person. Accordingly, Cohen states that God is "a reality Who exists in transactional relationship with me."[34] Such a transactional relationship can exist only between persons. Cohen continues:

> The divine-human continuum extends between persons. There is a modus of mutual address in which my aspiration is raised up to a person who hears, cares, is concerned, and in consequence seeks to energize the destiny of the historical.[35]

Thus, despite all his rhetoric and sophistication, Cohen's idea of God turns out to be not only that of a personal God but of a *person*.

Herein, I believe, lies the crucial difference between the term "encounter" and the term "transaction." The term encounter signifies that man meets or encounters a reality over against him. The emphasis is on the act or process of meeting. That which one meets or encounters could be a tree as well as another person. Buber, for example, could write of an encounter with a tree. It would be nonsensical, however, to speak of a transaction with a tree. The term transaction, unlike encounter, signifies a virtual certainty that the other *acts* as a person in a transaction with me.

Now most Jewish theologians seek to expound a concept of a personal God. It must be emphasized, however, that the term "personal God" is laden with ambiguity. It can mean a God to whom I can relate in a personal manner. It can mean a God who affects my destiny as a person. It can mean an idea of God which personally involves my being. But it does not necessarily imply, and, I believe, ought not to imply, the idea that God is a person.

The idea that God is a person is, in my opinion, a dangerous idea. It is dangerous because it leads to precisely the kind of thinking that Arthur Cohen states that he is assiduously trying to avoid—that is, creating God in man's image and playing the role of God. This danger emerges quite clearly when Cohen comments that

> the predicament of man in thinking about ultimate questions and particularly in thinking about ultimate questions which he believes to have substantive reality, requires that man think he were other than himself, as though he were in some sense coparticipant in the life of God rather than a man over and against and vastly inadequate to the ideas that he conceives.[36]

This statement bespeaks the danger of conceiving of God as a person. I am as interested in ultimate questions as Arthur Cohen. But it does not follow from my interest that I try to imagine myself as in some sense coparticipant in the life of God. I consider such a thought to be an expression of theological arrogance.

Cohen's attempt to identify with the life of God gives rise to an audacious description of how he conceives of this life: "Process within God is providence for man, unceasing actualization in God is destiny for man. . . . What we know as history is but an epoch in God's history."[37] Cohen states here that he is following in the footsteps of Lurianic mysticism, the German mystic Jacob Boehme and the Russian philosopher Nicholas Berdayev—all of whom attempted to understand the inner life of God. Despite these historical antecedents, I believe Cohen's conception of the theological enterprise to be ill conceived because of its highly anthropomorphic tendency.

Nevertheless, the virtue of Cohen's conception of God is that he attempts to deal with the problem of evil by emphasizing freedom. The essential nature of God, Cohen contends, is freedom. Creation, revelation, and redemption are free acts of God's outpouring into time, in the process of His actualization. Cohen is far too sophisticated a theologian to bluntly say that God needs man or that man actualizes God. Yet he does not altogether deny this possibility.

The following statement portrays this ambiguity: "This is not to say that man is the actualization of divinity; it is only to say that man is that creature through whose life the endless richness and variety of divine possibility is realized."[38]

We are presented, then, with a highly personalized conception of a God in process. This process within God is providence for man—that is, God's historical passion for consummation works itself out in history. God's final actualization or perfection and man's ultimate destiny, however, are metahistorical, or beyond history, in eternity. Therefore, in Cohen's view, the Divine historical process is not involved in every moment of human history. As Cohen writes: "There could be no movement in our world if the freedom of God and the goodness of God were allowed to determine us."[39]

The positive feature of Cohen's conception of God is that, just as God is free, man is free. Evil is thus a result of man's abuse of freedom and failure to recognize God as sovereign. Another virtue is that Cohen takes a long-range point of view, *sub specie aeternitatis*. God therefore is not conceived of as the sole determining cause of all historical disasters. The problem of Cohen's conception, however, is the extremely anthropomorphic manner in which God is conceived.

Typical of this is Cohen's conception of the supernatural. Cohen explains that he employs the term supernatural "in a principally atmospheric sense, as a term intended to describe the domain which God inhabits."[40]

Elsewhere, he describes the supernatural as "a substantial presence which is at the superficies of transcendence. In effect, we transcend toward the supernatural."[41]

Cohen admits that the supernatural dimension is not demonstrable by reason. It is, nevertheless, "seizable by the imagination."[42] Through imagination, the thrust of transcendence extends "beyond the natural."[43]

What is the basis of Cohen's contention that the supernatural can be imagined? The ground of his argument is what he considers to be the silence of nature. The infuriating and incommunicate silence of nature, Cohen contends, gives rise to an intuition of the supernatural. The basis of Cohen's argument is thus as follows: Nature is silent. Nature does not answer us. But man demands a transcendent answer. Therefore, the ultimate answer lies beyond nature.

Of course, nature cannot give Arthur Cohen the answer he

demands. However, there have been both poets and philosophers, physicists and biologists, who have not regarded nature as silent. The language of nature may be opaque to Arthur Cohen, but it has been evocative to thinkers like Thoreau and Emerson and poets like Wordsworth and Shelley.

Arthur Cohen is one of the most searching Jewish intellectuals of our time. I admire his passion for ultimate truth. But we cannot acquiesce in his demand for an answer. The problems with Cohen's theology, which I shall now summarize, center about his extravagant expectations. Quite simply, Cohen's demand for an answer implies nothing about the quality of the answer. Let us now assess the quality of his answer.

Critique of Cohen

From the point of view of inner consistency, Cohen's theology is by and large consistent if one is willing to accept his supernaturalist premises. There is, however, one major internal difficulty.

Cohen's major emphasis seems to be on eternity—on the eternity before history and the eternity beyond history. Final redemption can occur, for Cohen, only beyond history—in eternity. Meanwhile, in the here and now, the special destiny of the Jew is to witness to the evil man does, not alone to the individual, but to providence.

At the same time, Cohen argues that there is a relationship between Divine actualization and temporal history. We remarked that Cohen is not altogether clear on this point, that he does not go so far as to say that God needs man. Yet he does want to suggest that Divine possibility is to some degree realized through human life.

Now if the major emphasis is, as Cohen has argued, on creation and consummation, both of which occur in eternity, it is difficult to see how Cohen can at the same time argue for a relationship between Divine actualization and human history. To argue for such a relationship implies, at least, that human history, in and of itself, is immensely significant to God, anthropomorphically conceived. But Cohen also argues that history is but an epoch in eternity, and not intrinsically significant. That is to say, history is not significant *in itself* but only as a stage in "God's" evolution, between creation and consummation.

It seems to me that Cohen has drawn a conflicting antithesis between history and eschatology. If we are but an epoch in eternity, I fail to see how the individual, in his historical life situation, can be as important to God as Cohen wants him to be. The view that human history is but an epoch in eternity would seem to lead to the view expressed in Shakespeare's *King Lear*: "As flies to wanton boys are we to the gods." Such a stress on eternity seems to me to be inconsistent with Cohen's emphasis on the concern of God, as a person, for the individual.

In terms of the criterion of empirical reference, Cohen's theology, by his own admission, can be satisfactory only to one who shares his existential requirements. Discussing his own existential dogmas, Cohen defined his sense of empirical: "My dogmas are conclusions drawn from my understanding of the actual situation of the Jew—in this sense they are empirical."[44] This is, indeed, an unusual usage of the term "empirical."

To be empirical is, at least, to seek a common core of human experience before drawing any inferences or conclusions from these data. Cohen, however, is using the term "empirical" to refer to his subjective experience or understanding of the actual situation of the Jew. The problem is that the conclusions he draws from his experience are, in principle, unverifiable. His conclusions concerning transhistory and eschatological truth leave no room for those who have legitimate doubts concerning the existence of transhistory and the supernatural.

Cohen's distaste for the mundane and the empirical (as usually defined) gives rise to his imaginative and extravagant theological constructions and speculations. As purely imaginative constructions, they are finely wrought and aesthetically appealing. The problem is that Cohen means them to be taken as true and not fictive.

The result is that there is a blurring of distinction between fact and fiction, between reality and fantasy. Of course, Cohen could object that this assertion begs the question because, metaphysically, anything is possible.

Scientifically, however, it is not the case that anything is possible. Of course, this too is a metaphysical belief. But it is a belief that can be tested empirically, whereas Arthur Cohen's position is not amenable to empirical test.

Pragmatically, Cohen is to be commended for this intellectual defense of the Jew and Judaism. Although I cannot agree with the form and character of his defense, his effort is laudable and his writing is rich and suggestive.

As conceived by Cohen, however, the role of the supernatural Jew is nonpragmatic. He is to be a witness to the evil in the world. This is his present function.

In fact, Cohen has a decided aversion to the pragmatic. Anything that smacks of merely satisfying a human need is *ipso facto* suspect in his eyes. For Cohen, truth must transcend the pragmatic if it is to be truth.

I find this antithesis of truth and pragmatism to be false. The philosopher William Hocking has argued for what he calls negative pragmatism as a test of truth. By this, he means the following: It may not be the case that something is true if it works. But it is surely the case that if it doesn't work, it isn't true.

The problem of Arthur Cohen's theology is that any pragmatic application is foreign to it. It is, in the present writer's opinion, an impressive imaginative construction with little basis in reality.

Imagination can soften the often harsh impact of reality. Unfortunately, it cannot take its place. There are no substitutes, in the final analysis, for reason and reality.

The Rationalism of Jacob Agus

The thought of Jacob Agus offers a marked contrast to that of Arthur Cohen. Whereas Cohen emphasizes the imaginative, Agus stresses the rational. Whereas Cohen emphasizes Jewish exceptionalism—that is, a metaphysical qualitative distinction of the Jews from other peoples—Agus strives to demythologize this idea of the chosen people, which he calls a "meta-myth." Whereas Arthur Cohen has little use for the philosophical tools of analysis and epistemology, Jacob Agus seeks a synthesis of faith and reason.

Despite these differences, however, these two thinkers share one common aim. Both of their theologies culminate in a personalistic conception of God. The difference is that Agus employs an elaborate apparatus of philosophical argumentation to support his view. Our purpose in the rest of this chapter will be to analyze and evaluate Agus's arguments. First, let us meet this thinker.

Jacob Agus was born in Swislocz, Poland, in 1911. He was educated in *yeshivot* in Poland, Israel, and the United States.

He received his Rabbinical degree from Yeshivat Isaac Elchanan in 1935, and a Ph.D. from Harvard University in the history and philosophy of religion in 1939. He is the author of *Modern Philosophies of Judaism, Guideposts in Modern Judaism, The Evolution of Jewish Thought, The Meaning of Jewish History, Dialogue and Tradition,* as well as many essays in various magazines.

Jacob Agus has served as Professor of Rabbinic Judaism at the Reconstructionist Rabbinical College and as Adjunct Professor of Religion, Temple University.

The Necessity of Philosophy

Jacob Agus differs from most of the thinkers whose worldview we have examined, in one important respect. Agus has a positive attitude toward philosophy, in its traditional sense of a dispassionate search for ultimate truth and wisdom. In fact, Agus maintains the necessity of philosophy as a completion of faith.

Faith is the subjective, emotional, inner response of the individual to ultimate meaning. As Agus defines it, faith is "the response of my inner being to prolonged and anxious reflections on the meaning of life."[45] This response yields an awareness of being "embraced within a supreme design." And the awareness is subjectively felt rather than objectively proven.

Now most of the theologies we have examined are elaborations on the subjectively felt response of faith of the particular thinker. Agus, by contrast, is not content with faith alone. His is a faith seeking understanding. In fact, Agus asserts that faith "possesses also an inner reference to truth and to the objective realm of knowledge."[46] I consider this statement to be very important and therefore in need of comment.

I shall employ a technical term, "intentionality," to expound this concept. This term, which derives from the phenomenological studies of Franz Brentano and Edmund Husserl, signifies that emotional responses, like faith, refer or point beyond themselves to transsubjective reality. Our conscious acts are inherently directed toward objects. This does not mean that the referent actually exists as felt. Intentionality simply refers to that aspect of human consciousness whereby it is directed outward toward objects.

Let us now apply this concept to faith. Faith, in this view, is not only a subjective response. It possesses an inner reference to truth and to the objective realm of knowledge. That is to say, faith points beyond itself to an objective realm of truth and knowledge. And it is the task of reason, and of philosophy, to understand, clarify, and examine this objective realm, rendering it intelligible to the human mind. To summarize: Faith merely points beyond itself. It does not yield the nature of objective reality. This is the function of reason.

It can be immediately perceived that there is no conflict of faith and reason in Agus' thought. Rather, reason completes faith. Agus thus espouses the unity of the human mind—namely, a synthetic unity of faith and philosophy. In this spirit, Agus argues that philosophy is a natural extension of religion:

> Philosophy, in the Socratic sense, is an attempt to render the whole of knowledge intelligible, relating man's ethical and aesthetic value to his intellectual categories. Philosophy is, therefore, an essential expression of religion as is the fervor of ethics and the calm joy of esthetics.[47]

Agus thus follows the Hegelian doctrine that the truth is the whole, systematically interrelated by concepts. And he views the act of philosophizing as a religious duty, fostering the wholeness of man. The ideals he seeks are completeness and wholeness. His purpose is to elaborate as complete a world view as possible and to take into consideration all facets of the human personality, organically interrelated.

Moreover, he views his purpose to be in consonance with the classical current in Judaism:

> The union of faith and philosophy, exemplified in the thought of Maimonides, I consider to be the classical current in Judaism. My own thought is simply a modern development of the same basic approach.[48]

Accordingly, he opposes what he considers to be romanticist, as opposed to classical, tendencies in Judaism.

The distinction between classical and romantic religion was originally made by Leo Baeck. Agus correctly criticizes Baeck for the oversimplified dichotomy of Judaism as classical religion and Christianity as romantic religion. Quite obviously, there have been romantic trends throughout Jewish thought, emphasizing the mystical, the irrational, and the metaphysical uniqueness and stubborn particularity of Judaism and the Jewish people.

As against these romantic trends, Jacob Agus's philosophy, as he himself stresses, is "definitely classical."[49] He defines classical religious reality as "a basic endeavor to take account of life as a whole. Man knows that he reflects a reality which transcends his understanding."[50]

Again, we note Agus's Hegelian emphasis on the truth as a whole. Accordingly, he rejects romantic, particularist, and chauvinistic notions of the Jewish people. All such notions are adumbrations of what Agus pejoratively refers to as "the meta-myth." We turn now to Agus's discussion of the meta-myth and what he believes are its invidious consequences.

The "Meta-Myth": Agus and the Chosen People Concept

By the term "meta-myth," Agus means "the myth of Jewish metaphysical difference."[51] This myth consist of "the complex of fantasies about the peculiarity of Jewish existence—being blessed and cursed, set apart and made different from all the nations of the earth."[52]

Unlike Arthur Cohen who holds that Jewish metaphysical difference is a reality, Jacob Agus contends that it is a complex of fantasies. Moreover, Agus argues that there is no reason for a Jew to accept this myth. In point of fact, Agus holds that belief in this myth is downright pernicious to Jewish existence.

Quite obviously, beliefs have consequences. And beliefs ought to be evaluated, at least in part, on the basis of their pragmatic effect. The consequences of maintaining the meta-myth, according to Agus, cluster about the dehumanization of a people:

> Once a people has been de-humanized, in the fancy of the populace, lifted out of the common run of humanity, mysteriously set apart and made unique, there is no limit to the canards, malicious and fantastic, that will arise concerning its character and destiny. Myths and fantasies will cling to it like feathers to the tarred victim of a lynching mob. Anti-Semitism, as an enduring and pervasive ideology of hatred, is a direct consequence of the myth of Jewish metaphysical difference.[53]

In the Jewish religious tradition, Agus contends, the meta-myth was embedded within a context of ideas and ideals which mitigated its virulence. However, Agus argues, "with the breakdown of religious traditions in the modern world, the *meta-myth* was liberated from its ancient context and allowed to play a new independent role."[54] By this, Agus means that the stereotype of Jewish essential difference from other peoples was dissociated from religious tradition and combined with "the new myth of racialism to produce the mythology of Aryanism."[55] It follows from Agus's analysis that the myth of Jewish metaphysical sepa-rateness, originated by the Jews themselves, ultimately turned against them with virulent and violent consequences. Thus, an ancient theological concept, wrenched from its context, contrib-uted to the collective tragedy of the Jewish people in modern times.

Jewish thinkers with particularistic and exclusivistic orien-tations will not take kindly to Agus's exposure of the myth. His analysis has the clear implication that the Jewish people are, in part, responsible for their own tragic history. It is hard for a Jew to observe the course of events through universal spec-tacles. This is precisely what Agus tries to do. And his views will most assuredly be resented by those who cannot countenance his universalism. Unfortunately, those who would be wont to criticize his universalism fail to realize that truth plays no favorites.

It can be readily inferred that Agus rejects the exclusivist connotation of the chosen-people concept. Accordingly, he maintains that this concept must be reinterpreted in a way which "relegates its negative or exclusivist connotations to the dust-bin of history."[56] Agus thus follows Mordecai Kaplan in his assertion that the traditional chosen-people concept is an anachronism. Thus, Agus writes:

> Professor Mordecai Kaplan's call for a revision of this concept penetrates to the heart of the Jewish dilemma. We were chosen, as an *example,* not as an exception. All people are called upon by God to build His Kingdom on earth.[57]

The needed reinterpretation that Agus calls for is the extension of the concept of chosenness "beyond the boundaries of Jewry, to include all who seek God."[58] Like Mordecai Kaplan, Agus severely criticizes all attempts to retain the exclusivist connota-tion of the traditional chosen-people concept. Such attempts, Agus contends, are not excused by calling Jewish chosenness a burden. These halfway measures do nothing to eradicate the source of the problem—namely, "the self-removal of Jewry from the human family."[59]

Agus also follows Kaplan in reinterpreting the concept of chosenness in terms of vocation. The Jewish people, Agus argues, has "a task or a function."[60]

Being the heirs of a spiritual tradition and having a certain body of experience, the Jewish people has the obligation to make this heritage "serve the cause of advancing humanity."[61] Agus thus envisages the Jewish people as a progenitor of religious humanism. The task of the Jewish people, at the present time, is to demythologize its heritage and enter into dialogue with members of other religious groups and cultures. This revision of the ethnocentric emphasis in Jewish tradition, Agus maintains, ought to be "the first item on the agenda."[62] It is thus clear that Agus emphasizes the religiocultural aspect of Judaism rather than its ethnic component. This follows from Agus's underlying methodological principle: the unity of the human mind.

Therefore, Agus goes beyond Mordecai Kaplan's rejection of chosenness. Agus seems to reject, as well, any concept of Jewish uniqueness:

> As an axiom or dogma, Jewish uniqueness need only be analyzed into its separate components for its mystical aura to be dispelled and refuted. All analytical writing, in fact all logical thought, is based on the assumption of one mind, one way of logical thinking; the same pathways to error are open to all the children of men.[63]

The task of analysis, Agus holds, is to "separate the enduring, universal values from the ephemeral, historical phenomena."[64]

The above passage is the clearest statement of Agus's concept of the unity of the human mind and its implications for his view of Judaism and the Jewish people. It is evident that Agus stands at the opposite end of the spectrum from the Jewish existentialists. Of all contemporary Jewish thinkers, Agus most emphatically emphasizes *essence* rather than existence. His concern is with the universal rather than the particular.

Accordingly, Agus stresses the religious and cultural aspects of Judaism rather than ethnic and political elements:

> To me, as a man of faith, the religious-cultural phase of our

> heritage is enriching, compelling and fascinating. Others may
> find the ethnic-political phase of our collective existence more
> meaningful and challenging.[65]

Here Agus departs from the thinking of Mordecai Kaplan.

Whereas Kaplan's thought represents a dialectic of Jewish existence and Jewish essence, Agus's concern is almost totally essentialist. Kaplan is concerned with peoplehood and with Jewish uniqueness as expressed in its collective consciousness. Kaplan is furthermore concerned with the political status of the Jewish people as well as the theoretical and essentialist justification of Jewish existence. Kaplan, moreover, unites in his thought a faith in America with an awareness of the important role of Zionism in the reconstitution of the Jewish people.[66]

Agus, in contrast, views the ethnic-political aspect of Jewish existence as secondary to its religious-cultural essence. It follows from his methodological assumption of the unity of the human mind that the idea of a national Jewish collective consciousness is to be rejected because of its lack of universality. Concern with Jewish ethnicity, peoplehood, and Zionism is, for Agus, to be subordinated to the religious and cultural enhancement of American Jewish life. In fact, Agus criticizes Zionism as a kind of romanticism emphasizing the uniqueness and peculiarity of Jewish peoplehood:

> These elements of peculiarity and uniqueness are precisely the
> sentiments that the romanticists seek to foster, in order to keep
> the Jewish Diaspora from constituting itself as a normal compo-
> nent of the nations among whom Jews live.[67]

Here Agus stands in marked contrast to Arthur Cohen. Whereas Arthur Cohen sees Jewish existence as essentially abnormal, Agus maintains that the Jewish Diaspora ought to constitute itself as a normal component among the nations.

Agus is willing to go to great lengths to seek Jewish normalcy. This is manifested in his effort to find common ground with the historian Arnold Toynbee. He is extremely charitable in attributing Toynbee's scornful references to Judaism and the Jewish people, for the most part, to "the vein of poetic symbolism"[68] in his work. What he finds most sympathy with in Toynbee's writings is his stimulating and hopeful analysis of the Jewish Diaspora. Agus's common ground with Toynbee is expressed in the following anti-Zionist sentiment which Agus attributes both to Toynbee and himself:

> Thus, the Jewish Diaspora, if it succeeds in staying free from the virus of nationalism, can help to keep alive the one great hope for the future. It represents the pattern whereby an ethnic group transfers its collective ambition from the domain of politics to the ethereal spheres of culture and religion, from the horizontal pushing of elbows for an ever larger place in the sun to the vertical ascent of the spirit.[69]

This passage is the epitome of Agus's essentialism. He emphasizes the vertical ascent of the spirit and the ethereal spheres of culture and religion. And in seeking the universal, he too easily accepts a common ground with a historian who virulently attacks Jewish particularism.

Agus thus believes in the capacity of people to overcome the meta-myths through the application of the universal categories of reason. By ridding itself of stubborn particularistic notions, mankind can work to build the evolving great society. Thus, Agus displays a firm trust in the liberal, democratic instincts of man. This is, indeed, a great act of faith in our time.

Having rejected Jewish particularism, Agus now has to show the consistency of Jewish essentialism. The major burden of his thought is to develop a concept of God which justifies his essentialist approach to Judaism. If it is only the religious and cultural dimensions of Judaism that ought to be stressed, Agus must show how the conceptual structure of his system is knitted together in a viable idea of a God. Agus's thought, therefore, must yield a conception of God that does justice to the unity of the human mind, if his philosophy is to be rendered consistent.

Agus's Conception of God

The starting point for Agus's conception of God is the human spirit. Extrapolating from the human spirit, Agus strives to develop a conception of God which is neither naturalist nor supernaturalist:

> The concept of God that I assume is neither naturalist nor supernaturalist. It is not the personification of the forces of nature, or a force standing over, against and beyond nature. Its starting point is not force, but the human spirit.[70]

Manifestly, since Agus places such weight on the term "spirit," it is important that a clear definition be given.

Agus does not mean by spirit a kind of substance or soul-force.[71] Rather, spirit is "a realm of relations in respect of meaning."[72] Man, it has been said, is a symbol-producing animal. Through symbols, man is able to relate and connect disparate things. By so relating them, he endows them with meaning.

Meaning, in turn, is "the relation of any one event to a class, and that class, in its turn, to a more inclusive whole, reaching up to the ultimate Being that is God."[73]

Agus's conception of the universe is thus that of an ongoing movement toward transcendence. Just as the pebble cast into the river sends off its ripples, so does each event point to more inclusive wholes of meaning. Bearing in mind that Agus follows the Hegelian dictum that the truth is the whole, we can readily see how he develops his ontology as an ever-growing movement toward synthesis. And the ground of this synthesis is the ultimate universal Mind or Spirit—God.

Since Agus's position is neither naturalist nor supernaturalist, it is plausible to suggest that Agus is working toward a kind of transnaturalism. This becomes manifest when he writes that

> spirit is the polar opposite of a mechanical universe. While the latter is ideally understood through the interaction of the smallest conceivable particles, the former imposes the reign of meaning through the operation of the whole upon each of its component parts.[74]

We recall that transnaturalism is the view that the whole is greater than the sum of its parts. Applied to the concept of God, this means that God is manifested in the operation of the whole upon the parts as the process whereby nature functions as an organic whole. Agus's transnaturalism differs from Kaplan's, however, in that he is not content with the conception of God as the transnatural process. Agus maintains that the quest for transcendence can be fulfilled only through the conception of God as an Absolute Self or personality. What are Agus's arguments for this position?

First and foremost, Agus maintains that mind or spirit is the highest level of reality. Therefore, to conceive of God as anything less than mind or personality does not yield a suitable referent for worship. Agus clearly has Kaplan in mind when he writes:

> Conceptions of God as a power or as a process are altogether worthless for religion. The concept of power is derived from the science of physics, where it is employed to designate a potential force. Clearly, then, this term cannot be applied to God, since He must be an actual Being.[75]

What Agus fails to recognize is that the term "process" supplies precisely the connotation of actual or active in contrast to power, which connotes the Divine potential. And the term process has the additional virtue of implying that the Divine can be manifested in the human creative process. Moreover, it is dogmatic to assert that God "must" be an actual Being. What is the connotation, here, of "must"? Is this an *a priori fiat*? Or does it simply mean that God, to qualify as an object of worship, must be a Being?

Secondly, Agus argues for this concept of God on the basis of the principle of polarity—namely, God as Spirit or Absolute Self is the polar opposite of a mechanical universe. Here, Agus relies heavily on the philosopher Morris Cohen's concept of polarity. It is therefore important to take note of Cohen's idea.

By the principle of polarity, Cohen meant that

> opposites such as immediacy and mediation, unity and plurality, the fixed and the flux, substance and function, ideal and real, actual and possible, etc., like the north (positive) and south (negative) poles of a magnet, all involve each other when applied to any significant entity.[76]

Cohen maintained that this principle helps us to understand entities within nature. He did not, however, believe that this principle could be applied to the totality of all existence because the "whole" is not an object of knowledge.

Unlike Cohen, Agus is willing to extrapolate this principle to apply to the "whole." Agus attempts to justify his extrapolation on these grounds. He avers that "once we grant that it is not knowledge in the technical sense, that we seek, but grounds for faith, such an application becomes logically incontrovertible."[77] What is the logic of Agus's argument? Its basis is that the human self is the key to reality. Agus contends that "the whole, in a qualitative sense, is given to us in our consciousness of our own personality."[78] The human personality, according to

Agus, is "a chunk of reality and it is understandable only in terms of the polar concepts of purposiveness and mechanism."[79] Agus then extrapolates this polarity to extend to the universe: "May it not be then that God and the mechanical universe imply each other, even as the one and the many, space and time, point and the field?"[80] The important terms here are "point" and "field."

Agus maintains that the physical universe must be viewed in terms of a field and point polar relationship: "The field is the pattern of infinite relations to which every point in space is subject."[81] By this, Agus means to assert that things are not spatial events alone but "events" or units of space-time which are not static but dynamic pulsating tensions and rhythms. Thus, reality alternates between the "point," that is, particularity reaching down to a point in space, and the "field," or responsiveness to a total field of relations.

The result is that Agus arrives at "the conception of the universe, in which all parts exist in a state of tension—tension between the tendency to particularization and responsiveness to the total system of which it is a part."[82]

The human self is the highest exemplification of this tension. As Agus puts it, "The human personality presents the highest, observable field of individuation."[83] Man's capacity to reflect, reason and evaluate are all expressions of the field-building capacity or the power of freedom stored in the human personality. Man is the highest field-builder that we know, having the greatest degree of responsiveness to the total system of which he is a part. Yet human freedom is far from perfect, being subject to the mechanism of the body and the laws of nature.

Agus is not content to rest with this imperfect freedom. Logic requires, according to Agus, that there be an Absolute Self, the field-builder of all field-builders, representing that freedom of spirit which stands in continual opposition to the mechanistic universe. Agus sees this as a logical consequence of the principle of polarity:

> Applying the principle of polarity, we conclude that an Absolute Personality representing the highest measure of the field-building capacity, constitutes a pole of being, standing in continual opposition to and tension with the mechanistic universe. God and the physical universe are the two polar concepts of thought, and since logical thought is in correspondence with

reality, we are justified in concluding that the space-time con-
tinuum, as it exists in itself, and the Deity, as the projection
into the infinite of the field-making capacity, are the two poles
of being.[84]

The obvious question to be raised is precisely whether Agus
is justified in so concluding his argument. As impressive as the
architectonic structure of Agus's argument is, there are a number
of assumptions he makes which many would regard as gratuitous.

In the first place, Morris Cohen's reservations about applying
the principle of polarity to "the whole" cannot be so easily
dismissed. If "the whole" is not an object of knowledge, as Agus
admits, it is hard to see how his argument, as grounds for faith,
is logically incontrovertible. The phrase "logically incontrovertible" applies to knowledge, not faith.

In the second place, Agus assumes that the whole, in a qualitative sense, is given to us in our self-consciousness. Again, this
assumption is based upon an extrapolation from the self to
the "whole" of things. This movement from the self to the
totality of things is too great a leap from the known to the
unknown and would therefore constitute an unwarranted assumption to the scientific mind.

Finally, Agus assumes that the human self, as the highest
form of reality that we know, is the key to ultimate reality. The
concept of the human self as the key to ultimate reality and as
the model for the idea of God is a metaphysical assumption.
To be sure, it is an assumption shared by such philosophers as
Edgar S. Brightman and Peter A. Bertocci, and is known as
personalism. But this assumption is opposed by other schools
of philosophy. Naturalism, for example, holds that man is a
part of nature and not an external spectator standing outside
of nature. In this view, nature rather than the self is conceived
of as ultimate reality. And contemporary analytic philosophers
would argue that the expression "the whole of things" has no
definite empirical referent and is therefore meaningless.

Therefore, the conclusion of Agus's argument is a metaphysical
assumption and is not logically incontrovertible.

Why, we must now ask, does Agus make this assumption?
The philosopher F. H. Bradley has said that metaphysics is
the finding of bad reasons for what we believe on instinct.
Instinctively, Agus is motivated to defend his belief in a personal God, for his conception of Judaism is predicated on this

premise. Thus, despite his vehement insistence on the primacy of reason, it is obvious that Agus's conception of Judaism cannot be based on reason alone. Agus's rationalism must be complemented by a belief in revelation.

Needless to say, Agus does not argue for a fundamentalist conception of revelation. He rejects the idea of "Torah M'Sinai" —namely, the idea of the Divine origin of every word in the Torah. Moreover, as a philosopher, he rejects as immature a blanket belief in revelation without analysis and without "a comparative standard of revelation."[85] Rather (and on this point, he seems to be in agreement with Arthur Cohen), he regards the phenomenon of faith itself as an incontestable form of evidence:

> Thus, when I find within me the consciousness of the dependency or creaturely character of the physical universe and note everywhere the seal and stamp of a transcendent God, whose Will and Purpose permeates the whole range of existence, then this faith, in its multiple formulations, is an incontestable form of evidence.[86]

Agus here follows in the footsteps of Schleiermacher and Otto, two religious thinkers who sought to articulate the uniqueness of the religious consciousness. Schleiermacher held the essence of the religious consciousness to be a feeling of absolute dependence. Otto maintained that the religious consciousness is manifested in a feeling of "creaturehood," that is, in our awareness of being created. Agus follows these thinkers in holding that religion transcends the sphere of reason since the "religious consciousness is a realm of unique values, *sui generis.*"[87] Thus, Agus's concept of revelation is based on this analysis of the religious consciousness.

Since the possibilty of faith is present in every generation, being the outgrowth of the religious consciousness, Agus rejects past-oriented concepts of revelation. Accordingly, he avers that

> the belief in the historicity of a past event has nothing to do with faith in this sense, since there can be no inner correspondence between our present feeling and the events of several thousand years ago.[88]

Agus does hold, however, that there is an inner correspondence between "our deepest nature and the numinal world."[89] Namely, there is, in reality, a supreme Personality corresponding to our deepest longings.

How, then, does Agus conceive of revelation? He writes: "The concept of Divine revelation denotes the belief that truth and creative vision come to man from God, through channels other than physical senses."[90] Agus's concept of revelation is thus a direct antithesis of naturalistic philosophies which maintain that there is nothing in the mind that was not previously a matter of sense experience. What Agus seeks to include in his concept of revelation are "the creative novel elements in the course of evolution and the history of mankind."[91]

What, then, are the criteria or standards of revelation in Agus's view? These standards are "the principles of ethics and the feelings of piety; piety, as a psychic attitude, is conditioned by an historical tradition and therefore subjective in character. Hence subjective standards are valid within the boundaries of an historic faith."[92]

Does Agus's belief in revelation contradict his universal emphasis as a philosopher? Here Agus admits that religion, as a particular phenomenon, eludes the net of universal concepts: "Philosophy, like mathematics, is universal; religion, like speech, cannnot but be particularized."[93] And the Jewish religion, for Agus, is a classic example of revelation—of uniqueness and creative novelty.

Agus follows Yehezkel Kaufmann in affirming the uniqueness of Israel's faith—that is, the utter discontinuity of its God-idea with paganism. Accordingly, Agus maintains that in its non-mythological conception of Deity, "Judaism was a unique phenomenon. Therefore, all who share the conviction of its truth, cannot but regard it as a revealed faith in the highest sense of the term."[94] Thus, for Agus, it is the God-idea of Judaism that gives it its uniqueness and its revealed character.

It might appear that by virtue of his essentialism, Agus's approach is the same as that of classical Reform Judaism. This is not the case. Although Agus credits the classic founders of Reform for their emphasis on "ethical monotheism," he criticizes them for their failure to recognize that the practical elaboration of this insight through Jewish law, or Halacha, is integral to authentic Judaism. In the same manner as he seeks to evolve a nonfundamentalist belief in revelation, Agus argues for the Divine origin of the principle of Halacha, or Jewish law. As would be expected, Agus does not affirm the Divine character of all the minutiae of Jewish law as recorded in the *Shulchan Aruch.*

He argues for changes and new legislation in Jewish law. But the principle of *Halacha,* he insists, is of Divine origin:

> The revealed character of Jewish legislation refers to the general subconscious spiritual drive which underlies the whole body of *Halacha,* not to the details of the law. . . . It is of the very essence of the reasoning process to recognize that the particular is accidental and contingent.[95]

The above statement of Agus on *Halacha* reflects his general orientation—namely, truth lies in the universal and necessary, not in the particular and the contingent. Yet the uniqueness of the Jewish religion as a revealed faith is a particular and contingent fact, if it be a fact. There is, therefore, a tension in Agus's thought. If Judaism represents "the truth," as Agus admits, how, according to his own criteria, can a particular people be the bearer of absolute truth? Is Agus thoroughly consistent in his methodology? To these questions we now turn.

Critique of Agus

To begin with, it is important to note that Agus's thought has not heretofore been given the serious attention which it deserves. Jacob Agus is surely one of the finest philosophical minds in our midst. He employs reason, and exercises the rich tools of his philosophical background to a greater degree than most contemporary Jewish theologians. Agus is therefore to be commended for his courageous reliance on reason in an age replete with irrationalism.

Let us now analyze Agus's thought from the point of view of inner consistency. At this juncture, it is important to reiterate Agus' statement of his methodology—the unity of the human mind:

> As an axiom or dogma, Jewish uniqueness need only be analyzed into its separate components for its mystical aura to be dispelled and refuted. All analytical writing, in fact all logical thought, is based on the assumption of one mind, one way of logical thinking: the same pathways to error are open to all the children of men.[96]

Throughout the trajectory of his thought, Agus seeks to apply this principle to various subjects. He employs it to dispel the notion of the meta-myth and to revise the concept of the chosen people. He utilizes it in his development of the concept of God. But he fails to employ it consistently in his treatment of the Jewish religion. Again, let us recall Agus's statement that "Judaism was a unique phenomenon. Therefore, all who share the conviction of its truth, cannot but regard it as a revealed faith, in the highest sense of the term."[97]

Now it appears that Agus cannot have it both ways. If the methodological principle of the unity of the human mind requires that uniqueness be analyzed into its component parts, it is unclear how Agus can accept Yehezkel Kaufmann's idea of the total uniqueness of Israel's God-idea. To be sure, Agus consistently can accept a concept of uniqueness which does not preclude equivalences. When one uses the instruments which are common to all people in one's particular way, one achieves a kind of uniqueness. This does not mean that it is unique in every respect; it is unique only in the particular manner in which that capacity is utilized. Differences in the use of that capacity can be determined by heredity, environment, and particular circumstances. In this respect it is proper to say that every human being is unique, but there are equivalences. When one people develops a language and another people develops another language, each language is unique, but these people are united by their common need to communicate and by their common capacity to create language. This kind of uniqueness Agus can consistently accept. But the concept of uniqueness adumbrated by Kaufmann—namely, the utter unlikeness of Israel's God-idea and its discontinuity with the pagan world, cannot be incorporated into Agus's scheme without inconsistency.

More consistent with Agus's methodological principle is his later assertion that "divine Truth is so rich and many-sided that only fragments are found in any one faith."[98] Thus, when Agus says that Judaism is revealed truth, it seems that he really does not mean that Judaism is *the* revealed truth. Rather he means that Judaism as a revealed faith contains part of the truth, the truth being the whole.

The fact that Agus slips, at one point in his writings, into a concept of the total uniqueness of Israel's God-idea, however, is understandable. In point of fact, a totally essentialist conception of Judaism cannot be consistently maintained. At some point, the stubborn facts of Jewish particularity and the uniqueness of Jewish existence must intrude. At some point, Jewish uniqueness eludes universal categories. Uniqueness need not imply chosenness. Each person is unique. This does not mean that he is chosen. Analogously, the collective entity or corporate "personhood" of the Jewish people cannot be totally understood by universal categories alone.

It must also be understood from within, existentially. Therefore, as I shall demonstrate in my concluding chapter, existential and essentialist orientations are *both* necessary in contemporary Jewish thought. They are complementary rather than antithetical approaches. It is my opinion that the existentialist orientation has been overemphasized. Nevertheless, it cannot be ignored. But Agus is to be commended for redressing the balance, even though his essentialism, too, has its limits.

As we turn to the criterion of empirical reference, the subject that begs for evaluation along these lines is Agus's concept of God. I have already pointed out in my exposition of Agus's concept of God that his idea is arrived at through a process of extrapolation from the finite to the infinite. He employs Morris Cohen's concept of polarity, which, according to Cohen himself, has legitimate reference only to finite entities and not to the totality of things. This extrapolation, which Cohen held to be inadmissible, Agus regards as logically incontrovertible on the grounds of faith.

I cannot subscribe to the alleged logical character of this inference, because the term "totality of the universe" has, by definition, no empirical reference. It is a construction of pure thought alone. I therefore take issue with Agus's rejection of the empirical principle that thought must be based on sense experience. Eminently to the point is the Kantian dictum: Percepts without concepts are blind; concepts without percepts are empty.

On what empirical grounds, then, can we evaluate Agus's concept of God? Agus draws an analogy between the human self and God. He says that if we could know ourselves, we could know the Divine. There is some truth in this statement. Discovery of God is inseparable from self-discovery. As we deepen our self-knowledge, our concept of God becomes more profound.

But this is as far as the analogy can be drawn! To attempt to compare the human self to the "whole" of things is simply too much of an extrapolation from human experience. It therefore is deficient in terms of empirical reference.

The pragmatic value of Agus's thought lies in his courageous attempt to demythologize those elements in Jewish life which act as a barrier to mutual understanding between different ethnic and religious groups. Thus, his exposure of the meta-myth is well taken.

But the problem is that Agus's expectations are too high. He is too eager for a Hegelian synthesis and fails to reckon with the stubborn *otherness* and particularities that stand in the way of the acceptance of religious humanism by disparate ethnic and religious groups.

I share Agus's ecumenical ideals, but the road ahead is far more rocky and the terrain far more rough than he is willing to recognize. For this reason, Zionism is far more important than Agus admits.

Finally, then, Agus's thought can be conceived of as an idealistic quest for the unity of Judaism and truth. Agus's quest is noble, and his mind is profound. But in his idealism he does not always reckon sufficiently with reality.

What is needed, therefore, is a concept of transcendence that is both realistic and ennobling. The gathering together of the lines of development of contemporary Jewish thought and the explication of the resultant needed concept of transcendence is the task of the next, and concluding, chapter.

NOTES

1. Arthur A. Cohen, *The Natural and the Supernatural Jew* (New York: Pantheon Books, 1962), p. 9.
2. *Ibid.,* p. 6.
3. *Idem.*
4. *If Not Now, When? Conversations Between Mordecai Kaplan and Arthur A. Cohen* (New York: Schocken Books, 1973), p. 18.
5. *Ibid.,* p. 19.
6. *The Natural and the Supernatural Jew,* p. 5.
7. *Idem.*
8. *Idem.*
9. *Idem.*
10. *Ibid.,* p. 6.
11. *Idem.*
12. *Ibid.,* p. 297.
13. *Ibid.,* p. 304.

14. *Ibid.*, p. 294.
15. *Ibid.*, p. 6.
16. *Ibid.*, p. 6–7.
17. *Ibid.*, p. 7.
18. *Idem.*
19. *Ibid.*, p. 182.
20. *Ibid.*, pp. 184–185.
21. *Ibid.*, p. 187.
22. *Ibid.*, p. 187–188.
23. *Ibid.*, p. 300.
24. *Idem.*
25. *Ibid.*, p. 310.
26. *Ibid.*, p. 311.
27. *Ibid.*, p. 299.
28. *Idem.*
29. *Ibid.*, p. 300
30. *Ibid.*, p. 298
31. *If Not Now, When?*, p. 72
32. *Ibid.*, p. 22.
33. *Ibid.*, p. 35.
34. *Ibid.*, p. 27.
35. *Idem.*
36. *Ibid.*, p. 90.
37. *The Natural and the Supernatural Jew*, p. 298.
38. *Ibid.*, pp. 297–298.
39. *Ibid.*, p. 299.
40. *If Not Now, When?*, p. 90.
41. Ira Eisenstein, ed., *Varieties of Jewish Belief* (New York: Reconstructionist Press, 1966), p. 34.
42. *Idem.*
43. *Ibid.*, p. 35.
44. *The Natural and the Supernatural Jew*, p. 5.
45. *Varieties of Jewish Belief*, p. 3.
46. *Idem.*
47. *Ibid.*, p. 5.
48. *Idem.*
49. Jacob Agus, "Jewish Self-Definition," *CCAR Journal*, Autumn 1972, p. 11.
50. *Ibid.*, p. 6.
51. *Varieties of Jewish Belief*, p. 12.
52. *Ibid*, p. 11.
53. *Ibid.*, p. 11–12.
54. Jacob Agus, *The Meaning of Jewish History* (New York: Abelard-Schuman, 1963), Vol. II, p. 391.
55. *Ibid.*, p. 393.
56. *Varieties of Jewish Belief*, p. 12.
57. *Idem.*
58. *Idem.*
59. *Ibid.*, p. 13.
60. *Idem.*

61. *Idem.*

62. Editors of Commentary, *The Condition of Jewish Belief* (New York: The Macmillan Co., 1967), p. 14.

63. *The Meaning of Jewish History*, Vol. I, p. 32.

64. *Idem.*

65. *Varieties of Jewish Belief*, p. 15.

66. See Mordecai Kaplan, *The Future of the American Jew*, pp. 3–142.

67. Jacob Agus, "Jewish Self-Definition—Classicism and Romanticism: Our Basic Alternatives," *CCAR Journal*, Autumn 1972, p. 15.

68. Jacob Agus, *Dialogue and Tradition* (New York: Abelard-Schuman, 1971), p. 133.

69. *Ibid.*, p. 148.

70. *Ibid.*, p. 251.

71. *Idem.*

72. *Ibid.*, p. 252.

73. *Idem.*

74. *Idem.*

75. Jacob Agus, *Modern Philosophies of Judaism* (New York: Behrman House, 1941), p. 346.

76. Morris Cohen, *Reason and Nature* (New York: The Macmillan Co., 1931), p. 165.

77. Jacob Agus, *Guideposts in Modern Judaism*, p. 238.

78. *Ibid.*, p. 239.

79. *Idem.*

80. *Idem.*

81. *Idem.*

82. *Ibid.*, p. 243.

83. *Ibid.*, p. 247.

84. *Ibid.*, p. 248.

85. *Ibid.*, pp. 276–277.

86. *Ibid.*, p. 279.

87. *Ibid.*, p. 281.

88. *Ibid.*, p. 279.

89. *Ibid.*, p. 278.

90. *Ibid.*, p. 285.

91. *Idem.*

92. *Ibid.*, p. 291.

93. *Idem.*

94. *Ibid.*, p. 294.

95. *Ibid.*, p. 298.

96. *The Meaning of Jewish History*, Vol. I, p. 32.

97. *Guideposts in Modern Judaism*, p. 294.

98. Jacob Agus, "Revelation as Quest—A Contribution to Ecumenical Thought," *Journal of Ecumenical Studies*, Vol. 9, No. 3, 1972, p. 538.

11 Conclusion: Existence, Essence, and Transcendence

It is now time to gather together our evaluations of the leading figures in contemporary Jewish thought for the purpose of drawing specific conclusions concerning their strengths and weaknesses and some general conclusions and recommendations concerning the present state of this field and its direction for the future. First, let us summarize what our critique has disclosed concerning the specific thinkers discussed.

A Critique Based on Criteria

This study has been a critique animated by the aim of reconstructing contemporary Jewish thought. It has contended that the deficiency of contemporary Jewish thought lies in its lack of disciplined thinking. And it has argued that discipline can be injected into contemporary Jewish theology through the application of criteria of evaluation. Criteria are, by definition, standards or rules of judging. Application of the same standards for evaluating each thinker has been the method for clearing a path toward clarity and discipline in contemporary Jewish thought.

Three criteria have been employed in the evaluation of each thinker.

First, we have appraised each theology from the standpoint of *inner consistency*. We have endeavored to determine whether each theology is self-consistent or marred by internal conflict and contradictory statements.

Second, we have underscored the criterion of *empirical reference*. Accordingly, we have eschewed recourse to metaphysical speculation without a firm basis in some aspect of human experience.

Finally, we have employed the criterion of *pragmatic value*. We have examined the practical consequences of the doctrines espoused by each thinker. I have attempted to determine what difference it would make to one's life, both as a Jew and as an individual, to hold the various views expounded.

These three criteria—inner consistency, empirical reference, and pragmatic value—have been our measuring rods in this study. Only through the application of such rules and standards can a field of study become disciplined.

Critique of Jewish Existentialism

Let us now summarize the strengths and weaknesses of each thinker according to these criteria. We begin with the Jewish existentialists.

Existentialism, we recall, is that movement in philosophy which stresses the priority of human existence to objective and abstract thinking. Accordingly, the Jewish existentialists emphasize the experiences of the individual Jew and the collective experiences of the Jewish people. The religious existentialists tend to consider such experiences as the encounter with God and the Covenant at Sinai to be self-authenticating. For these thinkers, concepts of God are secondary. What is most important for them is the encounter or relationship with God.

Not all existentialists, however, are religious or theistic. Indeed, the most popular non-Jewish existentialists, such as Jean-Paul Sartre and Albert Camus, are atheists. These men contend that God is no longer experienced. What is experienced is the absurd—a universe supremely indifferent to the concerns of human beings. Because they emphasize the experience of nothingness, these thinkers are often called nihilists.

The most prominent contemporary Jewish thinker who espouses nihilism is Richard Rubenstein. Since the challenge of nihilism is so basic, this summary begins with Rubenstein's thought.

Just as the nihilism of Jean-Paul Sartre had its roots in the irredeemable evil and tragedy of World War II, so the nihilism of Richard Rubenstein is rooted in the Jewish experience of the Holocaust. Rubenstein's contention is that after Auschwitz, belief in a God of history is no longer possible for the Jew. The murder of six million Jews, Rubenstein argued, was an irredeemable evil. It signifies the death of God—that is, the end of any possible belief in God as the author of history and as the Supreme Being who maintains His covenant with the Jewish people. Let us now summarize our critique of Rubenstein's thought.

We found Rubenstein to be unremitting in his tragic, pessimistic vision of man. Rubenstein offers man no ultimate hope. At no time does he depart from this view.

As a theologian, however, Rubenstein is inconsistent. With all his argumentation for the death of God as a cultural fact, with all his documentation of the irredeemable evil of the Holocaust, Rubenstein nevertheless does not draw straightforward atheistic conclusions as does Jean-Paul Sartre. Instead, he reintroduces the term "God" to denote the referent of his nihilism—namely, God as Holy Nothingness.

Since this idea offers neither hope nor meaning to man, it is surely dubious to refer to this concept by the term "God." The concept of God, to be at all meaningful, must bear some relation to man's action in the world. But the chief problem is not merely the inadequacy of "Holy Nothingness" as a concept of God. The major difficulty is that this concept of God seems to be invoked merely to legitimize Rubenstein's theology as a discourse about God.

Rubenstein would have been far more consistent had he maintained a straightforward atheism. He is at his best in describing his own tragic experiences and those of his people. The major weakness of his thought is conceptual inadequacy

—that is, the weakness of his concept of God and the inconsistency of employing the term "God" in a view of the world so unremitting in its tragic vision of life.

Because of its rootedness in experience, Rubenstein's thought is stronger empirically than it is conceptually. Even empirically, however, Rubenstein is open to criticism because of his tendency to generalize and universalize his own experience. From reading Rubenstein, one could infer that the major psychoanalytical problem is the individual's fear of death. In fact, there is no such unanimity in psychoanalytic circles. Rubenstein makes the mistake, not uncommon to existentialists, of thinking that his own experience is applicable to others. In fact, his experience is unique and applicable only to those of like-minded temperament.

The pragmatic value of Rubenstein's thought is that it forces the Jew to confront the Holocaust as a major issue in contemporary Jewish theology. Rubenstein is surely correct in his insistence that Jewish theology, *to be contemporary*, cannot ignore the fact of the Holocaust. But pragmatically, Rubenstein's thought is deficient in not fostering man's will to improvement. Perhaps the best indication of this will to improvement latent in man is the fact that the Jewish people itself, after Auschwitz, did not succumb to Rubenstein's existential despair.

It is paradoxical that the thinker considered by may to be the greatest contemporary Jewish theologian did not live to confront the Holocaust.

The problem that disturbed Franz Rosenzweig (1886–1929) —namely, the role of Judaism in a world dominated by Christianity—seems remote to the secular Jew uninterested in any kind of transcendence. Rosenzweig's solution to this problem —namely, the metahistorical existence of the Jewish people (i.e., the Jew as witness to eternity or eschatological truth) — seems even more remote to the contemporary Jew. How, then, can we account for his undoubted influence on contemporary Jewish thought?

This influence is due, in part, to the dramatic quality of Rosenzweig's life: his vacillation between Judaism and Christianity, his return to Judaism, the writing of *The Star of Redemption* on postcards sent home from the front, and his heroic struggle to write despite the afflictions of his terrible illness.

But it is also true that Rosenzweig's influence can be attributed to his powerful mind—a mind exploding with ideas, a mind that enthralled his contemporaries and his disciples, and most important, a mind steeped in philosophy but seeking a way back to Judaism.

Rosenzweig's appeal to the contemporary Jew lies mainly in the fact that it represents the groping of an intellectual to find a rationale for a return to the Judaic faith. Rosenzweig's thought therefore is most applicable to the alienated Jewish intellectual seeking a philosophically justifiable way back to Judaism. Rosenzweig sought this philosophic rationale in existentialism. His effort was therefore to create an existential Jewish theology. How successful was Rosenzweig in this endeavor? This was the question posed by our critique.

Unfortunately, due to the brevity of his life, Rosenzweig's theology was incomplete. Doubtless, had he lived to develop his theology, he would have reconciled many of its inconsistencies. As it stands, however, we found Rosenzweig's theology to be inconsistent for these reasons.

Rosenzweig referred to his method as absolute empiricism. By this he meant a pure and complete description of experience without conceptual constructions. This aim is simply untenable. There is no such thing as a pure and complete description of experience without conceptual constructions. We are forced into them by the very nature of our sense equipment; otherwise we could not distinguish differences in space, depth, or the character of individual objects. Rosenzweig's illustration that "common sense knows that a chair is a chair" is also untenable. An infant looking at a chair would see something but wouldn't know that it is a chair.

The inadequacy of Rosenzweig's aim becomes manifested as he develops his own theology. Despite his alleged aim of absolute empiricism, his theology eventuates in a neat series of Hegelian triadic conceptual constructions—God, man, and the world; creation, revelation, and redemption.

Thus, writing about his triads, one of his distinguished disciples, N. N. Glatzer, noted: "These are clearly conceptual constructions, a method from which Rosenzweig could not free himself, though he considered them to be mere auxiliary concepts."[1]

The critical point is that Rosenzweig's inconsistency here was due to his untenable aim. The very attempt to be "free" of conceptual constructions, as Kant demonstrated, is impossible, for human experience is structured. Not realizing that conceptual constructions occur on the level of ordinary human experience, Rosenzweig introduced them as metaphysical concepts. Hence his theology became loosened from its existential moorings and developed into a metahistorical theory of Jewish existence.

Rosenzweig, therefore, did not succeed in developing a sustained existential Jewish theology. However, his writings do contain passages of acute existential import, such as his description of the finite individual's fear of death and the inability of idealist philosophy to rob death of its sting. The empirical reference of Rosenzweig's thought lies chiefly in such passages.

Theologically, the most important doctrine in Rosenzweig's thought is his concept of revelation as God's love. This concept functions as the bridge from subjectivity to objectivity in Rosenzweig's theology. Since this concept plays so great a role in Rosenzweig's thought, one would expect it to have clear empirical reference.

Unfortunately, this is not the case. Rosenzweig advocated a nonpropositional view of revelation. What is revealed is not a series of statements or propositions such as the Ten Commandments. What is revealed is simply God's love. Just as the love between two lovers cannot be communicated to a third party, so the human experience of God's love is incommunicable to a third party. Moreover, any attempt at such communication is dangerous because it makes the one who speaks of it vulnerable to the "psychologist's knife."[2]

This concept of revelation is too private to be significant. What has been the centuries-old experience of the Jewish people if not the ability to communicate "these words" to one's children, to the community at large, and even to the world? By making revelation so private, he destroys the very possibility of spreading love unless each individual Jew receives revelations from God. Moreover, Rosenzweig's reluctance to let this concept be categorized psychologically hardly represents an empirical, open-minded attitude.

Pragmatically, Rosenzweig's concept of metahistory has value predominantly for Jewish-Christian polemics. His theory gives both Judaism and Christianity significant roles to play in *Heilsgeschichte,* or sacred history. The Jew has his being outside of time, outside of history, anticipating redemption: "This people is denied a life in time for the sake of a life in eternity."[3] Thus, the Jew represents eternal life. The Christian is forever on the way, spreading Christianity to the pagan: "Christianity, as the eternal way, has to spread ever further."[4] Thus, Christianity represents the eternal way. Both Judaism and Christianity are therefore necessary, in Rosenzweig's scheme, for cosmic redemption.

Although Rosenzweig's treatment of the Jewish people may be profound *sub specie aeternitatis,* it seems that the Jews as an existential reality didn't appeal to him. It is strange indeed that Judaism emerges as the static, eternal life, whereas Christianity emerges as the dynamic, eternal way. This treatment neglects the historic conception of Judaism as a dynamic, evolving *way,* a way never complete, never finished—the way of *Halacha* and the way of *Torah.*

Rosenzweig's failure to treat the Jews as an existential group may have been due to his acquiescence in the submerged state of the Jewish people living in a Christian world. Moreover, Rosenzweig did not ascribe sufficient importance to the evolutionary character of Judaism. It seems as if, in the final analysis, Rosenzweig reverted to the pure philosophical approach that sees truth as eternal, unchanging, and immutable.

In accordance with this approach, Rosenzweig views Judaism and the Jewish people under the aspect of eternity. He therefore did not do justice to Judaism as an evolving, historical, existential reality. This is evidently the price he paid for not being a true existentialist.

In contrast to Franz Rosenzweig, Martin Buber was a true existentialist. In our discussion of Buber, we found his philosophy to be distinguished for its consistency. From the time that he first arrived at his doctrine of encounter, Buber consistently maintained the position that God can only be encountered and not inferred.

From the point of view of empirical reference, however, Buber's thought is more vulnerable. Buber insists that one who really, with his whole being, goes out to meet the world, will meet God. This was true in Buber's case, but it is decidedly not a universal human experience.

In terms of pragmatic value, the weakest doctrine in Buber's theology is that of the eclipse of God. Buber's theological response to the Holocaust was his assertion that we are living at a time when the Divine is in eclipse. It follows that our time is one of waiting for God.

Despite the sublime character of much of Buber's thought, his doctrine of the hiding God and man's waiting for His appearance is all too reminiscent of a children's game of hide-and-seek. Surely we are entitled to a nobler conception of God than "the cruel and merciful Lord whose appearance we await"[5] from a man of Buber's stature.

But that is precisely the problem of the true existentialist, like Buber. The true existentialist is committed to the view that God may properly only be addressed, not expressed.

Concepts of God are secondary in importance to entering into relationship with or encountering God. The question of the validity of this existentialist thesis shall be discussed shortly.

Two of the most prominent Jewish existentialists who have followed some of the doctrines of Martin Buber are Eugene Borowitz and Emil Fackenheim.

In our evaluation of the covenant theology of Eugene Borowitz, we found his thought to be marred by internal conflict. Whereas Martin Buber could be a true existentialist because he did not see Jewish law or Rabbinic tradition as normative, Eugene Borowitz attempts to espouse both existentialism and what he calls an "open traditionalism." As an existentialist, he emphasizes personal faith and individual choice. On the other hand, he is seeking a faith which is in consonance with the authenticity of Jewish tradition. Unfortunately, Borowitz cannot have it both ways. Once the individual becomes the arbiter of what is significant and required in Jewish life today, he becomes his own authority and is not acting under the authority of Jewish tradition.

In terms of empirical reference, we found that Borowitz utilizes such expressions as "God's will" and "God's responsibility" as if they were indubitable deliverances of human experience. Thus, the empirical reference of Borowitz's thought is for those who already have faith and are seeking to clarify its nature.

Pragmatically, Borowitz deserves credit for trying to awaken in the modern Jew a sense of the Covenant. What he fails to realize is that he will not accomplish this end by dubious and incorrect criticisms of scientific naturalism.

A personalistic faith, such as the one which Borowitz seeks, does not have to be erected at the expense of and by the disparagement of scientific inquiry. Furthermore, the concept of covenant needs far more reinterpretation than that provided by Borowitz. The Holocaust calls into question the traditional meaning of the Covenant far more than Borowitz realizes.

Unlike Borowitz, Emil Fackenheim is quite aware that the Holocaust calls into question traditional theological categories. Like Martin Buber, Fackenheim relies heavily on the doctrine of encounter. In his insistence on the immediate and not the inferred presence of God, Fackenheim maintains a consistent theological approach. Empirically, his thought is open to the same objections as was Buber's. Pragmatically, Fackenheim's response to the Holocaust calls for serious evaluation.

We noted that Fackenheim did not find Buber's concept of the "eclipse of God" to be satisfactory. For Fackenheim, God either is present or He is not. Thus, Fackenheim maintains that God's presence in the Holocaust manifested itself in a "Commanding Voice"—issuing an imperative of Jewish survival as a holy duty so as not to grant Hitler posthumous victories.

We remarked that the pragmatic value of this concept lies in its powerful emotional appeal. However, many secularists, especially the defiant among the Israelis, would resent being told that their fight for survival was in response to a supernatural Commanding Voice. And the Orthodox Jew would resent any possible analogy of Fackenheim's Commanding Voice with the Voice at Sinai. Thus, in his effort to unite the religious and the secular Jew, by a Hegelian synthesis, in a theological response to the Holocaust, Fackenheim could conceivably lose the staunchest proponents of both groups.

But the major weakness of Fackenheim's thought is the lack of a clear and articulate concept of God. This deficiency is manifested in Fackenheim's assertion that "we are here, exist, survive, endure, witnesses to God and man even if abandoned by God and man."[6] This statement makes no sense unless the first mention of the term "God" refers to some kind of a God concept.

Herein is exemplified the inadequacy of existentialism alone as an approach to Jewish theology. Existentialism alone, without a conceptual understanding of what we mean by the term

"God," is insufficient as a method for contemporary Jewish thought.

One can well understand that many of the Jewish existentialists are reluctant to spell out what they mean by the term "God" because they feel that such a clarification would vitiate the uniqueness of the personal encounter with God. As against this view, however, it must be pointed out that the effort to frame an intelligible concept of something does not mean that we are degrading the object of our discourse. On the contrary, it seems far more reverential to the Divine to clarify what we mean by this reality than to dwell in utter confusion and obfuscation.

The inadequacy of existentialism alone becomes especially poignant as we reflect on the response of some of these thinkers to the Holocaust. One thinker responds by an experience of the Divine as "Holy Nothingness." Another existentialist experiences the eclipse of God. Yet another hears a "Commanding Voice." And yet another tries to maintain the view of God as author of history by asserting that the Holocaust was shattering but not determinative.

These existentialist responses indicate a crying need to experience the reality of God. Yet they also show that this need, without the discipline of precise and articulate concepts, leaves contemporary Jewish theology in a state of fragmentation without intellectual integrity and wholeness.

The virtue of Jewish existentialism, therefore, is that it clearly shows the need for transcendence. Transcendence is needed to give the contemporary Jew meaning and purpose for his existence. But this existential need is not enough. Existential need must be complemented by conceptual clarity. Let us therefore turn now to a summary of our critique of some of the conceptions of transcendence promulgated by contemporary Jewish thinkers.

Critical Analysis of Conceptions of Transcendence

Realizing the insufficiency of existentialism alone, we then turned to an analysis of those contemporary Jewish thinkers who have been concerned with essence as well as existence. To these thinkers, experiences or encounters are not a strong enough foundation upon which to erect a Jewish theology. Concepts of God and ideational structures are viewed by these thinkers as equally important in theological discourse.

Naturally, when one considers the essentialist stand in contemporary Jewish thought, one thinks first of Leo Baeck and his classic work *The Essence of Judaism*. Let us recall what Baeck meant by essence. Baeck's approach was typological. It was the search for an inner essence or type of the phenomenon in question. Baeck's method was influenced by the philosopher Wilhelm Dilthey, who maintained that there are spiritual forms or types with their own structure and laws just as there exist natural laws in the universe.

Accordingly, in *The Essence of Judaism*, Baeck sought the inner spiritual core or typology which distinguished Judaism. Baeck saw the essence of Judaism in its ethical monotheism and ethical optimism. Baeck envisaged Judaism as a world-affirming religion, combining a practical awareness of the "commandment" with a metaphysical awareness of the mystery. Baeck maintained that just as Judaism consists of the polarity of mystery and commandment, so the concept of God in Judaism is the idea of the far yet near God.

Baeck's conception of transcendence, then, is the idea of a personal God who is, paradoxically, both far and near. Accordingly, Baeck wrote: "Judaism is filled with an anxiety because of the remoteness of God and with a longing for His proximity; but at the same time it is certain in the possession of Him."[7]

This conception of transcendence is based on a paradox. A paradox is what appears to be a contradiction which arises when the human mind attempts to deal with an object that is too great for its comprehension. The implication is that if we were really to understand the reality of God, the seeming contradiction would disappear.

To be sure, the reality of God is beyond human understanding. This does not mean, however, that logic is irrelevant to the explication of the concept of God. It seems to me that it is more reverential to the Divine to apply reason, as far as this is possible, than to begin with mystery and paradox. As a result of not adhering closely to the canons of logic and reason, Baeck does not avoid the pitfalls of inconsistency in developing his concept of God. The inconsistency centers about the fact that Baeck presses the tension between Divine transcendence and Divine immanence too far.

To be sure, Baeck emphasizes man's quest for God rather than God's quest for man. Moreover, Baeck's theology possesses great dignity. He views the Divine as manifested in the overall sweep and grandeur of Jewish history and the Jewish people's capacity for rebirth. Thus, in the area of *Heilsgeschichte,* Baeck displays a theological tentativeness which is admirable.

Yet, Baeck's theological tentativeness is not held to consistently. Thus he is capable of reverting to such a locution as "possessing God." Accordingly, there is no doubt that Baeck believed firmly that the commandment derives from God.

To be sure, a certain amount of tension between the categories of transcendence and immanence as applied to God is understandable. As much as we attempt to identify the Divine as manifested within human experience, we must always be aware that our categories are metaphors and cannot fully capture the transcendence of God. Yet this tension between transcendence and immanence must not be pressed so far that it borders on a contradiction. Thus, when God is conceived of both as remote and as within man's possession, paradox simply becomes a theological term for what in logical terms would be a contradiction. Concepts such as paradox and polarity, therefore, must be used with circumspection in theological discourse. To summarize, then, it must be said that Baeck's concept of the far yet near God, although extremely suggestive and poetic, needs more clarification and defense to avoid the pitfalls of inconsistency.

In terms of empirical reference, Baeck's theology will appeal to those who have experienced the mystery or heard the commandment. Baeck's thought has the power to awaken in the Jew a response of ethical activism if the latent spirit or feeling exists. But there is not sufficient argumentation to convince or persuade those who are dubious of the premises upon which Baeck builds his theological edifice.

Pragmatically, it is interesting to note that, eventually, Baeck came to the realization that essentialist considerations are a necessary but not a sufficient condition for a Jewish theology. This is evident in the title of Baeck's later book *This People Israel: The Meaning of Jewish Existence.* To be sure, Baeck was still primarily concerned with essence—that is, the meaning of Jewish existence. Yet in this work, he views the people of Israel as the revelation of God and the living experiences of the people as their way of working out the details of the revelation. Thus, revelation is placed into the continuous experience of the Jewish people. It is not the special content of a special moment in the past. The Jewish people itself is revelation. Accordingly, the existential reality of the Jewish people came to occupy a more significant role in Baeck's theology.

Baeck's renewed awareness of the existential reality of the Jewish people and his concept of the continuous capacity of this people for rebirth give his writings a moralism and heroism that reflect his character. The pragmatic value of Baeck's work lies in its thesis of hope in man as exemplified in the Jewish people's perennial capacity for rebirth.

From the theology of Leo Baeck, we see that essence and existence are both necessary factors in the development of a Jewish theology. Yet, what we seek, and do not yet find, in the theology of Leo Baeck is a correlation of Jewish existential reality with a clear and consistent concept of transcendence that endows this reality with meaning and significance.

In contrast to Leo Baeck, Abraham J. Heschel's emphasis is not upon man's quest for God but upon God's quest for man. Unequivocally, Heschel states that "we have not chosen God; He has chosen us."[8] He states this as though it were a known and verifiable fact. Our discussion of Heschel's thought centered around an attempt to discover the source of Heschel's certainty on this issue.

Unfortunately, a clear and consistent methodology is not delineated in Heschel's thought. At times, he argues on the basis of religious experience. In other instances, he argues on the basis of reverence for the past. Throughout, he seeks to awaken in the reader a religious sensitivity to respond to what he believes is the essence of the Biblical message—namely, that God is in search of man.

Heschel succeeds in awakening in the reader a sense of the ultimate questions, an awareness of the mystery of existence, and a feeling for the majesty and grandeur of creation. The problem is that Heschel's answer will satisfy only those who operate with his initial premise—namely, that our questions presuppose the reality of God seeking out man in general, and the Jewish people in particular.

The idea that God needs man might be interpreted symbolically to mean that Divine ideals such as truth, goodness, and righteousness require human effort to be realized. If this is what Heschel is saying, it is clear and comprehensible. However, it does not appear that Heschel intended such a concept as God in search of man as a metaphor in the usual sense of the term. Rather, it is a metaphor only in the sense of being an understatement about God. What Heschel seems to be saying is that the reality of God is so overpowering that no concept can do justice to it.

This does not prevent Heschel, however, from adumbrating the concept of God as "togetherness of all beings in holy otherness."[9] Again we are faced with the concept of polarity applied to God—this time the polar concepts are uniqueness and togetherness. In this view, God is essentially transcendent and accidentally immanent. All is "in" God; yet God surpasses or transcends the "all" or the universe. This view is known as panentheism, as distinguished from pantheism. Whereas pantheism is the doctrine that identifies the totality of the universe with God, panentheism is the view that God includes, yet surpasses, the totality of all that is.

In order for this view to be defended philosophically, it must be indicated how God surpasses or transcends the universe. Process philosophers such as Alfred North Whitehead and Charles Hartshorne introduce concepts of God similar to the one suggested by Heschel. The difference is that they take great pains to suggest how God transcends the universe.

What we find, then, in Heschel's theology are suggestions, allusions, metaphors, and understatements—not a developed and consistent theology.

Lacking a sustained and fully argued philosophical foundation, the concept of God in search of man can be viewed as a purely anthropomorphic notion. Heschel was not unaware of this difficulty. Thus he attempted to defend his notion of Divine concern in this manner:

> In ascribing a transitive concern to God, we employ neither an anthropomorphic nor an anthropopathic concept but an idea that we should like to characterize as an anthropopneumism *(anthropos + pneuma)*. We ascribe to Him not a psychic but a spiritual characteristic, not an emotional but a moral attitude.[10]

Now a concept such as Divine concern requires more philosophical justification than coining a new term. To call it an anthropopneumism rather than an anthropomorphism does little to mitigate the difficulty of finding adequate empirical reference for this concept.

In terms of pragmatic value, it is important to reiterate that Heschel's greatest philosophic contribution was to awaken in the modern Jew a sense of depth and a feeling for ultimate questions. For him, Jewish existence was inseparable from essence. This essence involved, as we saw, the spiritual order of Judaism and the Jew's kinship with eternity. Heschel succeeds in awakening a sense of mystery. But the seeker after truth is still left in a state of perplexity about the character of the meaning beyond mystery.

The quest for the meaning beyond mystery is pursued in two different ways by Arthur A. Cohen and Jacob B. Agus. In considering these two contemporary Jewish thinkers, one is confronted with the choice between dogmatic and definitive theological statement versus dispassionate philosophic inquiry.

Cohen is definitive and dogmatic in his supernaturalism. It is no coincidence that he refers to his theological beliefs as existential dogmas.

As was pointed out, Cohen's theology is by and large consistent if one is willing to accept his supernaturalist premises. The one major internal difficulty, it was noted, is the incompatibility of Cohen's emphasis on creation and consummation with his existential need for God's concern with the historical situation of the person in the here and now. If we are but an epoch in eternity, it is difficult to see how the individual, in his historical life situation, can be as important to God as Cohen wants him to be.

In terms of empirical reference, it must be remarked that Cohen uses such terms as creation, consummation, and eternity as if they were indubitable deliverances of experience. There seems to be no room in his conception of Judaism for those who have legitimate doubts about the existence of realities beyond history and beyond nature.

Pragmatically, Cohen is to be commended for his intellectual defense of the Jew and Judaism. Although the character of his defense is rather unempirical, his effort is laudable and his writing is rich and suggestive.

The thought of Jacob Agus stands in marked contrast to that of Arthur Cohen. Whereas Cohen emphasizes the imaginative, Agus stresses the rational. Whereas Cohen emphasizes Jewish exceptionalism—that is, the metaphysical qualitative distinction of the Jews from other peoples—Agus strives to demythologize this distinction, which he calls the "meta-myth." Whereas Arthur Cohen has little use for the philosophical tools of analysis and epistemology, Jacob Agus seeks a synthesis of faith and reason.

In evaluating Agus's thought, it is important to bear in mind his methodological principle—namely, the unity of the human mind. According to this principle, all analytical writing is based on the assumption of one way of logical thinking common to all men. Therefore, Jewish uniqueness need only be analyzed into its separate components for its mystical aura to be dispelled and refuted. The task of analysis, as conceived by Agus, is to separate the enduring, universal values from the ephemeral, historical phenomena.

It is thus evident that Agus stands at the opposite end of the spectrum from the Jewish existentialists. Of all contemporary Jewish thinkers, Agus most emphatically stresses essence rather than existence. His concern is with the universal rather than the particular.

How consistent is Agus in the application of his essentialist methodology? Agus is consistent in his vitriolic criticism of the meta-myth or the belief in the metaphysical distinction of the Jewish people *qua* people. Throughout his writings, Agus is consistent in his criticism of the chosen-people concept as an assertion of ethnic or political superiority.

However, Agus does introduce the category of uniqueness in his discussion of the Jewish religion. He launches a vitriolic attack against Jewish metaphysical differences in terms of peoplehood but admits the concept of the uniqueness of Judaism as a revealed faith. Now to be totally consistent in his methodology, Agus cannot admit any total qualitative uniqueness applied to Judaism as religiocultural phenomenon and not applied to Jewish peoplehood. The fact that Agus does see fit to introduce the concept of the particular uniqueness of Judaism as a religion indicates that a completely essentialist position is unworkable.

From the point of view of empirical reference, it must be said that Agus does not give sufficient weight to the existential reality of Jewish peoplehood. He is not critical enough of

Toynbee's attacks on Zionism. In short, Agus fails to realize that a strong sense of peoplehood (which need not involve the concept of the chosen people) is a *sine qua non* of Jewish existence today.

In terms of pragmatic value, Agus is to be commended for his attempted synthesis of faith and reason. Contemporary Jewish thought has tended too much in the direction of a fideistic, almost irrationalist, existentialism. Agus has redressed the balance toward essentialism.

Yet, as we have seen, essentialism alone, devoid of existential particularities, is also insufficient. Thus, it is clear that neither existentialism alone, nor essentialism alone, offers an adequate methodology for contemporary Jewish thought. The following conclusion can therefore be drawn. It is clear that an adequate contemporary Jewish approach to transcendence must include both existential and essentialist elements. It must be existential in the sense of faithfully representing the particularities of Jewish experience. But it must also be essentialist in underscoring the necessity for the ideas of Judaism, however they be conceived, to be evaluated according to the universal standards of reason and truth.

The singular virtue of Mordecai M. Kaplan is that he has given the best use of his cognitive powers toward clarifying the meaning of Jewish peoplehood, toward explicating a concept of God palatable to the modern mind, and toward evolving functional concepts for modern Jewish life. Thus, it is in Kaplan's thought that the goal of a synthesis of existence and essence is most closely approximated in contemporary Jewish thought. Kaplan has described this synthesis as follows: "In terms of contemporary philosophy, Judaism as an evolving religious civilization is *existentially* Jewish peoplehood, *essentially* Jewish religion, and *functionally* the Jewish way of life."[11]

Kaplan therefore combines in his thought an acute awareness of the existential reality of the Jewish people and the existential needs of the intellectual Jew, a searching and painstaking effort to evolve a meaningful concept of God (essence) and functional concepts such as *sancta,* to make Torah a living reality to the Jew.

In our critique of Kaplan, we noted various inconsistencies in his conception of God and how they might be reconciled. The major problem, as we saw it, is how the unity of God can be maintained in the face of Kaplan's repeated assertions that God is the sum total of all the forces in the universe that impel man to self-fulfillment. It was demonstrated that despite the frequency of such phrases, it is abundantly clear that Kaplan conceives of God as a unitary creative process that makes of the universe a *cosmos,* or ordered totality. And it was noted that Kaplan attempts to steer a middle course between supernaturalism and naturalism through his concept of the transnatural.

Obviously, it is possible to attack Kaplan's concept of the transnatural as a *tertium quid*—as an unnecessary category from the point of view of strict naturalism. The intellectual openness of the Reconstructionist movement is testified to by the fact that Kaplan's theology of transnaturalism is not accepted by all Reconstructionists.

For example, Ira Eisenstein, President of the Reconstructionist Foundation, argues that what is divine is the nature of nature, —that is to say, that aspect of nature which calls attention to creativity, to organicity, and to polarity. It is not something apart from, but rather the quality of, nature.[12] He maintains that by introducing the concept of the transnatural, we create a category for which there is no room. The fact that living beings add up to more than the sum of their parts is still, he argues, a fact of nature.

The issue here seems to be whether or not the God-process transcends nature. According to Eisenstein, the God-process is within nature. According to Kaplan, the God-process transcends nature, but not as an entity or being.

Here we come upon the major difficulty of conceptions of transcendence—namely, does it make any sense to speak of God as transcending nature? The problem revolves around the definition of the term "nature."

If we mean by "nature" the totality of the universe, it is obvious that we do not know the totality of all that is. Therefore, we cannot say anything meaningful about Deity transcending nature. Eisenstein defines nature as the totality of the universe. According to his concept of nature, transcendence of nature is patently a difficult concept.

However, if we mean by "nature" the mechanical functioning of the universe, then it does make sense to refer to Deity as transcending nature. Kaplan seems to be using "nature" in this sense. Thus, by the transcendence of nature, he means the belief in the existence of a creative process which makes nature interrelated and organic and is the source of human values and ideas. The significant point that is worth remarking is the lively interchange of ideas and open-minded inquiry that is manifested within the Reconstructionist movement.

In terms of empirical reference, Kaplan continually endeavors to find in human experience the basis of the conceptions he propounds. Thus, his conception of Judaism as an evolving religious civilization is one that fits the facts of modern Jewish life. Pragmatic value is the main criterion operative in Kaplan's thought. In all areas of his thought, he seeks those conceptions that best foster human self-fulfillment. And he has done more than any other contemporary thinker to foster and enhance Jewish life in America. Kaplan's contribution to American Jewish life is not merely that of a solitary thinker. Of the contemporary Jewish thinkers studied, Kaplan alone has founded a school of thought and a movement. To be sure, some of these other thinkers are associated with various move-ments—be it a school of philosophy, such as existentialism, or a movement within Judaism, such as the Reform movement. But the unique feature of Mordecai Kaplan is that his writings actually produced a new movement—Reconstructionism.

Does Reconstructionism, then, provide the synthesis of exis-tence and essence which we have been seeking? In the sense of promulgating a world-view that unites a consideration of the existential reality of the Jewish people with a sense of the need for a clear essentialist concept of God, Reconstructionism provides the sought-for synthesis. The problem is whether it speaks to the existential reality of the individual Jew—namely, the Jew who seeks a relationship with God.

We have seen that the Jewish existentialists emphasized the relationship or encounter with God. Is an encounter with God possible for a Reconstructionist?

The point is that an encounter with God is possible but far less likely. A Reconstructionist would be far more circumspect about drawing conclusions about God's relationship to him than would be an existentialist. But it is surely possible for a Recon-structionist to have an encounter with God.

It is important to note that God need not be conceived of as a person in order for an encounter to be possible. Even Buber speaks of a dialogue with Being and an encounter with a tree. But, it will be said, to Buber, God is a reality and not merely an idea.

At this point, it must be reiterated that to the Reconstructionist, God is no less a reality. The difference is that Reconstructionists pay far more attention to our ideas about God than do existentialists. And the reason is simple. There is no such thing as a "mere" idea. Our ideas of the universe are the most important things about us. Furthermore, is not a person related to his own ideas? How, then, can any idea of God not be "personal" in the sense of person-related? An individual's idea of God reflects his personal existential needs. And a people's idea of God reflects its deepest needs. Thus, Kaplan distinguishes between *Elohim*, the cosmic God, and *Yahweh*, the particular way in which the Jewish people has conceived of this cosmic God, as reflected in their collective *conscience*.

It seems, then, that the main feature of the Reconstructionist theological position is its intellectual modesty. Reconstructionists prefer to speak of our ideas of God rather than God Himself. They speak tentatively rather than definitively. And they are willing to revise and adapt their views.

If it takes definitive and dogmatic theological utterances to awaken the American Jew, Reconstructionism is not the answer to his existential needs. But if it takes philosophic and patient inquiry, Reconstructionism, with more metaphysical emphasis, has in it the germ-idea of the needed synthesis of existence and essence in contemporary Jewish thought.

A major program for future Jewish thought is thus the formulation of a synthesis of existentialism and essentialism. The goal of seeking this synthesis would be the ability to perceive universal truth in the particular phenomenon of Judaism. This is the fundamental task ahead for Jewish theology in our time.

NOTES

1. In his Foreword to Franz Rosenzweig, *The Star of Redemption,* trans. William Hallo (New York: Holt, Rinehart and Winston, 1970), p. xiv.

2. Nahum Glatzer, *Franz Rosenzweig: His Life and Thought* (New York: Schocken Books, 1973), p. 243.

3. *The Star of Redemption,* p. 304.

4. *Ibid.,* p. 341.

5. Martin Buber, *On Judaism,* p. 225.

6. Emil Fackenheim, *God's Presence in History* (New York University Press, 1970), p. 97. It is important to note that Fackenheim is not unaware of the problematic nature of existentialism as a means of explicating Judaism. But, unfortunately, this awareness does not give rise on his part to an effort to clarify his concept of God. On the contrary, it paradoxically leads him to an even more radical anticonceptualism and antiessentialism expressed in such a statement as the following: "Jewish existence today overwhelms existentialist and indeed all philosophical thought" Fackenheim, *Encounters Between Judaism and Modern Philosophy* (New York: Basic Books, 1972), p. 228. The doctrines of encounter and of the primacy of existence to essence therefore become even more pronounced in Fackenheim's thought. In this sense, he remains an existentialist despite his effort to transcend this approach.

7. Leo Baeck, *The Essence of Judaism* (New York: Schocken Books, 1961), p. 103.

8. Abraham J. Heschel, *God In Search of Man* (New York: Octagon Books, 1972), p. 245.

9. Abraham J. Heschel, *Man Is Not Alone* (New York: Octagon Books, 1972), p. 109.

10. Abraham J. Heschel, *Between God and Man* (New York: Free Press, 1965), p. 111.

11. Mordecai M. Kaplan, *The Purpose and Meaning of Jewish Existence,* p. 300.

12. A similar position is adumbrated by Jack J. Cohen in *The Case For Religious Naturalism* (New York: Reconstructionist Press, 1958). In this work, Cohen states that his idea of God is "that quality of the universe, expressed in its order and its openness to purpose, which man is constantly discovering and upon which he relies to give meaning to his life" (p. 130).

SELECTED BIBLIOGRAPHY

Agus, Jacob. *Modern Philosophies of Judaism*. New York: Behrman House, Inc., 1941.

Baeck, Leo. *The Essence of Judaism*. Translated by Victor Grubenweiser and Leonard Pearl. New York: Schocken Books, Inc., 1948.

Borowitz, Eugene. *A New Jewish Theology in the Making*. Philadelphia: The Westminster Press, 1968.

———. *The Mask Jews Wear*. New York: Simon and Schuster, 1973,

Buber, Martin. *I and Thou*. Translated by Ronald Gregor Smith. New York: Charles Scribner's Sons, 1958.

———. *Between Man and Man*. Translated by Ronald Gregor Smith. Boston: Beacon Press, 1961.

Cohen, Arthur A. *The Natural and the Supernatural Jew*. New York: Pantheon Books, 1962.

Cohen, Jack J. *The Case for Religious Naturalism*. New York: Reconstructionist Press, 1958.

Dewey, John. *A Common Faith*. New Haven: Yale University Press, 1934.

Eisenstein, Ira, ed. *Varieties of Jewish Belief*. New York: Reconstructionist Press, 1966.

Fackenheim, Emil L. *God's Presence in History: Jewish Affirmations and Philosophical Reflections*. New York: New York University Press, 1970.

Friedlander, Albert H. *Leo Baeck: Teacher of Theresienstadt*. New York: Holt, Rinehart and Winston, 1968.

Friedman, Maurice. *Martin Buber: The Life of Dialogue*. New York: Harper Torchbooks, 1955.

Glatzer, Nahum N. *Franz Rosenzweig: His Life and Thought*. New York: Schocken Books, Inc., 1973.

Heschel, Abraham Joshua. *Man Is Not Alone*. New York: Farrar, Straus and Cudahy, Inc., 1951.

———. *God in Search of Man: A Philosophy of Judaism*. New York: Octagon Books, 1972.

Kaplan, Mordecai M. *Judaism as a Civilization*. New York: Reconstructionist Press, 1957.

———. *The Future of the American Jew*. New York: Reconstructionist Press, 1957.

———. *The Meaning of God in Modern Jewish Religion*. New York: Reconstructionist Press, 1962.

Kaufmann, Walter. *Critique of Religion and Philosophy*. New York: Harper and Brothers, 1958.

Kaufman, William E. "The Relation of Man to the World in the Philosophy of John Wild." Ph.D. dissertation, Boston University, 1971.

Rosenzweig, Franz. *The Star of Redemption*. Translated by William Hallo. New York: Holt, Rinehart and Winston, 1970.

———. *Understanding the Sick and the Healthy*. New York: The Noonday Press, 1953.

Rubenstein, Richard. *After Auschwitz: Essays in Contemporary Judaism*. New York: The Bobbs-Merrill Company, Inc., 1966.

Wild, John. *Existence and the World of Freedom*. Englewood Cliffs, New Jersey: Prentice-Hall, Inc., 1963.

Index